Who Said That?

THE
EMPIRE
CLUB
OF CANADA

CELEBRATING ONE HUNDRED YEARS

Who Said That?

Memorable Notes, Quotes and Anecdotes

Selected from The Empire Club of Canada Speeches 1903–2003

By Russ Merifield

Editor Mary Byers

Foreword by Michael Bliss

ISBN 0-9734345-2-X

© Copyright 2003
The Empire Club of Canada

Royal York Hotel
100 Front Street West
Toronto, Ontario M5J 1E3
(416) 364-2878

Published by
The Empire Club Foundation
Chairman, David Edmison
Yearbook Editor, Edward Badovinac

Design by Fine Impressions, Toronto, Ontario

Printed and bound in Canada by
Gandalf Graphics Limited
Toronto, Ontario

Table of Contents

Foreword

Flying With the Blinds Up:
The Empire Club's Trip Through History

Wouldn't you agree that the worst airplane flights are the long trips on beautiful days where you're told to keep your window blinds down so everyone can watch a crummy movie? It's like spending a whole day pushing paper at your desk, with nothing but a sandwich from the food cart for lunch. Or it's like going through life without ever leaving your home town, without ever meeting anyone you didn't know in high school.

For one hundred years people have come to the luncheons of The Empire Club of Canada because they treasure the opportunity to open the blinds, look up from their desks, and get to know new and interesting people and learn about the problems and opportunities of a wider world. Perhaps even more than its sister organization, the Canadian Club, the Empire Club was formed to look outward, beyond the borders of Canada, to the British Empire, then the Commonwealth, and nowadays the globe. The sun never sets on topics of interest to Empire Club members. It's one of the delights of living and working in Toronto, Canada, that we have luncheon clubs with such long histories, rich traditions, and vital connections at the start of the twenty-first century.

The Empire Club has always prided itself on preserving the records of its meetings in the annual volumes of addresses it publishes. This centenary volume is an overview, the best of the best, snapshots from a hundred years of travelling with the blinds wide open. Like any good album, it's meant to be a browsers' delight. You can open this book anywhere and find an interesting snippet. Perhaps it's the marrow of an address by a Prime Minister of England on the state of the Empire; perhaps it's a joke—not always a good one—made by a journalist; perhaps it's an exhortation about democracy or the need for social compassion; perhaps it's a policy statement by a Prime Minister; perhaps it's greetings from a president.

When I open these pages at random, I find us introduced in March 1936 to the country doctor who delivered the Dionne quintuplets; in April to an American talking about the greatness of the Great Lakes; in October to the Canadian monument at Vimy Ridge; in November to Grey Owl, that strange Englishman who pretended to be an Indian; and in December to a lament against lobbyists. And so it goes, year after year, page after page, never knowing what's coming up next—quick images seen through the windows that Empire Club luncheons afforded on the whole history of the twentieth century.

The verbal geography changes over time, as the landscape of Britain and the Empire gives way to more varied terrain, and the Club never forgets that its home is in Canada. If you read the book from beginning to end you travel through the greatest period of change in human history, and you see those changes reflected in the distance the book takes us from Alexander Graham Bell to Canadian astronauts, from Methodist ministers to Marshall McLuhan, from Stephen Leacock to Margaret Atwood, and from George Drew to George W. Bush. The Empire Club is older than the provinces of Alberta and Saskatchewan and Newfoundland, but as young as Prince Andrew, and as young as next month's guest speaker. As the club president says in 1975, "It is not good because it is old. It is old because it is good."

The bookcases in my study groan under the weight of the thick history books that are the tools of my trade. Some of these volumes are well-thumbed, others a bit dusty; everything is practical and utilitarian. But I also have several shelves by my bed, where I keep my browsing books, the ones I leaf through late at night—not just to put me to sleep (though sometimes that happens)—but as a kind of last gaze out the window as a day comes to an end. *Who Said That?* goes on the bedside shelves. To change the metaphor, drawing on a hundred years of downtown luncheons the editors have put together a book of rich late-night snacks. Enjoy.

Michael Bliss, University of Toronto

Acknowledgments

This book was produced as a centenary project by The Empire Club of Canada Foundation in celebration of the 100th anniversary of The Empire Club of Canada. The Foundation is indebted to Russ Merifield who spent countless hours researching speeches from the volumes of Empire Club books dating back to the Club's founding in 1903 and extracting what he felt were the most memorable quotes. Russ was greatly assisted in his efforts by Mary Byers, a director of the Foundation, who agreed to edit his work and format the presentation. Mary also wrote all of the historical vignettes introducing each decade. Thanks are also due to Michael Bliss, noted historian, who wrote the foreword to this book.

The Foundation is also indebted to the following donors for their generosity in bringing this centenary project to fruition.

The Empire Club of Canada
(Through the Centennial Gala Luncheon,
whose sponsors are listed on page 339)

Col. The Hon. Henry N.R. Jackman

The Bank of Nova Scotia

Jackman Foundation

The E.W. Bickle Foundation

As well as several donors who wished to remain anonymous

David Edmison
Chairman
The Empire Club of Canada Foundation

Preface

When I attended my first luncheon meeting of the Empire Club as a new member I found myself seated beside Sydney Hermant, a sage past president and an avid historian. He told me that he had learned more about Canadian history by coming to these luncheon meetings than in any other way—the subjects were varied, the speakers challenging. This idea was echoed by Hal Jackman, former Lieutenant Governor of Ontario, who flatly said that one would be a better Canadian for attending and listening. This was an invitation to a feast of current thought. Sometimes it triggered a nod of agreement, sometimes a mental rebuttal.

But now, when asked to travel back to 1903, to enter the thoughts of the famous and articulate as editor, the past became present. It was possible to sit with the perspective of time as an advantage, hearing a debate to which the conclusion was history, but wondering what would have been my own opinion then—a fascinating experience. There was Winston Churchill ripping off the microphone in Maple Leaf Gardens when the public address system broke down, that great voice carrying to the audience with not a stir among them; there was Alexander Graham Bell musing about inventing the telephone; there was a young man just returned from the trenches in the First World War, bringing those horrors home.

The Empire Club has always brought speakers from diverse fields to the podium.

From the inception of the Club in 1903 to its one hundredth anniversary in 2003 there have been over 3000 men and women who have been heard, then, as years went on, been seen on television, and always from the beginning, their thoughts have been published in the annual yearbook. They covered days before income tax (that temporary inconvenience) to the days before the millennium when disaster was expected and on to the disasters of a different sort that opened the 21st century.

In my essays at the beginning of each section I have tried to follow the issues most on the minds of speakers of the day. It was tantalizing to taste the most popular of the delicious morsels from this feast for the mind, sometimes home grown, sometimes exotic, sometimes prescient, sometimes not. This then is an invitation to those who have tasted the appetizers of the century in this volume to visit the Empire Club website at www.empireclub.org. This will be a moveable feast as it courses through the years of this century. You are urged to taste and then to make your own choices. The menu is varied and inviting.

Mary Byers

Note:

The honours and post-nominals etc. listed after a speaker's name are as they appeared in the yearbook of the date and reflect usage at the time.

In the Beginning

The Empire Club of Canada was formed in 1903 with remarkable speed. The catalyst was a majority decision by the International Boundaries Tribunal in October 1903 which settled the Alaskan boundary by awarding a large strip on the Pacific coast of Canada to the U.S. The six-member Tribunal consisted of three Americans, two Canadians and one Britisher (Chief Justice Lord Halversham). The British delegate sided with the Americans, giving them the decision by 4 to 2. The Canadian delegates refused to sign the award and the Canadian press printed many articles harshly critical of the English sell-out to the Americans. The Canadian Club of Toronto promptly invited one of the Canadian delegates, Sir Allan Aylesworth, to address the Club immediately upon his return to Canada. Many in the Canadian Club felt that such action was inflammatory and divisive, to say the least. Sir Allan's address, which received full page coverage in the Toronto newspapers, was tactful and statesmanlike and concluded with his declaration of loyalty to the Empire.

Nevertheless, many Canadian Clubbers were not appeased. Furthermore, in other circles there were proponents for greater independence of Canada and even amalgamation with the U.S. Some deprecated the wide-open character of the Canadian Club which permitted independence men and even annexionists to be members. A prominent group of local leaders felt there was need for a new popular organization that supported Empire union.

Within two weeks, on November 18, a small meeting was held in Webb's Restaurant, Toronto, mainly on the initiative of Lieut-Col. James Mason, for purposes of preliminary discussion. Those present were: Lieut-Col. Mason, G.A. Stimson, Messrs. W.E. Lincoln Hunter, F.B. Fetherstonhaugh, J. Castell Hopkins, J.P. Murray, Robert Junkin, Capt. R. Wyly Grier, Charles Elliot, James R. Code, Wallace Jones, E. Strachan Cox, J.F.M. Stewart, Noel Marshall, Major J.B. Miller and Major J. Cooper

Mason, D.S.O. The Chairman briefly pointed to the desirability of an organization, following the plan of weekly luncheons, to be addressed by prominent men or men speaking with authority upon the issues of the day, and having also a distinctive basis of British unity in its work and policy. Others spoke and then a committee was formed to organize a new association along these lines. It comprised Lieut-Col. Mason, Lincoln Hunter, J.P. Murray, F.G. Fetherstonhaugh, Noel Marshall, E. Strachan Cox and Castell Hopkins. Although the nucleus of the proposed new club was comprised of dissatisfied Canadian Club members, Col. Mason was not himself a member.

The Committee met the following day and appointed the previously mentioned Mason, Grier and Hopkins, together with Wallace Jones, to draft a Constitution and Bylaws for approval by a general organizational meeting.

The organization meeting was duly held November 25, 1903 at a luncheon held in Webb's Restaurant, about seventy being present. Lieut-Col. Mason presided and J.F.M. Stewart acted as Secretary. After a discussion of proposed names, such as The British Canadian Club, The British-American Club, The Dominion Club (the name suggested by the organizing committee), the name The Empire Club of Canada was approved by a large majority. The policy of the Club was declared to be summed up in the words "The advancement of the interests of Canada and a united Empire."

The first officers elected were

President	Lieut-Col. Mason
1st Vice-President	Prof. William Clark
2nd Vice-President	Hugh Blain
3rd Vice-President	J.F. Murray
Treasurer	Major J. Cooper Mason
Secretary	J.F.M. Stewart

Executive Committee	Frank Darling,
	F.B. Fetherstonhaugh,
	Alex Fraser, Capt. E.I Wyly Grier,
	W.E. Lincoln Hunter, Wallace Jones,
	R.G. Junkin, Noel Marshall,
	H.C. Colborne and F.B. Polson

The draft Constitution and Bylaws were approved by the general meeting with few changes. Membership was open to any man of the full age of eighteen years who was a British subject. The Annual fee was $1.00. One of the early amendments was to limit the number of members to 500. Membership candidates had to be proposed and seconded by two members and approved by a two-thirds vote of the Executive Committee. Within a few months the membership quota was filled and there was a waiting list.

The inaugural weekly luncheon meeting, held in Webb's Restaurant, December 3, 1903, was addressed by the Reverend Professor William Clark, 1st Vice-President. More than 100 members attended and 58 new members were proposed. The Empire tradition started immediately with the election of the Rt. Hon. Lord Strathcona and Mount Royal (1820–1914) as Honourary President and the Rt. Hon. Joseph Chamberlain, MP (1836–1914) leading British statesman and champion of Imperial unity, as the first Honourary Member. Lord Strathcona, born Donald Smith, started his career as an 18-year-old apprentice with the Hudson's Bay Company and rose to become Governor of this great enterprise. At age 83 he was still Governor and was serving as High Commissioner for Canada in the U.K. He amassed an enormous fortune in his activities as trader, manager, banker, promoter, railway promoter and politician, and became one of Canada's most influential individuals. Best of all, from the Club's standpoint, he was an enthusiastic supporter of Britain and the Empire.

The Club held 20 luncheon meetings in the 1903–04 season

that ran from December to May. More than half of the speeches had titles relating to the British Empire. They included:

The Empire Club and its Ideal of Imperialism

Preferential Trade Within the Empire

Imperialism in Education

What Makes a Good Citizen of the Empire

The Relations of Canada, the Motherland and the United States

The Loyalty of French Canadians to the Empire

Imperial Ignorance

Imperial History

Imperial Unity

Practical Imperialism

Two Pillars of the Empire

Of course, Canadian problems were also discussed, and many of them are still with us. They included education defects, railway transport, manufacturing, Canadian character and taxation. The great Canadian scientist, Sir Sanford Fleming (inventor of standard time) announced that the undersea cable network was almost completed. This would enable Empire countries to communicate within minutes instead of relying upon delivery by ship that often took several weeks.

Lest some infer that the Empire Club was conceived in the ambiance of a dirty spoon, a brief description of Harry Webb's restaurant is in order. A book entitled "Toronto Illustrated" published near the end of the 19th century contains the following eulogy: "Harry Webb … is the leading representative of the catering business in Toronto (and we may safely say in the Dominion). His wedding cakes and dinner outfits are sent not only through all Canada, but throughout the United States and occasionally across the Atlantic. At 445 and 447 Yonge Street he has one of the best equipped catering and confectionary establishments in Canada. He delivers his celebrated brands of bread to over 1,600 houses in the city daily. He also carries on a restaurant at Yonge and Melinda Streets and in connection with this a spacious ballroom and banqueting hall, which is by far the most attractive and best of its kind in Canada. It is well patronized by the elite of Toronto." This site was demolished about 1917 to make way for one of Toronto's first skyscrapers, the 20-storey Dominion Bank Building at the south-west corner of Yonge and King Streets.

The Club's first President, Lieut-Col. James Mason (1843–1918) was a leading member of the Toronto "elite." Always a Torontonian he attended the Model School where he became Head Boy. Upon graduation he started at the bottom rank with Toronto Savings Bank, which merged with Home Savings and Loan Company and eventually became the Home Bank of Canada. By 1903 Col. Mason had risen to the office of General Manager. A leader in business and community activities he was a director of several corporations, served terms as President of the Red Cross and the St. John's Ambulance Society and was one of those chiefly responsible for the establishment of the Toronto Public Library. He also belonged to several of the leading clubs in the city but his prime interest was his life long military service which began with the Queen's Own Rifles at age 19. He served in the North West Rebellion in 1885, suffering severe wounds at the Battle of Batoche. At the time of his election as first President of the Empire Club his rank was Lieutenant Colonel, but in later years he became a Major General. He was appointed to the Senate in 1913.

An early key person in the Empire Club was John Castell Hopkins (1864–1923). In addition to being the founding Secretary he was appointed as the officer responsible for recruiting guest speakers. He was on the first editorial committee for publishing the annual volume of addresses given at meetings and took over the editorship commencing with the second volume (1904–05). He continued as editor until 1911 when he became Club President for the term 1910–11. Hopkins was a highly regarded Canadian historian and writer who turned out an enormous number of books, articles and pamphlets. His chief work was the Canadian Annual Review of Public Affairs, which he founded and published, mainly assisted by his wife, who carried on the publication after his death. This large annual volume earned praise as a unique reference book in the world as a source of information on questions of importance to a country. He literally wrote every line and at the time of his death had been credited with writing 18,000 pages of Canadian history.

Russ Merifield

1903–1913 Early Days and the Pre-War Years

Plus ça change

"This Club….is founded upon a distinct and well understood and realized principle, namely that the highest interests of the Dominion of Canada are identical with the interests of the British Empire."

"I do not seek to belittle the great Republic alongside of us….But that is all very well. You may be on good terms with your neighbours without having them live in your house or you living in theirs….I esteem and respect the United States without desiring to be one of them."

With the first words of the opening luncheon, December 3, 1903, the speaker, the Rev. Professor William Clark, struck two themes that have resonated over one hundred years—the extent of our ties with Great Britain and, to an even greater extent, our ambivalence concerning our relations with the United States. And to follow the thoughts of those who stood after him at the podium of the Empire Club in the years immediately after its founding is to hear a litany of comments, some of which could come from that same podium in 2003.

Thus the 20th century started—and continued in the same.

"The French-Canadian knows too well that Independence would be, for the present, a mere Utopia, in which would be lost the safeguards that the existing Constitution has established for his interests, his laws and his language; he knows that a national or political alliance with another country would mean the forfeiture of the same advantages."

"If imitation be the sincerest form of flattery, we sometimes flatter the United States….We can well afford to share their alertness, their enthusiasm, their strongly patriotic spirit but I think we can do without some things which their own best citizenship repudiates….I see no particular reason why we should court the peril of their form of democracy."

"Well, ever since any one here can remember, the Canadians have been doing great promise-work in connection with the militia….we have 40,000 rifles in Canada to arm 200,000 men….our Canadian cannon are cemeterial monuments….We have a toy army, which by repeated skeleton camps and 50-cents-a-day inducements, is becoming an imaginary army."

As well as the themes that were to resonate for one hundred years, there were issues that galvanized a new nation and aroused pride or controversy. The state-owned railway, the Canadian Pacific, had been the recipient of John A. Macdonald's aggressive support in the form of cash and land grants. A state-supported railway was called "a system of defence," "the best means for a systematic development of the resources of the country," "patriotic," one that "does not discriminate in favour of preferred interest or preferred customers." On the other hand there were those who found it a boon mainly to central Canada as well as an unfair monopoly. The West, with Alberta and Saskatchewan having achieved provincial status in 1905, was raising its voice. This community of communities was shouting its regional character aloud. One speaker called Confederation, less than forty years old, "a bugle call to rally parties who were not at all prepared to rally."

Opening and developing the West was a recurring topic as were the growing-pains of multi-culturalism. One speaker asked "Why do men carry implements and wives into the far country of the Peace River, when a thousand miles nearer the best market for their produce there are a thousand square miles of fertile land to be obtained for the asking?" He answered his own question, stating that it is "the re-assertion of the elemental quality in virile mankind which….founded colonies and transplanted empires across the face of the planet." There were statistics. "Up to the end of June, 1907, it may be conservatively estimated that over 30,000,000 acres of land have been granted by the Crown to legitimate settlers in Manitoba, Alberta and Saskatchewan." As well as applauding the manhood of the new immigrants, there were concerns expressed either guardedly or openly about the health and suitability of those who were "pouring into our country, and especially into our great North-West, by the tens of thousands almost every day, people from every nation under Heaven," as opposed to the days when immigration was, as one speaker succinctly put it of "mainly British-thinking, British-speaking, British-acting citizens."

And, at the other end of the country a British colony was agonizing over its destiny. "It is a matter which the Dominion of Canada ought to deal with, and I for one am tired of hearing Party after Party saying they are favourable to it and yet doing nothing….Newfoundland ought to be part of Canada….Canada ought to go to the Imperial Government and say that we consider the outstanding of Newfoundland as a menace and as an act of hostility to the Dominion: The union of Canada and Newfoundland is not a new idea. It was advocated by Lord Durham in 1839." The speaker's remarks were made in 1903. That union would not happen for another forty-six years.

And that eternal debate about the national character of Canadians was in fact settled by one speaker as early as 1903. He described us as "a blend of energy, vigour, aggressiveness, loyalty to the past, considerateness of tradition, with the national attributes and knowledge of philosophy, science and art, language and manners, courtesy and politeness," and then directed a searching question to Plato, "Do you not think, in Canada, Plato, we have the chance of combining what you want to combine in your ideal state—the many-sided virtues of a perfect character?" The philosopher's answer to this modest question remained a mystery!

True to its name, the Club analysed The Empire from every angle. Sentiment towards "the Mother Country" was positive, intense, and emotional. Of all available themes chosen by speakers "The Empire" was by far the most popular, including "Toronto and the Empire," "Ontario and the Empire," "Canada and the Empire," "What Makes a Good Citizen of the Empire," "The Loyalty of French-Canadians to the Empire," "Milton as an

Empire-Builder," "The Irishman's Place in the Empire," "Sir Walter Scott as an Empire-Builder." In 1909 alone there were eleven speeches about the Empire. Eloquence knew no bounds and resulted in such as, "And today that flag which floats through the four quarters of the globe, from the rocky bastions of Gibraltar, up the Nile, along the great rocky scarps of the north-west frontiers of India, from Hong-Kong, from the antipodes in the east and in the west, in the north and in the south; that flag which there is no sea so lonely that it does not flap to the breeze; that flag today stands as the emblem to hundreds and thousands and millions of all that they aspire to in the way of progress, in the way of equity, and….in the way of square-dealing."

Trade with the United States was a sensitive issue and agreements were hotly debated. In 1910 when Sir Wilfrid Laurier was advocating the reciprocity agreement that would have removed or lowered duties on "natural" products, those of the farms, fisheries and forests, reaction at the Empire Club podium was "it is the duty of the people of this country…to show the farmer that his position under Reciprocity would not be [as positive] as he was led to believe….this is the thin edge of the wedge." "We want them [the United States] to distinctly understand this, that if they expect Canada at any moment to forego her rights and her interests as a Dominion in order to meet any demand they may make, we are not prepared to do anything of that kind." During negotiations it was reported that "Sir Wilfrid has stated that Canada has shown her face in Washington for the purpose of negotiating better trade relations for the last time, and we all hope that policy will continue." It didn't, and caused Laurier's defeat in the 1911 election.

Certain statements, however, belong strictly to their time—pre First World War, in particular…."We are the lowest taxed people that you can hunt up in any part of the civilized world."

"I remember in 1889 or 1890 the Parliament of the Province [Quebec] introduced a Bill whereby the father of twelve children was to be entitled to one hundred acres of land....we soon found that we would not have enough acres to satisfy the demand, and....we reduced the grant....to one of cash— $50 to each parent of twelve children....we soon found we would be entirely bankrupt if we continued to do it, and we passed a law to the effect that after the 30th June at twelve o'clock at night no father of twelve children would be entitled to the $50....It was almost enough to upset the government."

Mary Byers

"GETTING STARTED"

CLUB CONSTITUTION 1903
The active membership of the Club shall be limited to five hundred, and membership shall be open to any man at the full age of eighteen who is a British subject.

THE EMPIRE CLUB OF CANADA AND ITS IDEAL OF IMPERIALISM
December, 1903
The Rev. Professor William Clark, DD, DCL, LLD

I have not the least doubt that this Club will become of great influence and power in this Dominion, because it is founded upon a distinct and well understood and realized principle, namely, that the highest interests of the Dominion of Canada are identical with the interests of the British Empire.

IMPERIALISM IN EDUCATION
January, 1904
The Rev. Nathanael Burwash, STD, LLD, Chancellor, Victoria University, Toronto

For many generations the world has been alive to the importance of patriotism in education. You will find it away back in the days of ancient Greece and Rome, and you will find it in the earliest development of the nationalities of the Old World—that is, of Europe.

CANADIAN SENTIMENT BEFORE AND AFTER CONFEDERATION
January, 1904
Mr. Benjamin Sulte, FRSC, Vice-President of the Royal Society of Canada

You remember when the first talk about Confederation came, that it sounded like a bugle call to rally Parties who were not at all prepared to rally....I remember those days. I was twenty-seven years old, and I had ten years of journalism. I remember how often we thought it was not made at all....As for Confederation, this we had, and it was agreed that the people did not like it, but that they accepted it under these conditions....It might last five years, ten years, three months, we did not know. The least little thing might break it asunder.

OUR EMPIRE CABLES
February, 1904
Sir Sandford Fleming, KCMG, LLD

The sentiment in favour of an All-British system of state-owned cables is a matter of education and that it will become more popular every year I have no doubt whatever....Only a month or two ago a remarkable example was furnished of its efficiency. During the course of the British-Australian cricket matches last autumn and December a determined effort was made to cut down the records, and illustrate the potentialities of the new all-British route from England to Australia via Canada....The score of Australia's cricket champions, at the close of their first innings, handed in at the Sydney office at 2:40, was delivered in London at precisely 2:43.5 [Greenwich time]—that is to say in 3.5 minutes. Imagine transmitting a message around the circumference of the globe—15,000 miles in 3.5 minutes!

THE LOYALTY OF FRENCH-CANADIANS TO THE EMPIRE
March, 1904
The Hon. L.P. Brodeur, KC, MP, Dominion Minister of the Interior

The French-Canadian knows too well that Independence would be, for the present, a mere Utopia, in which would be lost the safeguards that the existing Constitution has established for his interests, his laws and his language; he knows that a national or political alliance with any other country would mean the forfeiture of the same advantages.

THE UNIVERSITY AND THE PEOPLE
March, 1904
The Very Rev. Dr. Daniel M. Gordon, DD, LLD, Principal,
Queen's University, Kingston

The true scholar should not only know some one subject pretty well, but he should be familiar enough with other subjects to see how his own is related to them.

IMPERIALISM IN CANADA
Beware the Crystal Ball
November, 1904
W. Wilfred Campbell, FRSC, poet, novelist, columnist

We should not see too far into the future; as to do so would paralyze our effort here.

RELATIONS OF THE UNITED STATES WITH CANADA AND GREAT BRITAIN
January, 1905
The Hon. Eugene N. Foss, Boston, Massachusetts

You are aware of the great disappointment in the United States over the memorable decision which gave Canada the great valley of the Columbia River and her outlet to the Pacific. More recently you have had your own disappointment in the award of the Alaskan Boundary Tribunal. Whatever Canada may have had to complain of in the cry of "54-40 or fight," or in the personnel of our representatives upon the Alaskan Commission, this must not be charged to the spirit of the people of the United States. When we lost a large portion of what we considered to be our North-West Territory, our people accepted the verdict and refused to fight; and when, more recently, "impartial jurists of repute" were not appointed to the Alaskan Tribunal, through the influence of our overpowering Senate, this breach of faith was publicly rebuked in the United States on more than one distinguished occasion. I am sure you agree with me that this record ought to allay any suspicion or fear on your part that we of the United States have political designs on Canada.

THE DEFENCE OF THE EMPIRE
February, 1905
Colonel Sam Hughes, MP, Opposition military critic

If time permitted I could point out by figures that there is no nation on the face of the earth that pretends to have any commerce to defend but what spends millions on a Navy for the defence of that commerce. Canada, ranking about sixth in the tonnage of the world, is the only nation that does not contribute one dollar to the defence of that tonnage, and we are content to live hanging on to the skirts of Great Britain, and letting the British tax-payer do our defensive work.

OCCIDENTAL JAPAN
April, 1905
The Rev. Egerton Ryerson, MA, Missionary in Japan

But our respect for Japan should not be based simply upon her military and naval achievements; it should be based more upon her achievements in peace; upon her great progress in Western civilization and her commercial achievements of a peaceful kind. Japan has been in the past perhaps backward in commerce. The Japanese in the old days were not accustomed to business. In fact the business man was looked upon as being of the lowest class. First came the soldiers, then the farmers, then the artisans and last of all the merchants. But today that has been changed and people are going into business from the nobility down, but still, as business was despised in the old days, the business methods are not altogether ideal, and it has been hard for Japan to change them altogether quickly.

THE EVOLUTION OF CANADIAN SENTIMENT
May, 1905
The Hon. George W. Ross, LLD, MPP, former Prime Minister, Ontario

It is only, Sir, within the last few years we knew we were Canadians. I am sorry to say in Great Britain they hardly know we are Canadians yet. They generally speak of us as Americans.

RECENT DEVELOPMENTS IN PARLIAMENTARY INSTITUTIONS
November, 1905
Mr. Robert Laird Borden, KC, DCL, MP, Leader of the Conservative Party in Canada

The trend of the last sixty or seventy years and more especially, perhaps, of the last thirty or forty years, has been to shift...power from Parliament to the Cabinet...Much of its [Parliament's] efficiency has passed to other agents. Its supremacy is qualified by the growth of rival jurisdictions. Its own servants have become, for some purposes, its masters....Thus we have the curious fact that nearly one-half of the Legislature are not legislators at all, or only legislators on sufferance and on matters of no moment.

NEW DEVELOPMENTS IN EDUCATION
Looking Back
November, 1905
James L. Hughes, Public School Inspector, Toronto

I remember when, about fifteen years ago in this City, it was proposed to introduce the trolley service and one man, who was afterwards Mayor of the City, objected to it because he said if they erected the trolley wires they would shut out the sun at noonday....The world moves on. A little over 100 years ago there were 223 crimes for which the criminal might be hanged. We have been making progress in all departments.

THE NEW CRIMINOLOGY
January, 1906
W.P. Archibald, Dominion of Canada Parole Officer

The tendency of the parole system is to change the atmosphere of the Prison. The convict, when his opposition to our penitentiary discipline has once been overcome, comes to regard it as the abode of hope, not of despair.…When he learns the meaning and intention of the law, and becomes reconciled to it, like a wild animal tamed, his reformation is achieved.

CANADIAN JOURNALISM
March, 1906
E.J.B. Pense, MPP, Editor and Proprietor, *Kingston Whig*

Quebec and Ontario would be warmer national colleagues but for feelings of hostility rising from a too serious consideration of occasional vagaries of party journalism—baseless as evidence of public feeling. A few heated expressions are remembered and a thousand just and friendly articles are forgotten.

CANADA AND IMPERIAL DEFENCE
March, 1906
Major E. Wyly Grier

In every country there is a certain section of the public who are reluctant to admit that war is a possibility. I dare say that every gentleman here will remember that when the South African war was imminent a number of our personal friends didn't believe it would come to pass. I heard it stated by a man of no small gifts that the Spanish-American war could not take place, but the *Maine* was blown up about two days afterwards, and the war followed very rapidly. Now there have been other rumours of war which fortunately never developed into actual hostilities.…I contend that a war in which we would take a prominent part, or a lesser part, is eminently possible if you look at the condition of Europe today.

RESOURCES AND PROGRESS OF QUEBEC
The Present and Future
April, 1906
The Hon. W.A. Weir, KC, MPP, Speaker, Quebec Legislative
Assembly

There is one thing that is perfectly sure, as sure as the sun shines
over all the land, and that is that the people of Quebec are loyal
to the core to the country in which they live....While the English
population of Quebec may be increasing, that increase is almost
totally confined to the cities, while in the rural districts the
English population is dying out very rapidly; and that, as I say, is
the only black point of view that I have to refer to in connection
with the future of the Province.

THE NEWFOUNDLAND FISHERIES QUESTION
A Speaker Forty-Three Years Ahead of His Time
November, 1906
The Hon. A.B. Morine, KC, former Leader of the Opposition in
Newfoundland

Newfoundland ought to be part of Canada. Her interests ought
to be represented by the Government of the Dominion and the
Government of Canada ought to take some active steps to bring
about the Confederation of the two colonies.

CIVIL SERVICE REFORM
November, 1906
The Rev. Father L. Minehan, Toronto

The man who obtains his office simply and purely by merit has a
more exalted sense of his duties and is likely to do his work better. A man who obtains his office by political intrigue knows that
his advancement must depend on the same thing and he is more
likely to think of currying political favour than of entering heart
and soul into his duties.

THE UNION JACK OF THE EMPIRE
December, 1906
F. Barlow Cumberland, MA

Here is a flag which carries such a history as no other flag in the world.…The flag tells us whence we came; the flag tells us from whom we obtained it; it tells us that we are to keep it not only for those who are living here, but for those who are loyal to it around the world. Well, then, may it fly upon the school-houses of Manitoba; well has that Government taken the foremost step in saying that all those varied nationalities which are coming within their lands shall be taught by the visible emblem which they have placed above their schoolhouses, that they are coming under the influences and under the charge of the Union Jack. So, too, may we have them over all our school-houses in Ontario. 'Well done' to those men and to those people who would spread the use of these flags among our Canadian school-houses, for they are the signals not only of our own union; they are the signs of a nationality wider than the country in which we live; they are a sign of brotherhood with our fellow peoples around the world.

RAMBLES THROUGH THE BRITISH EMPIRE
War
January, 1907
J. Graham Gow, New Zealand Government Trade Commissioner in Canada

War is a serious thing, so hit hard and finish it as quickly as possible.

NIAGARA POWER AND THE FUTURE OF ONTARIO
January, 1907
Major-General Francis Vinton Greene, Buffalo, N.Y.

I believe the day is not far distant when practically every house in Ontario within two hundred miles of the Niagara River will be lighted by electricity supplied by the power of the great Cataract [Niagara]. It will be running the sewing machines, the churns, the ice cream freezers, the ventilating fans, the house pump, the knife cleaner and sharpener, the dish washing machine, the clothes wringer…and a host of other domestic utensils not yet invented.

THE MACHINE IN HONEST HANDS
January, 1907
Herbert. B. Ames, MP, Montreal

The Germans have a proverb that 'To be well soaped is half shaved,' and nothing is truer in elections than that proverb. To have your lists in good shape is half the battle in an election fight.

A FORCED SPEECH
1907

At a meeting featuring McGill's Professor Leacock, a head table guest was called upon unexpectedly to introduce the speaker. He compared his position to that of the unprepared bridegroom suddenly called to respond to a toast to the bride. Rising with embarrassment, his hand on his new wife's shoulder, he blurted "Ladies and gentlemen, this thing has been forced on me."

EDUCATION AND EMPIRE UNITY
March, 1907
Professor Stephen Leacock, PhD, McGill University

It has been said that the hand that rocked the cradle ruled the world. I think we might revise that and make it read, 'The hand that rules the blackboard rocks the world': for it is our [teachers'] privilege to deal with the youth of the country; to inspire in them those ideas which afterwards will bear fruit; to implant in them the morality of the school which shall some day become the morality of those in public places....Let us settle with ourselves in Canada as to what our country is going to be, let us find what are the future aspirations we can teach to those who come after us.

THE BUSINESS MAN AND THE CHURCHES
February, 1908
The Rev. J.A. Macdonald, Editor in Chief, Toronto *Globe*

The life of a man...is too abundant, to be confined...to the making of money.

BRITISH POLITICIANS
March, 1908
Duncan C. Hossack

It appears that British politicians of both parties do not cling so desperately to office as politicians in Canada. The darkest pages of our history had not been written, had leaders been willing to resign when popular favour had departed. Such desperate attempts as have been witnessed on this side of the sea have not been made in Britain to sustain by unworthy means governments which have forfeited all right to popular support. Perhaps for this reason the average British parliamentary term is brief. It may be said that in the main the British politician will do his duty rather than strive for personal benefit or power. In this we see not the least of the factors which have made the British Parliament the greatest the world has ever known.

IMPERIAL DEFENCE
September, 1908
Howard d'Egville, Hon. Secretary, Imperial Federation
(Defence) Committee, London, England

Therefore, loyalty to our own individual countries is not inconsistent in the least with the true Imperialism which, while recognizing that each country must have the fullest scope for the development of its own individuality and for the conduct of its own affairs, recognizes that there must be an equal co-partnership for common Imperial objects. For that to take place the United Kingdom must cease—in fact, has ceased to regard the great Dominions as children. She recognizes that they are great nations; that they are sons which must be taken into partnership and added to the efficiency of John Bull & Sons; otherwise they will set up as independent houses. Now, gentlemen, one of the first indications of this would be the establishment, I venture to think, of separate Colonial navies, under separate Colonial control.

PRESENT CONDITIONS AND FUTURE PROSPECTS IN INDIA
November, 1908
Professor G.S. Brett, MA, Trinity University, Toronto

It is impossible for the British Government at the present time to give up its administrative superiority simply for the sake of the Indian. Take the Civil Service. It is open to a native who can qualify, yet he cannot occupy a civil post as an Englishman can occupy it. He must be on one side or the other, and if he is on neither he is looked upon as a hypocrite by both parties. It is impossible for such administrative power to be vested in Indians born and bred. On the other hand, there is a large sphere of development possible in local and municipal administration which would afford positions for many natives.

BRITISH DIPLOMACY
November, 1908
R.S. Neville, KC

Great Britain has been, as the British Empire is today, the greatest secular force for good that ever existed in the history of the world. In her diplomacy abroad, as in her system of government at home, she has opposed tyranny, befriended freedom, and lighted the paths of progress. Under her international leadership, since the fall of Napoleon and the establishment of the doctrine of Balance of Power, there has been no general war though such wars were common before, and the world and every human interest have advanced more in 100 years than in any 1,000 years of previous history.

THE GERMANY OF TODAY
King Edward and the Threat of Germany
December, 1908
Professor L.E. Horning, PhD, University of Toronto, Victoria College

I am probably safe in saying that few of us dreamed that our King Edward would develop into such a thorough-going diplomat as he has proved himself to be....Without shedding a drop of blood, he has cemented Europe into what may be called a peaceful family of nations, first of all encircling and isolating the only nation from which there is today any real trouble to be expected. That is a terrible thorn in the side of the Germans.

THE MENACE OF SOCIALISM
February, 1909
E.J. Kylie, MA, Toronto University

Socialism means, in essence, either robbery or religion....As it is proclaimed by the ordinary street orator, it means robbery, it means confiscation, it means the plunder of the rich for the benefit of the poor. This kind of socialism...is justified...by the economic theories of Karl Marx....Intellectual socialism, for which, as you will perceive, I have very great sympathy, is a religion, is a creed, a faith, a belief in the future of mankind as an ideal democracy....It is said that out of 1000 people who die in Great Britain, 941 leave less than 200 pounds. I am not concerned with the 941. They are dead. But I am concerned very much with the children of the 941 in their struggle with the children of the 59.

A WEAK LINK IN THE IMPERIAL CHAIN
November, 1909
Lieutenant-Colonel W. Hamilton Merritt, Governor General's Body Guards, President, the Canadian Military Institute, Toronto

Suppose we liken the British Empire to a chain girdling the world, composed of alternate links of blue and brown—sea and land—we then have a symbol of the Empire. One weak link and the chain is gone. The blues would all go together, but each brown link might perchance exist alone. Canada is a very, very, weak link, and the best and first work Canada can do for the Imperial chain is to make the brown link of Canada strong. This should be her first duty to the Empire. Let us begin at the bottom, the land safety first, then we can look out for the sea. We got the worst of it on the water in 1812, but we did not lose Canada. If the United States took Canada tomorrow could the Empire wrest it from her if it held the sea? I think not. Don't let us risk it at any rate. Let us make our link strong by training the manhood of Canada, every man training to fit himself to serve at sea or on land in defence of his beloved country should it become necessary.

THE PSYCHOLOGY OF THE SUFFRAGETTE
January, 1910
Professor Andrew Macphail, MA, McGill University

Suffragettes are mistaken if they suppose that their labour is ended when they pause in the weary round of visits to the dressmaker, manicure, and masseuse, or interrupt their social and domestic duties, for so much time as is required to place a dainty ballot in a box. When they adventure into the booth they plunge into the world of politics and of crime, unaware that their innocent act may be the means of depriving a rich corporation of its booty, a poor man of his food, a worker of the right to live, a woman of her profession, or a criminal of his prey. They must not expect that, upon beholding the spectacle of a suffragette about to vote, all these forces of self-interest and evil will run backward and fall to the ground as dead men....When women place themselves in situations for which they are not qualified by their nature to fill with obvious advantage, they become a ridiculous caricature of themselves.

ENGLAND'S PLACE AMONG NATIONS
The Threat of War Identified
March, 1910
The Rev. W.H. Hincks, LLB, DD, President of the Methodist Conference of Toronto

One of the most serious reasons to fear war is because of the belief in both countries that war must come. An Anglo-German war is regarded as probable in almost every Chancellerie in Europe....We all know that the colossal German navy is not built for a floating museum, for the fun of fireworks. To ignore the danger is only to lay a plaster on an open sore.

THE EVOLUTION OF A GREATER TORONTO
April, 1910
William Houston, MA, Associate Editor, *The Globe,* Toronto

The population [of Toronto] at the beginning of my period of residence [1865] was not more than 50,000; today the population is close to, if not quite, 400,000. A fair way to exhibit the rapidity of increase of population is to take the statistics of school attendance. In 1865 Toronto had 90 public school teachers; in the present year we have 901....In 1865, four years after the street railway was started, there were only four miles of single-track horse-car railway, now we have 407 miles of electric railway....When the late Mr. Howard offered 200 acres to the city on easy terms of payment—practically a gift—it was only after long discussion and much hesitation that the offer was accepted. It is now Howard Park [High Park]. Prior to the acquisition of that great pleasure ground the City's only park was Queen's Park, which it has from University of Toronto at a nominal rental and on easy conditions; yet the lease was forfeited for non-fulfillment of these conditions, and in order to secure the park again it had to pay $6,000 a year in perpetuity.

THE BOY SCOUT MOVEMENT
August, 1910
Lieutenant-General Sir R.S.S. Baden-Powell, KCB, KCVO

Scouting, as you know, may be taken from a military point of view, but we take this scouting entirely from a peace point of view. The aim is to cultivate the principles which actuated the pioneers of civilization in nearly all corners of the globe, that is to say, trappers, explorers, frontiersmen, backwoodsmen, soldiers, and such men as you have in your North-West Mounted Police. These men promoted civilization under exceptional difficulties of climate or surroundings, relying entirely upon themselves to carry out their work, full of resource, energy, endurance, hope and pluck. Such men do their work far away from all applause simply because it is their duty, full of chivalry and self-sacrifice, possessing the best type of manliness in our race. These are the types we hold up to these lads as their ideals to follow, whatever class, city or country they may come from, or whatever religion or nationality they may be. Therefore, I believe the training and elementary work begun, and the supplementary work they are to receive, as the Scout masters gradually introduce these other attributes of frontiersmen and backwoodsmen and so on, will tend to make for manliness of character and good citizenship among the boys.

TORONTO AND TOWN PLANNING
March, 1911
W.D. Lighthall, MA, KC, FRSC, Metropolitan Parks Commission, Montreal

Now with regard to our Canadian cities....There is a sort of crisis at this particular time. The next ten years, most of us agree, will be the greatest growing time for Canada....Cities like Montreal, Toronto, Winnipeg and Vancouver are large enough to feel more than the beginnings of the slum and the non-planning disease....You are not actually carrying out a really large plan for the city of Toronto...every postponement of a year during the next ten or fifteen years is a very great mistake for the city of Toronto.

THE WIDER PATRIOTISM
Promoting the Empire
April, 1911
Castell Hopkins, Club President

We [The Empire Club of Canada] have, in the past eight years, had 218 speakers of whom 117 dealt with Imperial topics.

IMPERIALISM
Canada's Future Growth
May, 1911
The Rt. Hon. James Bryce, OM, British Ambassador at Washington

...and when the population [of Canada] has reached—as it will in the lifetime of many here present who are still in middle life—perhaps forty or fifty millions, you will be an immense power in the world.

THE DICKENS CENTENARY
February, 1912
Thomas O'Hagan, PhD, Editor, *New World*, Chicago

When [Dickens] had written "Pickwick" at the youthful age of twenty-four, he woke up one morning and found himself famous. There has been no other example of such early ripening in our day.

A STATE-OWNED ATLANTIC CABLE
February, 1912
Major M. Archer-Shee, DSO, MP, London, England

In 1902 the Pacific Cable [Vancouver to Australia] was laid…there has been…only one fault in the whole nine years…although that cable was laid over practically an unknown ocean bed at that time, and against the advice of people who said it would be eaten by torpedoes, destroyed by coral insects and so on.…Mr. Chamberlain stated the cable scheme would be completed by laying a cable across the Atlantic. That has not been done, and my object in addressing you today is to put before you the urgent necessity of laying that cable at once.

AUSTRALIA AND HER RELATIONS TO THE BRITISH EMPIRE
Germany's Intentions
September, 1912
The Rt. Hon. Sir George H. Reid, KCMG, High Commissioner for Australia

There is a great people, sixty millions and more, one of the finest peoples the earth has today—I allude to the German People, a people for whom I have the most unbounded admiration. We are kith and kin with them.…Don't let us talk of the Germans as if those sixty millions of people were all inspired with a hatred of our Empire, or a desire to destroy it. In that country, as in every other country, there is a peace party, and there is a war party, and I honestly hope and believe that the peace-loving millions of Germany exceed in number, if not in official rank, the war-loving people of Germany.

ARE WE EQUAL TO THE OCCASION?
January, 1913
J.H. Burnham, MP, Peterborough

There is growing up in this country undoubtedly a disposition among people who should know better, to forsake their duties and responsibilities as men and as members of this great Empire, whose privileges have come down to them and have enabled them the freedom and civilization which they have today. But I regret to say that there is one man enjoying the Senatorial dignity and this is his conception of the duties of citizenship....He [Senator Cloran] says he is in favour of the United States protecting us, rather than having us tying ourselves up to Downing Street in any way. I say the man should be stripped of his senatorial dignity....The point...is whether Canada shall continue to float along under protection of the British flag without incurring any expense or risk.

OUR NORTHLAND, ITS PEOPLE AND RESOURCES
February, 1913
Vilhjalmur Stefansson, Arctic explorer

Measles, syphilis, increase of pulmonary consumption, diseases from unhealthful food, all have co-operated in the Mackenzie District to bring down the Eskimo population in sixty years from two thousand to forty.

TWO TOKENS OF NATIONAL PROGRESS
In Praise of Riches
February, 1913
The Rev. R.E. Knowles, DD, Galt

I think it is a good thing we are having some men and corporations who are becoming very rich....For the development of the
nation we must have great wealth; it lies back of all progress in
architecture, in science, in education, in domestic life itself....All
we have in our national life above the mere materialistic has had
its roots in money....The money may be made in steel, but it
blossoms in literature.

THE INSPIRATION OF BURNS
1913

The Hon. Sam Hughes, Minister of Militia, then rising in power
and popularity, received enthusiastic laughter from his audience with the following story; he was conducted on a tour of
Robby Burns' home by a very nice young girl. She drew his
attention to a particular verse in Burns' own handwriting.
Hughes was immediately inspired to compose:

Gin a body, meet a lassie
In this gran' old toon,
Gin a body kiss a lassie,
Need a lassie froon?

"How would that do?" "I guess it's all right" she said.
Later, after hearing this story, his friend interjected "Well?"
Hughes said, "Well, what?"—"Well, did you kiss her?" "Good
gracious" said Hughes "I thought she meant the poetry was all
right."

THE EFFICIENCY OF THE CANADIAN MILITIA FOR DEFENCE

January, 1914

Major General Sir William D. Otter, KCB, CVO

The idea that the time is fast approaching when all national disputes will be settled by peaceful arbitration appears to me an extremely fallacious one and most dangerous of adoption....Peace can only be secured through ability to resist aggression...I feel duty bound as a Canadian to urge to the full extent of my power the necessity for the development of the Militia in accordance with that precept.

World War I and Post-War Conditions through the 1920s

In December, 1914, Prime Minister Sir Robert Borden spoke to the Empire Club about Canada's immediate response to the declaration of war. "We offered them an expeditionary force on the first of August,".... then...."I asked the Chief of the General Staff how many men could be efficiently trained in Canada at one time. He told me that....30, 000 was as many as could be trained at one time. We determined forthwith that 30,000 should immediately be put in training, and as soon as 15,000 or 20,000 should be required by the War office....we would send them and immediately enlist more, so that the number of men should be kept up to 30,000; and with that idea, until the termination of this war....we would keep men continuously in training in that way." Shortly thereafter the speaker was the Hon. Arthur Meighen, Solicitor General of Canada. He said "The world knows we are not fighting for territory. The stake is a thousand times bigger than that. The stake is as big as the conflict, and the conflict is a world convulsion. The stake is the destiny of mankind."

During the war speakers, one and all, referred to its anguish, to the courage and honour of the troops, to the resolution and solidity of The Empire, the contribution of women. And one, expressing in January, 1915, the country's total preoccupation with the horror, said that it seemed to be such as long time since the struggle began—that the period before the war seemed to be a remote time indeed, so that when looking back to the things with which we were all preoccupied before war broke out they seemed very trivial.

It was suggested at one meeting that as well as singing "God Save the King" those present should sing "Rule, Britannia." The speaker cited an inspiring incident when "thirty-one transports were gathered at the Gaspe awaiting the arrival of the British fleet that was to escort them,"....then...."They saw battleships and battle-cruisers of the Old Mother's navy coming over to convoy them across the ocean....One of the captains of one of our Ontario battalions said 'What about Rule Britannia?' No sooner suggested than done and with greater volume than ever before the grand old song rang out from the *Cassandra* and spread to the other troopships....[the British] never had such greeting from any of the sons or colonies or sister nations as they had on that memorable occasion when 31,000 vibrant, virile young Canadians welcomed them in song." The Empire Club meeting that day closed with the robust singing of "Rule, Britannia."

As the war progressed the Club began to hear from men who had been in the trenches including a private, simply entitled Private Peat, part of the first Canadian Contingent, who, wounded, with one arm useless and one lung infected, was sent back to Canada. He in turn sent for the girl he had met and fallen in love with in a hospital in England. They were married, and, with a total capital of $15.00 set out so Private Peat could talk to those back home about the war. He came to the Empire Club with the message that no one who went "knew what they would see when they got there." Some went for love of King and country, some even for what they thought would be the "fun of the thing....But....I never knew a man to go 'over the top' for the fun of the thing." While bringing home the true horror of the trenches he dwelt on the true heroism. He told the story of a young soldier, not more than seventeen, who stumbled into a field station with dreadful shrapnel wounds, a shattered jaw and a broken arm. He was without his greatcoat and shivering. When asked by a nurse why he had no coat he said his buddy had just been killed and as he lay there on the ground he looked cold, so "I just covered him up, and it doesn't make any difference if I do die; that is a very little thing."

The Rt. Hon. Sir Robert Horne, Chancellor of the Exchequer in the Lloyd George Government paid tribute to Canadian Colonel John MacRae, who wrote "In Flanders Fields."

And quoted:

To you from failing hands we throw
The Torch; be yours to hold it high!
If ye break faith with us who die
We shall not sleep, though poppies grow
In Flanders fields.

In August, 1919, General Sir Arthur Currie, Commander-in-Chief of the Canadian Corps, spoke about "The Last Hundred Days of the War." He told of the tenacious courage of the Canadians at the Battle of Ypres. A British General said that when he heard of the retirement of their troops on the left he anticipated disaster until he heard that the Canadians were holding on. Their commander said "It was your sons and brothers who saved the situation for the Empire." Currie followed by saying that there is no glamour or glory about a battlefield. "War is simply the curse of butchery." And at the end of his speech he added an emotional appeal "These men have come back....For them I appeal to every business man here present, I appeal to every woman here present, that they do everything in their power to see that not a single soldier goes without work....These men do not want sympathy, or something for nothing. They were an asset before they left the country. They are a greater asset now....Their bodies have been exposed as a living bulwark on the battlefields of Europe to save for you this nation of Canada....It will call for patience and tolerance on the part of the employer but I appeal to you to give these men jobs and pay them better than you ever paid them before."

But if his words were heard, conditions were changing and jobs were not there. The very year that Currie was advocating job creation, industrial strife was erupting throughout the country with strikes and lockouts as unions were fighting current working conditions and pay. The Winnipeg General strike, started for union recognition, spread into a sympathy strike by other workers in the city, resulting in arrests and civic disruption for weeks. Now the current issues brought to the Club by its speakers were such as the International Labour Conference in Washington, the "eight-hour day," the Minimum Wage bill, the "Open Shop," with opinions on both sides of the question.

Some jobs were created when, in 1920, five insolvent, over-built railways were taken over by the federal government, leading to the formation of the Canadian National Railway. The new president, Sir Henry Thornton, noted that there were those who, in a quest for competition took on the most formidable of obstacles, like climbing Mount Everest, or undertaking "the task….to try and make our Canadian National Railway system not only pay, but also meet the transportation requirements of the community and become the pride of the people of Canada."

And while the world wanted peace, one speaker, a British journalist, saw what he called "Peace complications" and gave a prescient look at Europe after the Armistice. He spoke about the Treaty of Versailles, hammered out amid fear that Communism would spread and complicated by nationalist movements within ethnic majorities. He claimed the treaty "made no provision for peace." It contained, instead, he felt, the germs of international jealousies and strife. Its main weakness was that it entirely ignored economic conditions. It cut up vast territories that had formerly been economic units, and "set them at loggerheads." He spoke of the Austro-Hungarian Empire, "A very rotten affair politically, but it was an economic unit….Now, when we set up the Jugo-Slavs and the Czechos, and Austria and Hungary and Roumania, and drew the new boundaries for Bulgaria, the whole economic unit was smashed to pieces." The new units became adversaries, set up tariffs and blocked communications. "They were independent. They had leaped from the Middle Ages—some of those people like the Slavs—and become a democracy leaving one leg in the Middle Ages." Noting that France had been convinced for four years that when the war was won it would draw on what it considered "an inexhaustible fund of gold "in Germany.

He said there was no such fund now…."France is in a very deplorable financial position." He paid tribute to Lloyd George, noting that "It was due to him that the delegates from Poland and Russia met. He is now the greatest personality in European politics." And he blamed President Wilson for ceasing to support the Allies in peace. "Neither as a party to post-war settlement nor as a member of the League of Nations has the great republic given the world the benefit of its help."

Then the Right Hon. Lloyd George came to the Club and, with Armistice barely five years old, voiced an eerie warning. "I don't quite like the look of Europe four years after the spree. When she [Germany] limped along into the Palais de Glace, hobbling on her crutches, she was willing to sign any covenant. She signed a solemn pledge that she would have no more war. But now she is mended, and she is filling her cellars with the deadliest and most destructive explosives and I am afraid that unless something intervenes there may be in the world again a catastrophe….human ingenuity is expending the whole of its diabolical power in inventing and perfecting and developing the machinery of destruction….That is why I want to see the British Empire strong and mighty, so that when her arms go up and when she cries 'Halt' these deadly weapons of war will fall down. (Loud and continued applause followed these remarks.)

General Sir Arthur Currie, who had spoken so urgently in 1919 about the necessity of finding jobs for veterans, returned to the Empire Club podium in 1925 to speak about the conquest of fear, not in war, but in peace. Since his earlier speech, full of hope, industrial strife had caused the loss of a million working days. Now he spoke of "a definite fear with regard to the present state of the country and with regard to our future destiny…" He mentioned rumblings of discontent and pessimism. "The fires of unrest were lighted soon after the war and instead of doing everything within our power to extinguish them there are many among us who are today trying to add fuel to those flames." He mentioned taxation, cost of living, unemployment, problems with railways, immigration, labour, provincial jealousy and misunderstanding, of the fear that our united country would come apart, fear that "the Maritime Provinces will secede to independence, the prairie provinces will pass to the United States. It is very much in common….to decry our country." But again Currie was optimistic with the strength of our history in mind, the courage of our people in war and said "if we open up the gate of our moral energy and our pride and effort, then will the tide come sweeping in to carry forward our hopes to the ocean of triumphant destiny….For no harm can come to our country if we conquer our shadowy fear and unworthy terror and if we keep our fathers' faith."

Fears were indeed conquered as the 20s continued with industrial development in the automotive, pulp and paper and mining industries. William Lyon Mackenzie King's new Liberal government introduced the old age pension, farmers' incomes looked up and national spirits rose—that is until October, 1929.

These were serious days but there was the odd light touch: There were numerous speeches on the subject of Australia, comparisons with Canada as the two young countries, similar in many ways, strove to outdo each other as part of the Empire. One Australian speaker, noting that he had heard nothing but kangaroo jokes since he came to America, gave considerable time to a comparison of the qualities of the kangaroo and the beaver. He extolled the virtues of the kangaroo, an animal that does not move in inches, but only in yards, like Australians, a peace-loving animal but one who, if challenged and backed against a tree, would put up a fight worth watching. "It is the only animal," he said, "the Lord ever made that cannot put its tail between its legs." Briefly praising the beaver for its teamwork, he returned to the problem of kangaroo jokes, claiming that he had spoken twenty-two times since he came here and had repeatedly heard the same story. An Irishman visited the New York zoo and inquired about that very strange animal in a cage. When told that it was a kangaroo, a native of Australia, he said "Great heavens, my sister married one of those."

It would have been interesting to attend the meeting at which a professor gave, whether intentionally or not, a stand-up comic act on the subject of "Public Speaking—Good, Bad, and Indifferent." There were, he said, four parts of good speaking. The first is position, which he illustrated by "standing steady." The next is breathing, and the trick is to breathe through your nose. For the edification of the meeting he stood on a chair with a paper and a mirror to show correct and incorrect methods of breathing and breath control, vibration and voice control. Vocalization and articulation came next and all were asked to watch the rise and fall of his diaphragm while he articulated "ch" and "sh" and "st" and the hissing and puffing required to do justice to "k." At this point he turned his back to the audience so they could see the movement of his lower body. He concluded with this advice to budding speakers. "Stand up, speak, up, and shut up."

EMPIRE
International Aid
January, 1914
The Hon. William Howard Taft, former President of the United States

My political experience on an issue that the title of your club suggests, makes me a little doubtful—or would if I were in politics—of my present association with you....We have reached a time in this world when nations and peoples are neighbours—and a great powerful nation with a surplus, who is thrust by circumstances into a position of trusteeship for another people, owes it to that other people, whether that other people realizes the necessity or not, to put an arm under its arm and help it on.

WAR AND EMPIRE
April, 1914
Sir John Willison, LLD, FRSC

The influence and authority of a nation, its power to defend its rightful interests, depend ultimately on that fighting strength in war, which it nevertheless may never be called upon to use. See...what is happening in Europe today. International boundaries are being altered. Solemn treaties are being torn up. Yet not a shot has been fired, probably not a shot will be. The strong will prevail and the weak will go to the wall without any such necessity.

CANADA AND THE GREAT WAR
December, 1914
The Rt. Hon. Sir Robert Laird Borden, KC, MP, Prime Minister of Canada

It is fitting I should speak to you of that which is uppermost in the hearts of men, the great trial and stress through which this Dominion is passing, in common with all the Dominions of the Empire at the present time. And I desire to emphasise in the first place my conviction, my supreme conviction, that the statesmen of Great Britain strove most earnestly to find an honourable way by which peace might be preserved and war avoided. And I believe no people more earnestly desired to avoid war than the people and nations that compose this vast Empire. Why is it that war has been forced upon it? The public journals today, the information you have got from many sources, make it unnecessary that I should say much about this. But I do desire to say this: it seems to me this war was inevitable. The policy of the German Empire under Prussian domination is foreshadowed in the words which found expression by the great Prussian statesman Bismarck in 1862, "These great questions are not to be settled by speeches and majority votes, but by blood and iron."

THE WAR
December, 1914
The Hon. Arthur Meighen, KC, BA, MP, Solicitor-General of Canada

At bottom it is a conflict of two schools of thought. There is the German school of Frederick the Great, of Nietzsche, of Bismarck, of Treitschke, and of Jagow, fed on the doctrines of Nietzsche for the most part, who worshiped force, who hated the ordinary virtues which applied, as he said, only to the herd and had no meaning when applied to the masters; in other words where applied to the nations. On the other side the British school of Bacon and Burke and of Pitt and Canning, Asquith and Lincoln and Wilson that pins its faith to public law....the school that believes...that the state was made for man, and not man for the state.

SIR JOHN A. MACDONALD, EMPIRE BUILDER
Reflections on the 100th Anniversary of His Birth
February, 1915
The Rev. Byron H. Stauffer

Of his early life we know but little, and for good reason—his youth was so short. He fairly leaped into maturity. He was a lawyer at twenty-one, and bounded into fame at twenty-three....I remember seeing him come down King Street. Spying a couple of men on top of about our only three-storey building that we had in town, and seeing them wave flags, Sir John jumped to his feet and took off his cap and answered the salute vigorously. It was enough for me; it was such an unconventional thing that I found myself in the skating rink in the afternoon well up at the front. Up rose Sir John to his feet. His rising was very deliberate; he took a long time to get square on his feet and as he was swaying back and forth with his hands in his pockets my Grit neighbour...whispered, "The old man is drunk." And our Tory neighbour in the next row in front of us said, "Drunk is he? Well he knows more drunk than Ed Blake ever knew sober, anyway"....Sir John's career, like a summer express train, ran in two sections....The first half ended in 1873; the second half began in 1876....The greatest test of life is in its power to resurrect itself after failure....What amazes us is when a man rises phoenix-like from his ashes, and continues his career and augments his power....He died poor, and that is the best testimony you can give a preacher or a statesman....The faults of some great men look great because their souls are great. Warts appropriate for a giant would deface a baby.

THE WAR AND THE CHURCH
March, 1915
The Rt. Rev. W.T. Herridge, DD, Moderator of the Presbyterian Church of Canada

As I daresay you know, in his earlier years the poet Coleridge was a Unitarian clergyman, and though he soon left the pulpit he never lost his pompous oratorical manner. One day he asked his fellow author and friend Charles Lamb "Did you every hear me preach?" Lamb chuckled in reply "I never heard you do anything else."

SOME WAR REVELATIONS
March, 1915
Chancellor A.L. McCrimmon, MA, LLD, McMaster University

A colonel stood before his mounted troops and said, "Let me give you this order; when you get on those horses, do not get off till I give the order to do so." They saluted and mounted. Murphy was pitched headlong to the ground. He picked himself up as the colonel turned around and said, "Didn't I tell you to stay on?" " Yes, Sor." "And you dismounted?" "Yes, Sor." "Orders from headquarters, I suppose?" "No," he says, "from hindquarters."

BRITAIN AT WAR
April, 1915
J.M. Dent, Esq., Publisher of *Everyman's Library*, London, England

One incident I found in reading through the law news in the American courts, where a German ship was brought up for not delivering its cargo. It was sent over before the beginning of the war with specie for England from America, so many millions of gold. It turned back when war was declared and secured its cargo in an American port. For this dereliction of duty it has been condemned, I believe, in a very heavy fine. Why did it turn back? It was a German ship, and the captain confessed that he had had a sealed envelope containing instructions given to him when he went on his first voyage, which he was not to open until he received a wireless message with the word "Siegfried" in it; he was to understand when he received that, that he was to open the package and get the message interpreted. He did so, and he found it to be: "Germany at war with France, Russia, and

England; turn back." Gentlemen, that letter was deposited with that ship in 1912, two years before the world ever thought or dreamed of war with Germany....there is a...poet whom the Germans have lately claimed as their own, they say that Shakespeare is far more German than he is English. Somehow, though they know him well, they have overlooked a few things he has said which we English people remember, and as Shakespeare spoke for England then he speaks for England today when he says:

> "This England never did and never shall lie at the proud feet
> of a conqueror,
> But when it first did help to wound itself.
> Now these her princes are come home again,
> Come the three corners of the world in arms
> And we shall shock them. Naught shall make us rue
> If England to herself do rest but true."

RUSSIA: BRITAIN'S ALLY
December, 1915
Lieut. V.V. Utgoff, Russian Naval Aviation Corps

I think that this war is good, not for Germans, but only for us, for Russia, because during this war our people begin to understand which is the best way to civilization; and I think that when the war will stop, our people will be together with all civilized countries of this world....Our government is willing now to give more liberty to our people. And even the Czar Nicholas, he is making also steps to help our people, to give them more liberty....Our Czar himself is a very good man, only he has not very much strength to himself, and now that the Germans are away he makes very good things.

WITH CANADA AT THE FRONT
January, 1916
Lieut. G.R. Forneret

Our transports went over in three lines and we were convoyed by certain battleships. One of them was *The Princess Royal*, a magnificent ship, absolutely the last word in battle-cruisers. She had been keeping some distance to our left flank. In the afternoon, about five o'clock, the cry went about the ship "*The Princess Royal* is coming in." Sure enough she was. We crowded the rail to watch her as she lazily overtook us. She was paying us the compliment of an afternoon visit. On she came, looming larger and larger. Now we could make out the great guns in tiers protruding from the forward turrets; now we could see the crowded fighting-tops; now the decks, stripped to the steel plates for action. Now we saw the crew, hundreds of them, lining the decks. Now she was up to our stern. Her band was playing "O, Canada!" As she started to draw abreast there was a broadside of British cheers from her—crash, crash, crash—with a vibrant human note of patriotism and fellowship. Then we went clean mad. We scrambled to deck, breaking for points of vantage, and cheered and cheered until we were hoarse and dizzy. So she sailed past, proud, rugged, ugly, huge and magnificent. Our ensigns dipped, and the deep-throated greeting crashed and echoed from ship to ship till she passed on and we stood gazing devouringly after her. There wasn't anything to say. It was just British glory on the sea—and we were British. A senior officer clinging to the davit next me, kept repeating hoarsely to himself, his eyes shining through his tears, "My God, My God," like that....The most unreal sensation for a beginner in the trenches is when morning comes, you look through the periscope towards the enemy trench to see the source of the danger—and none is visible....You are so apt to trust your eyes that one man always has to be the goat to prove to his comrades that there is danger. One of my men, after observing, went back to get his cap which was near a loop-hole that had been left open. I remonstrated with him, but he said nothing was going to happen to him. He took about three steps and crack! He was shot clean through the head from 200 or 300 yards distance.

PRACTICAL CONSOLIDATION OF THE EMPIRE
Women in the War
August, 1916
Sir George Perley, KCMG, Acting Canadian High Commissioner for Canada in London

[In Britain] we see women occupying all kinds of positions which have been vacated by the men who have gone to the front....Nearly all the men of military age have gone from the shops and their places are taken by women. Women are doing a great deal in the manufacture of shells and other munitions....Not long ago my wife and I saw in the north of England five young women, well-bred girls, working on the farm, milking, looking after the pigs and chickens....They were working from six to six for a pound a week...and the father of the chief one among them is one of the very highest officers in the command of the army in Mesopotamia....I understand that some Canadian women are offering to do this kind of work, and I see that the Munitions Board say they are getting short of men. Well, I hope that a way will be found by which the offer of these women to take the places of some of the men may be utilized in this country.

THE PRUSSIAN MIND
March, 1917
The Hon. William Renwick, LLD, Supreme Court of Ontario

I have been taking a course in Nietzsche and Treitschke, as also in the German Denkschrift, illumined by excerpts from the German papers in this country and the official utterances of Chancellor von Bethmann-Hollweg. The result has been most disastrous. It has utterly destroyed my capacity for judicial consideration. I can only say that if what I find in those sources is the capacity to think Germanically, I would rather cease thinking at all. It is the absolute negation of everything which has in the past tended to the elevation of mankind, and the installation in place thereof of a system of thorough dishonesty, emphasized by brutal stupidity. There is a low cunning about it, too, which is to me in the last degree repulsive.

CANADA'S PLACE IN WORLD POLITICS
In the Perils of Pacifism
March, 1917
The Rev. Charles Aubrey Eaton, DD, LLD

You cannot have a nation except through the travail and pain of sacrifice. There is nothing great in the world that can be bought at a cheap price, and that is why I consider pacifism, per se, to be a delusion and a snare. The pacifist thinks you can get results that are a power in life without sacrifice. It cannot be done.

EMPIRE CLUB WAR RESOLUTION
Annual Meeting, May, 1917
Resolved: That in the opinion of the Empire Club, each and every Government, corporation and person throughout the Empire should spend no money except for necessities and the vigorous prosecution of the war: and each person particularly should not purchase luxuries or other articles which will divert labour from the work essential to the production of munitions, supplies and other means for winning the war; and that all such persons should save as much as possible and utilize such savings for war purposes; and that the Empire Club urge the Dominion Government to take such steps as may be necessary to prohibit the importation of luxuries into Canada during the war.

HISTORIC TREASURE OF EMPIRE CLUB SPEECHES
Dr. Alfred Hall, Hon. Editor, Volumes 1915–17

First, observe the varied persons who speak; then note the places from which they come; then survey the subjects upon which they have spoken. Statecraft and Economics, Religion and Science, The Farm and the Battlefield, the Bench and the Bar, the Navy and Army, Homeborn and Foreign allies, Leaders of our Manhood and our Womanhood—all are here. The ringing notes of this lofty eloquence will live on to mould the public sentiment of the Dominion and to shape the public policy of our glorious Empire. Our future leaders must consult these pages.

THE SUBSTANCE OF MY LATEST RESEARCH
November, 1917
Professor Alexander Graham Bell, LLD, SCD, PhD

When I come to look back upon the history of the telephone, it seems almost like a dream that I was connected with it at all, so long is it since I have had anything to do with telephones—and I do not have a telephone in my own house within reach of my ears. So much of the practical development of the telephone has been in the United States that I think the fact that the telephone was invented in Canada should be more widely known than it is—at least in the United States. Until within the last few days, I have never been able to give a more definite date of the conception of the telephone than that it was somewhere in the summer of 1874. At that time I was residing in Salem, and went into Boston every day for my professional work in the Boston University. I spent the summer vacations, and also the Christmas vacations, at my father's home on Tutela Heights, near Brantford Ontario, and all that I have been able to say hitherto has been that the telephone was invented in Brantford some time during that summer vacation of 1874. But in looking over some old material, I came across a little pocket journal—a sort of day-a-line book—kept by my father, and I looked for any reference to his only son's appearance at Tutela Heights. Of course, when I went home, I discussed with my father all the various ideas of which a young man's brain is full, and I very well remember that I had a great electric motor which was to revolutionize everything; then I had this telephone, and I found that my father had made a little note in his diary on the occasion of this conversation. It was dated July 26, 1874. It contained very few words: "New motor; hopeful. Electric speech?" (with a big query mark on it) However, that gives us the date. I had described the telephone to my father on July 26, 1874, and many friends in Boston have preserved little drawings of the telephone that were made during the autumn of 1874. The telephone devised in Brantford was not made until 1875, when it appeared in Boston; so that the telephone was conceived in Brantford in 1874, and born in Boston in 1875. But Canada was also associated with a very important development of the practical telephone in the early days. It was in Brantford that the first transmission of speech to a distance occurred. That was in August, 1876. Previous to that, speech had been transmitted from one room to another in the same building, but the attempts to get speech on the rural telegraph line with one instrument in one place and the other in another place miles away, had been unsatisfactory; however, in Brantford, for the first time, speech was actually transmitted to a distance. The experiments on the 10th of August, 1876, were especially important, for they enabled me then to work out the division of parts that fitted the telephone to work on the long line. I can remember very well that by the kindness of the Dominion Telegraph Co. we had the loan of a line from Brantford to Paris, with a battery in Toronto here—a pretty long journey! The transmitting instrument was in Brantford under the charge of Mr. Griffin, who was manager, I think, of the local office at that time, and who is still living. The receiver was in Paris, eight miles from Brantford. I put my ear to the receiver, and arranged for people to sing and speak into the transmitter in Brantford. The instruments I had were only adapted for transmission one way, so we had to use two lines, transmission from Brantford to Paris being by phone, and transmission from Paris to Brantford being on another line by telegraph. When I put my ear to this receiver in Paris, I heard a perfect storm of noises—explosive sounds like distant artillery—in fact a hurricane of noises, all due to some peculiar electrical condition of the atmosphere. All persons connected with long distance telephoning now know what these noises mean. But mixed up with those storms, I heard the faint sound of a singer's voice in Brantford. The sounds were very faint. I could understand the words because I knew the song, but when sentences were uttered which were unknown to me before, it was a little difficult to make out the sense. Still, there were these faint human voices mingled with the electrical storm to which I was listening. The purpose of the experiment was to ascertain the conditions that would yield the best results. It is all very well to try parlor experiments, but the practical thing is to get on a long line. So I came, provided with coils of varied sorts—coils with a few turns of thick wires, coils with many turns of fine wires, and so on, and I had arranged with Mr. Griffin to change the coils in his instrument when I gave the signal. So I telegraphed to Brantford to change the coils, and instead of putting on the thick, coarse wires we had been employing, to put on coils with many turns of fine wires. I did the same thing in Paris. Then I listened again; and the vocal sounds came out loud and distinctly, and I could even recognize the speakers and the singers by their voices. I had been told by my father that he would not be there, and yet one of the voices sounded so like my father's voice that I telegraphed to Brantford, inquiring whether my father was there, and it turned out that he was—his voice was recognized by telephone.

THE WAR AND THE SONS AND DAUGHTERS OF THE EMPIRE
September, 1918
Mrs. Emmeline Pankhurst

A few years ago, when women were fighting for their enfranchisement, one of the arguments against them was that women should not have power of citizenship because they could not understand Imperial questions, and their coming into citizenship would be very dangerous for the integrity of the Empire. Is it not strange that, now that that question is settled, I should be here today as the guest of an Empire Club? Whether women are competent to deal with the vital questions of Empire as citizens remains to be seen; we are still young in citizenship; but the women of the Empire have shown that whether their brains can deal with those complicated questions or not, their hearts and their hands have been ready to take up the burden of Empire and to sustain it equally with the men.

WAR CRY
Annual Meeting, 1918
F.J. Coombs, President, Empire Club

The Great War is still upon us; the armies of the Hun are still plying their diabolical trade of murder, fire and pillage; our sons and brothers, and those of our gallant Allies on the Western Front...are still shedding their blood and laying down their lives in checking the enemy's attempts to break through their unconquerable lincs. God grant that the time may soon come when the beast will be hurled back over his own frontiers and the world be forever free from the menace of militarism, and such awful frightfulness as has been seen in Europe during the past four years.

WOODROW WILSON AND THE DOCTRINE OF SOVEREIGNTY
October, 1918
Darwin P. Kingsley, President, New York Life Insurance Co.

In all the Babel of voices discussing the future relations of nations the one great voice that is clear and prophetic and powerful is the voice of Woodrow Wilson. It takes us no whither to say that we should have entered the war sooner. Most of us will regret so long as we shall live our long period of hesitancy. Our delay in getting into the war will be costly. How costly to you and to me in money and in hearts' blood we do not yet know. But under the President's leadership we have been through that travail of soul which enables us now to say to the Government "Slay the great reptile, no matter what it costs." President Wilson in my opinion moved as rapidly as public opinion moved, he led it, and finally crystallized it by his timely and inspiring eloquence. We are all very wise now. It is easy, always easy, to be wise afterwards. But in his vision of a post-bellum program, in his prophetic forecast of what must be done, if all this precious blood is not to be spilled in vain, the President stands above all other leaders of nations and in really constructive utterances, unhappily, almost alone. He has said that after this war Democracies must unite, not as States, not as Sovereignties, not as mere governments, but as peoples. There sounds the prophetic voice. In that lies the only process by which victory can be made worth all its dreadful cost.

THE TURNING OF THE TIDE OF WAR
Fighting God's War
October, 1918
Dr. Russell Wakefield, Bishop of Birmingham

I trust that you will believe that every word I say is said by one who is satisfied of this—that the Allies of this war are fighting God's battle and are fighting for humanity.

FRATERNAL RELATIONS
January, 1919
The Hon. William Howard Taft, former President of the United States

Now, I did not come here to talk about the United States, or what she has done in this war, although of course, we as Americans are proud of the demonstration of our ability to raise a great army, and of what part of that army was able to do on the plains of France and Flanders. I feel that we may well be modest in outlining what we have done in this war, in the presence of an audience like this, of citizens of the city of Toronto and of the Province of Ontario, in view of what they have done for four long years in this war. Your history is remarkable.

THE FOUR PARTIES TO INDUSTRY
March, 1919
The Hon. William Lyon Mackenzie King

I have chosen [my topic] in order to emphasize a truth which seems to be fundamental in any attempt to cope with the industrial unrest which has followed so closely, and, one might add, so inevitably, in the wake of the war. If there is to be release from the thralldom of fear in which men's minds are everywhere held, it is the Truth that shall set us free, and the enforcement of the Social Justice which the Truth demands.

POST-WAR CONSTRUCTIVE PERIOD FROM A WESTERN VIEWPOINT
Post-War Euphoria
May, 1919
R.C. Henders, MP, Winnipeg

The clash of arms is past; the glorious days of peace with a complete and everlasting triumph of the forces of justice and liberty are here....Autocracy has received a blow from which it will, please God, never recover; democracy is completely triumphant;

and the real reign of the people is beginning to be established in the world....I say without hesitation that, if we face the aftermath of the war as we faced the war itself, there will be no difficulty at all.

THE LAST HUNDRED DAYS OF THE WAR
August, 1919
General Sir Arthur Currie, GCMG, KCB

I am going to tell you briefly something that I think will interest you. That is the story of the last hundred days of the war. I want to preface that by making one reference to the first engagement in which the Canadians fought, the Second Battle of Ypres. I remember after that engagement took place the commander of the Second Army, Gen. Smith Dorrien, came to me and said "I can never tell you General what the stand of the Canadians meant. When I heard of the retirement of the troops on the left I foresaw the greatest disaster that ever overtook British arms. And when I pictured men, transports, guns all trying to get across the Yser canal I shuddered with horror. Then the message arrived that the Canadians were holding on. I refused to believe it. I sent out my own staff and every succeeding report I received was better than the one before it." And the Commander-in-Chief of the army, General French, was good enough to say, "It was your sons and your brothers who saved the situation for the Empire." And the traditions which they established, traditions for not giving up, for determination to win, for endurance, were carried on and built upon by the succeeding men who came from Canada. We were able to build up in the Canadian corps what was universally conceded to be the hardest hitting and fighting force of its size on the Western front. I know the modesty of the men and I know that you would never gather that fact from them. But I think it is only fair that I should say it.

IMPRESSIONS OF MY CANADIAN TOUR
November, 1919
His Royal Highness, The Prince of Wales

The welfare of the whole Empire is, after all, the big question for all of us, and it has taken a new shape since the war. Because of their whole-hearted participation in the great struggle, the Dominions have entered the partnership of nations by becoming signatories of the peace treaties, and members of the Assembly in the League of Nations. The old idea of an Empire handed down from the traditions of Greece and Rome was that of a mother country surrounded by daughter states which owed allegiance to that mother country. But the British Empire has long left that obsolete idea behind, and appears before us in a very different and far grander form. It appears before us as a single State composed of many nations of different origins and different languages, which give their allegiance, not to the mother country, but to the great common system of life and government....The Dominions are therefore no longer colonies; they are sister nations of the British nation.

A UNITED CANADA
November, 1919
Leon Mercier Gouin, Quebec lawyer, son of the Premier of Quebec

We are still very far indeed from national unity, and from interracial harmony....Read our Canadian newspapers—your papers from Toronto, ours from Montreal and Quebec—and you will see how divided we are, how bitter still are our racial controversies, our class and clan antagonisms....We are divided because our aspirations have not been coordinated; because we have lacked national pride; and it is a virtue more necessary than any other...patriotism must be broad enough to include every one of us, to allow every one of us to remain true to the ideal of his particular race and faith and at the same time preserve undauntedly this blessed land of ours, our beloved federation.

CONDESCENSION

Prime Minister Arthur Meighen made a surprise visit at the Annual Meeting of December 20, 1920. President Hewitt, in introducing him as the Premier, expressed appreciation that the first citizen of Canada had condescended to come and say a word or two to members of the Empire Club. Responding to loud, standing applause Mr. Meighen chaffed the President for using the inappropriate word "condescension." "I hope the time will never come, that my life will never be so long, nor the office I hold so high and dignified that an attendance at the Empire Club will be anything in the way of a condescension." President Hewitt was not subdued and in thanking the Premier said…"and notwithstanding his dislike of the word 'condescension,' I know many a man who would not even have condescended; but the Premier did." As the Premier departed for another engagement the audience rose with loud applause.

"PROFESSIONALS IN POVERTY"
January, 1920

Rev Canon Cody, leading Toronto clergyman, spoke of the inadequate payment to ministers of the churches and teachers in the schools, the two great groups most vital to the heart life of Canada. He quoted a comment specifically directed at teachers, but equally applicable to both professions. "It would seem that one of the prime requisites…is the possession of a sound constitution and the ability to fast unostentatiously and meekly."

THE QUEBEC CODE AS A CANADIAN ASSET
November, 1920
Louis S. St. Laurent, KC, LLB

Mr. Stappells wrote to me the other day asking me to give him a short sketch of what he was pleased to call my career. I had in all frankness to tell him that so far it had been most happily uneventful and that I was still privileged to consider myself just an average Canadian with the average Canadian's healthy interest in the various problems which confront us these days of our young nationhood, and the average Canadian's sturdy confidence that the average men and women of Canada have it in them to at least blunder successfully through these problems, no matter how serious they may at times appear on the surface to be. I certainly esteem it a very high privilege to be your guest today and I appreciate that I owe it to your own desire to bring about better understanding between the French-speaking Canadians of Quebec and the English-speaking Canadians of Ontario....Your own Club is devoting some energy to bringing about more complete understanding between the Canadians who speak your language and the Canadians who speak my language, not because you or I expect personally to derive any immediate benefit from it, but because we both hope that those who come after us may avoid some of the petty quarrels we have had....Nevertheless, I might still hold to some pessimism, did I not hope and confidently expect from meetings such as these, that when we have come to know one another better, to recognize more fully in each other preordained partners in a necessary society, we will realize that if we have much to develop in Canada, we also have much to conserve, and that the national heritage can be and is the richer by counting in its assets the traditions and culture of two great races, the institutions and private laws of two great civilizations and, I venture to add, as inseparably linked up with both, the two great languages through which these traditions, this culture, these institutions and these laws have been turned down to us.

THE RELIGION OF IMPERIALISM
December, 1920

The following concluding paragraph, in a speech by Ellis Powell, author and historian of London, England, in December

1920, inspired a standing ovation plus three cheers and was quoted as a highlight of the season at the 1920 annual meeting:

"And you Canadians…looking out across your own vast Dominion…and then remembering that even your own magnificent Empire is but an Empire within an Empire and that that larger Empire of which you are a part, an indissoluble part, as it is set upon the loftiest ideals of human liberties and progress, can you stay bound to what you can achieve so long as that lofty vision inspires you, and so long as in the background of your lives and in the background of the Empire itself there is that Imperial Personality, that Imperial soul pouring down its inspiration upon your sons and daughters, and going on to a fate more splendid than any which has hitherto gladdened the eyes of the sons of men?"

OUR INTERNATIONAL OUTLOOK
February, 1921
Jacob G. Schurman, DSc, LLD

Historians are very apt to be blinded to the importance of events in their own day.…There is not a Government in the world today…that is not spending more money than it ought to spend, bringing it, as it does, from the pockets of the people. There is not a Government in Europe, with one exception, that is living within its income.…If it comes to competition in arms and competition in armament between Japan and the United States, Japan sees ahead of her only economic exhaustion. I think the Japanese are the quickest of all nations of the world in perceiving international relations, and soundest in their judgment, and the quickest to act upon it; and for these reasons I believe that Japan will be just as anxious as the United States and Great Britain to forward a policy of disarmament.

THE LEAGUE OF NATIONS AND THE FIRST ASSEMBLY AT GENEVA
February, 1921
The Rt. Hon. Sir George E. Foster, KCMG, DCL, LLD

The League of Nations was really launched with the adoption of the covenant or draft at the Peace Conference. After six thousand years of toilsome progress....After six thousand years of the trial of other methods, the power and might of armed force, the alliance of one country with another for selfish or partly selfish purposes, the dominations of great conquerors....All these methods have been tried with the result that at the end of them all the culmination was found in the unparalleled war of the five years from 1914, and the unparalleled and almost unparallelable disaster which has resulted from that war. The war is over, men; the armistice has been signed; the peace treaties are being signed one by one; but the effects of the war remain with us, deep in our hearts, deep in our homes, deep in every activity—economic, business, or other, as you please—and the trail of the serpent of war will remain with us for many, many years. In the face of this object lesson is it not time that the world tried something else? And is not this something that the world may well try? For if disaster and the trail of consequences which you know so well, and which so many have personally experienced, have followed this war which has just ended, what may be said of the trail that would follow another great world war? We cannot conceive it; we cannot face it; we do not want it; we will not have it.

THE STORY OF LABRADOR MEDICAL MISSION
November, 1921
Wilfrid T. Grenfell, CMG, MD, MRCS, LLD

Now, it takes a very long time for any man to work out his own vision of how he is to introduce a better condition of things; and it is exactly thirty years since I landed there in a sailing boat from England. I was a young surgeon, and my idea was that my contribution to life should be through the healing of the human machine.

In the opening remarks to his topic, "Our Nation Considered as an Ethical Idea," in January 1922, the Rev. Trevor Davies, pastor of the Metropolitan Methodist Church, Toronto, presented some sage advice!

There are three elements present in a successful speech. In the first place it ought to have something good at the beginning; in the second place it ought to have something good at the end; in the third place these two things should be brought together as quickly as possible.

PUBLIC SPEAKING—GOOD, BAD AND INDIFFERENT
April, 1922
Professor J.C. Newlands

Stand steady, use the diaphragm, articulate clearly, use spirit and don't be too long-winded. Stand up, speak up, and shut up.

THE OUTLOOK FOR CANADA
Work, Work
April, 1922
The Rev. J.C. Hodgins

A statement was made by one of the provincial ministers which ought not to have been allowed to pass unchallenged. Addressing a farmers' club up in Western Ontario he had the absolute stupidity to advise them to work only eight hours a day and take Saturday afternoon off. At a time like this when the world is short $300 billion of commodities, 25 million of the flower of the human race, with its potential manhood; a national debt of $2.5 billions; the markets of Europe closed to us; the only possible hope is that we shall work as we never worked before in our lives to pay our honest debts. To tell farmers at such a time as this to work only eight hours a day and take Saturday afternoon off is not only unmitigated foolishness, but almost a crime against the well-being of this country. No one will ever convince me that the sound axiom—that the more you produce the more there will be to divide—is false.

EMPIRE BUILDERS
November, 1922
Miss Effie Bentham, Barnardo Homes

More than eighty percent of the 27,000 settlers who have come from the Barnardo Home own their farms. That is good enough in itself, but the work is done because from the bottom of my heart I believe, and my friend, Dr. Barnardo believed, that if we wanted to do the greatest amount of good we must win the children for the Lord of all empires; and it is of vast importance to you, as Canadian citizens, that you should thank God for the magnificent contribution that God Himself has given to your Canadian citizenship through that divinely-led student, Dr. Barnardo, who was the pioneer of children's homes of this sort. I know of no other such homes in the wide world from whose door no single destitute child has ever been refused admittance for nearly sixty years. Do you know the reason why? Because Dr. Barnardo did refuse a little lad just after the homes were opened. This lad was so hungry and tired and forlorn, and absolutely homeless, that Dr. Barnardo said: "My little son, I have three and four in a bed, and I will get into trouble for overcrowding; I just can't take you now, but I will give you a meal, and will send for you when I can make room." In a week that little lad was found frozen to death, and Barnardo swore that with God's help never again should a single destitute child be refused admission.

THE BUSINESS OUTLOOK FOR 1923
November, 1922
Roger Ward Babson, International economist and financial consultant

Russia is in anarchism; Germany and Austria have collapsed; Italy is on the point of collapse; France is struggling under her burden; England alone is carrying the burden. Men have made maps, drawn boundary lines between nations, but in the sight of God and in the sight of economists these boundary lines are not recognized and ultimately, whatever our nation, whatever our creed…we must all suffer and prosper together in the end.

Attitudes, English and American

William Sowden Sims, Rear Admiral U.S. Navy (retired) spoke to the Club in November, 1922, and entertained members with some quips re the English, Scots and Americans.

It is said that the Englishman walks into the drawing-room as if he owned it, and the American walks in as if he didn't give a damn who owned it.

The Scotsman said to the American "And what part of the world do you come frae?" And the American said "Why I come from the greatest country on God's earth." And the Scotsman said "Well, it seems to me you have sort o' lost your accent."

A SPONTANEOUS SPEECH
January, 1923
The Rt. Hon. Sir Robert Horne, PC, Chancellor of the Exchequer in the Lloyd George Government

Apologizing for his informal remarks, Sir Robert told of the Scottish minister who suddenly realized he had forgotten to bring his carefully written sermon "I shall just have to tell you whatever the Lord puts into my mouth," explained the minister, "But I hope I will have something very much better to say to you at the afternoon service."

THE LLOYD GEORGE MEETINGS
War Clouds
October, 1923
The Rt. Hon. David Lloyd George, MP, PC, former Prime Minister, UK

I don't quite like the look of Europe four years after the spree. When she limped along into the Palais de Glace, hobbling on her crutches she [Germany] was willing to sign any covenant. She signed a solemn pledge that she would have no more war. But now she is mended, and she is filling her cellars with the deadliest and most destructive explosives and I am afraid that unless something intervenes there may be in the world again a catastrophe....The last was terrible; the last was full of horror; the last devastated and disrupted; but it was nothing to what will happen if there is another war....The next war might well destroy civilization unless something or somebody intervenes. That is why I want to see the British Empire strong and mighty.

SOME CANADIAN PROBLEMS
January, 1924
Edward W. Beatty, KC, President, CPR

Ever since Fate ordained that I should occupy my present position, I have been asked for expressions of opinion on everything under the sun, and a good many things besides....Economy is not an attractive word, nor an exhilarating slogan. People are never disposed to cheer the speaker who advocates retrenchment....We will never, perhaps, escape the necessity of large expenditures, but....We should spend for the purpose of development or for the purpose of securing greater economy.

CONFESSIONS OF A NEW CANADIAN
January, 1924
The Rev. Dr. J.R.P. Sclater

My acquaintance with Canada as a body, a community, was not made here or in Britain, but on the sand fields of Flanders. The first vision I had of Canadians directly…[was] in that tragic moment…during the first gas attack that was made outside Ypres.…A dying Canadian Engineer Officer was brought in; he was still conscious…in a whisper he repeated the same sentence over and over, "Cut off my buttons!" Fortunately somebody there was alert enough to understand what he meant.…He meant that the gas oxidized on the metal buttons.…So the buttons were cut off and sent home to a famous chemist…and the gas was analyzed and in an incredibly short time gas masks were sent to the front.

ON BEING SORRY FOR OURSELVES
January, 1924
Professor Bernard K. Sandwell, Queen's University

It is astonishing how easy it is to hear people discussing Prohibition, and I think that everybody is grieved about it. People who approve of drinking are grieved about Prohibition because they say it prevents men from drinking. People who approve of not drinking are grieved because it does not prevent men from drinking.…If my friends who are in favour of drinking would only realize the beauty of the fact that Prohibition, while it satisfies those who like a law against drinking, does not prevent men from drinking, then they would be perfectly satisfied; and if only my friends who approve of laws to prevent people from drinking would concentrate their attention on the fact that they have a law to prevent people from drinking, they, too would be satisfied.

THE PROPER LIMITATIONS OF STATE INTERFERENCE
March, 1924
Professor Stephen Leacock, BA, PhD, McGill University

What I am going to say, Sir, will give offence, I trust, to many present—otherwise it would not be worth saying to such a large gathering as this. It is too often the fate of associations such as this that the speaker spreads before them an after-dinner banquet of platitudes, offending nobody and pleasing few. My task is different. I am to speak on a controversial subject in which I cannot hope to agree with all of you, but I know that you will give me at least that respectful sympathy which you always extend to the people who come from our spacious and hospitable Province of Quebec. And therefore, for greater certainty, I think it wiser to say to you in a few words the substance of what I have to say. I will give you my whole wit in a word; and it is to try and establish this—that at the present age and in the present country we are in danger of over-government; that we are suffering from the too-great extension of the functions of the State; that it is doing already great harm to our economic life, and threatening greater still; doing a great deal to undermine the sounder principles of morality and self-reliance, and doing much to imperil the older and sterner spirit of British liberty on which our commonwealth was founded.

HISTORY AND LITERATURE
March, 1924
George Macaulay Trevelyan

There is nothing that more divides civilized from semi-savage man than to be conscious of our forefathers as they really were, and bit by bit to reconstruct the mosaic of the long-forgotten past. To weigh the stars, or to make ships sail below the sea, is not a more astonishing and ennobling performance on the part of the human race in these latter days, than to know the course of events that had been long forgotten, and the true nature of men and women who were here before us. Truth is the criterion of historical study; but its impelling motive is poetic. Its poetry consists in its being true. There we find the synthesis of the scientific and literary views of history.

THE FIRST LABOUR GOVERNMENT OF GREAT BRITAIN
January, 1925
Mrs. Philip Snowden, wife of The Rt. Hon. Philip Snowden, Chancellor of the Exchequer

I am not so foolish as to imagine that you have chosen that I shall address you briefly upon the topic of the first Labour Government of Britain because you are supporters of the principles and ideas which that Government represented; but I do not care in the very least about that. The only thing that matters is that the facts shall be known, and that if we cannot agree about those we shall—honest and sincere people all—agree to differ, which is almost the whole of the law and the prophets....Nobody was more surprised than the Labour Leaders themselves when the first Labour Government came into being. Not one of them desired it; not one of them sought it. I know most of them personally and how real and deep is their sense of responsibility; and had the choice been theirs they would have preferred, on personal grounds, a little longer period in opposition before taking up the duties of Government. But it was not theirs to refuse the opportunity so amazingly thrown in their way. You know how it came about. The Prime Minister of the last Conservative Government, to the astonishment of many of his followers, threw away a majority of more than eighty, when he might have held office for the allotted span of five years. He chose, as Mr. MacDonald chose later, to fling his unhappy country into the turmoil of a General Election, in order, it was said, to test public opinion upon the question of Protection; but really, as it is believed, because of the appalling difficulties, national and international, with which the Government was faced. He did not see a way through the difficulties which, later, unmanned his successor in office.

CANADIAN ART

February, 1925

A.Y. Jackson, RCA, OSA

There are a great many people interested in Canadian art today—more than ever before. That interest is sometimes like that of the old lady who was hurrying rapidly out of one of our Group exhibitions, and when asked why she was in such a hurry she explained, "I hate these pictures, but I am afraid that if I stay around here longer I am going to like them." Today art is becoming rather a fashionable and well organized commerce which is parading itself as culture, when art should be to us an expression of emotion. So the academic bodies, instead of looking forward, look backwards....Even fifteen years ago Canadian art was a vague term that brought to mind paintings which bore a strange resemblance to French, English and Dutch works. I do not wish to diminish its virtues; Paul Peel, Blair Bruce, Barnsley and many others won distinction abroad but they were not creating a native art. They lived abroad and made their contributions to European art in the fashion of the day. We have no record that they showed any peculiar colonial qualities of daring or originality. Nor do we see much mention of them in the history of European art today....In 1910 the Royal Canadian Academy sent an exhibition to England and I remember the disappointment expressed in the English papers in expecting to find something breezy and virile from a young country and finding only a tame acceptance of their own convictions....But the pioneer spirit in this country is second nature. We have had to find our own way of doing almost everything and, while we may admire the way they do things in Europe, we realize our way is the way for us and it was obvious that Canadian artists were not going to stand around forever in humble admiration while our bankers turned the spotlights on their cows....Any great part of Canada can be painted; it is full of character everywhere. We found beauty in it—at least we think so, though a lot of other people think we didn't....Another thing—the pictures which our critics and would-be experts have been most scornful about were the pictures they took most seriously over there. The modern painter is supposed to have no respect for tradition because he does not humbly ape it, remembering as he does that earlier schools only rose and survived because they departed from the tradition of their day. Millet was scorned in his day because he painted country clods in his pictures, stupid, boorish, unpaintable, unfit for the drawing room; and today the class who scorned them would pay hundreds of thousands of dollars to possess them....Now, a last word on modern Canadian art, because tomorrow we shall all be academic. When the last cow is taken from the drawing room and the walls are alive with red maple, yellow birch, blue lakes and sparkling snow-scapes, I can hear the young modern painter up north say to his pal, "There's the trail that those old academic Johnnies, the Group of Seven, blazed."

Montreal in Winter
December, 1925

Professor Bernard K. Sandwell of Queen's University, later editor of the then prestigious *Saturday Night*, amused his audience with a poem he had recently composed. In retrospect it gives some revealing insights to Canadian city life in the twenties.

The winter is a pleasant time;
The sun comes down and hides the grime;
The grime comes down and hides the snow;
By June they both begin to go;
That's winter.

The furnace coal goes up in price;
But the refrigerator still needs ice;
Girls wear wool stockings under silk;
Tall ice-caps grow on bottled milk;
The young take out their skates and skis;
The old, insurance policies.
In winter.

The kids upon the sidewalk slide
The cat is all electrified;
The car is full of antifreeze;
The Church congregations loudly sneeze,
In winter.

The winter is a pleasant time
In Florida or some such clime;
To Florida, I fain would go
To write these poems about the snow
In winter.

CANADIAN DIPLOMACY AND RESPONSIBILITY
February, 1926
Professor H.A. Smith, MA (Oxon)

[A] suggestion is this—that we should maintain, so far as we can
do so, separate diplomatic services of our own....But there is
this further question: What is our diplomatic service at Ottawa
and abroad to do? It must either agree with the British
Ambassadors or it must disagree. There again you have the old
dilemma. You know the old story of the burning of the library at
Alexandria many centuries ago, when Caliph Omar laid down
the rule that either the books agreed with the Koran, in which
case they were superfluous, or they disagreed, in which case they
should be destroyed. We are faced with a similar dilemma; if our
representatives only say "Ditto" to the British Ambassador...they
are superfluous. If, on the other hand, they disagreed...are you
prepared to push the disagreement to the point of independence?

PROGRESS IN CIVIL AVIATION
March, 1926
Sir Sefton Brancker, KCB, British Air Ministry

I remember an amusing case of a Colonial officer who had to
proceed to Baghdad, and was told to go by air from Ameer,

which is beyond Jerusalem across the desert, which would save three weeks travelling time. He had never flown, fearing that it was unsafe. It was a muddy day, and at the airdrome, the machines were having trouble getting off. The official became fussy and said to the pilot, "Who is responsible for the machine if it is overloaded?" The pilot replied, "I don't know, you had better ask the commanding officer." The official repeated his question to that officer, who very grimly replied, "Well, that is settled at the inquest."

LABOUR'S CONTRIBUTION TO COMMUNITY PROGRESS
Want Amidst Plenty
April, 1926
Tom Moore, President, Trade and Labour Congress of Canada

In spite of [her] boundless resources, Canada has her hungry thousands, her unemployed, and her industries idle. She has forests of timber, but not enough houses for her people; Tremendous yield of wheat, yet many are hungry; extensive possibilities of industrial development, but with many idle hands. Is it not a pity that someone could not fittingly and truthfully boast of a nation of homes, a well-fed and well-educated people, free from the burden of debt and fear, and want? That is really what the Canadian people would like to see, but cannot.

CANADA AT THE CROSSROADS
October, 1926
Charles W. Petersen, Calgary

During the last two census periods, between 1901 to 1921, Canada made a total gain in population of 3,417,000. During the same period we received 3,340,000 immigrants. Canada must apparently look almost solely to her immigration to augment her population....With one difficult problem; we have, as a matter of fact, two; 1) to get the people and 2) to hold the people we get.

EDUCATION IN BUSINESS
The Basics
January, 1927
Dr. Otis Randall, Dean of Brown University

There are only a few subjects that need to be taken in our schools and colleges for their value as education....It is not the subject-matter that counts, it is the influence that study has upon the student....Everyone must study English, because we must know our language, which is the tool we use in our work, the channel through which we express our thoughts....Then every man should have some knowledge of mathematics and general science, with some foreign language, some social science, which shows us how to live with one another. Philosophy and history are also essential for we must know where we stand, what went on before us, in order to know how to go on in life....But outside of these subjects it does not make much difference what you study....These are simply agencies though which we are building men and women....Something else...the cultivation and development of those qualities that make you and me worth while to ourselves and to our fellow men. I know no better name to use that to call it the spiritual. Germany developed their men physically and mentally to the extreme, but they lacked the third element, and that lack was the cause of the world disaster. If you leave out the cultivation of these spiritual qualities you simply make dangerous men.

EDUCATION IDEALS
August, 1927
The Rt. Hon. Stanley Baldwin, PC, MP, Prime Minister of Great Britain

The whole world today, with one or two exceptions, is singing loudly the praises of democracy. The whole world renders lip service to democracy. They have learned that cry from the English-speaking peoples. Our great task in the future is to show the world what democracy can mean. There have been democracies in the past; there are democracies today, but I like to think that no democracy today is even a shadow of the democracies that our children's children may see in years to come. Freedom, which you guard so well in Canada, freedom can only be maintained, as has often been said, by a constant vigilance. A democracy can only be maintained when every man, woman and child in that democracy means to do everything in their power to make that community better, stronger, freer. The reason so many democracies in the past have fallen is because democracy is always in the old world on a knife edge, or, as I have often expressed it, it is a certain point in the circumference of a wheel, and how often has mankind travelled on the circumference of that wheel working their way with infinite labour to a point they call democracy, but when they are there, go but a little further, democracy becomes license, license becomes anarchy, anarchy becomes tyranny; and man has to fight his way out of tyranny once again. We are convinced that we are on that part of the wheel, secure for the moment from either license on the one hand or tyranny on the other. It is our task to keep it there. We cannot keep it there without an educated people, educated not only in letters but educated in those deep, profound and moral truths on which our forefathers first of all built up the British Isles and went out to build up the Empire. You in Toronto, as much as in any place in the Empire, are the children of these men. From your position your influence on this great continent must be great, and must increase. Resolve, every one of you that you will all give your best thought, your best work, not only to the furthering of the interests of each individual among you, which, of course, is necessary, but to that greater community of which each of us is but a unit. Work for yourself, work for Canada, work for the whole Empire, and determine that so long as we speak the same tongue, obey the same God, obey the same laws, wherever we be situate, we remain to the end of time one people as the only hope of this world.

INDUSTRIAL CONDITIONS IN THE HOMELAND
The Tree of Good and Evil
September, 1928
The Rt. Hon. Hugh P. MacMillan, PC, KC, former Lord Advocate of Scotland

I [visited] one of the great paper mills in the north of your province, and there I saw the process whereby the immemorial forests of Canada are being converted into newsprint. I think hereafter we shall have to regard the spruce as being the tree of good and evil.

ABOLISHING THE ARCTIC
The Canadian Climate
October, 1928
Vilhjalmur Stefansson, MA, LLD, Arctic explorer

The point is, there are two kinds of good climate—there is a good loafing climate and a good working climate. I suggest that it is not a good climate where bananas and yams flourish, if men decay. Canada, except Victoria B.C., has a working rather than a loafing climate.

A GILBERT AND SULLIVAN REPERTOIRE
October, 1928
Frederick Hobbs and The D'Oyly Carte Opera Company

A Recital [was performed and it was closed] by Mr. Griffin singing, on special request, "The Englishman" from Pinafore, the audience joining in the chorus with greatest enthusiasm. The applause was so loud and long that the song was repeated, the whole audience rising and joining in the chorus, and cheering.

THE IMPERIAL SIGNIFICANCE OF GAMES
March, 1929
The Rev. Dr. J.R.P. Sclater recited a verse, with apologies to Wordsworth

Breathes there a man with soul so dead
As never to himself hath said
I'm sick of working for my bread
I'll go and play at golf instead

PALESTINE TODAY
March, 1929
Colonel Frederick H. Kisch, CBE, DSO

I am in Palestine as a Jew engaged in the task of establishing what we call the Jewish National Home in Palestine, under the auspices of the British Mandate....Perhaps I can introduce the subject well by quoting a phrase from my friend, Col. Wedgewood, who said "England has provided the picture frame, but the Jews are painting the picture." That is what is intended, what we are trying to do....Then I should say a word or two about the Arabs. It is sometimes suggested that the idea of Zionism is to interfere with the Arabs of Palestine. In the first place I would say to that that the Arabs have shown neither the desire nor the ability to develop the Holy Land. Their production in the field of agriculture was just enough for their own minimum needs. The country went steadily back. I think it is generally recognized that the world is too small to justify a country being left in an undeveloped and deteriorated condition if there is a people ready to develop it. In this case, also, we are dealing with a people that has come from this ancient land. I was once asked by one of the Arab leaders, the king who formerly ruled in Mecca, how he, an Arab, should be expected to accept the Balfour Declaration. I will give you my reply, which explains something of the historical background of Zionism. I told him I thought even he as an Arab leader would accept it, that the Balfour Declaration was merely the recognition of certain historical facts. The first fact was that the Jews were once the people of Palestine; the second fact was that the Jews were driven from Palestine by might, by the Roman Empire. The third fact was that the Jews throughout the two thousand years during which they have been scattered throughout the world, have retained a love and a race-consciousness for this Palestine. And the fourth fact was that what the Jews have given to the world comes from this very connection with this land.

WHAT IS A CANADIAN CITIZEN?
April, 1929
The Hon. William Renwick Riddell, LLD, DCL, Justice of Appeal, Ontario

There is no such thing, in strict terminology, as a "Canadian Citizen," just as there is no such thing as the "British Empire," or the "British Commonwealth of Nations." But—qui haeret in litteris, haeret in cortice—and he who is a stickler for the literal may miss the substance—there is no difficulty in understanding what is meant by the expression "British Empire...."

AUSTRALIA
April, 1929
Major J.J. Simons

Our emblem, as you know, is the kangaroo; your emblem the beaver, both are animals with adorable qualities. I think there was something in the minds of the early colonists of your dominion and ours when they selected peace-loving animals for their emblems, not animals that tear and claw and devour the other fellow. Take the kangaroo, one of the most graceful creatures that God ever made; it never kills a living thing in order to live. It is peace-loving; it never fights unless it is forced to, and when it has to fight it puts its back up against a forest tree and then the fight is worth looking at. And, gentlemen, the natural historians tell us that the kangaroo is the only animal which the Lord ever made that cannot put its tail between its legs....It goes ahead by leaps and bounds.

BRITISH IMPERIAL INTERESTS
August, 1929
The Rt. Hon. Winston Churchill, CH, MD

Here is a stronghold of the United Empire Loyalists. Here too are
many of those who have cherished affection and affinities with
Northern Ireland, with Ulster. I have had many ups and downs
with Ulster. I remember in the bitter party struggles which in
Great Britain preceded the Great War, that I had a quarrel with
Ulster, but I have been forgiven. I have renewed a friendship
with Ulster that I might have inherited from my father, and I
know that when Ulstermen make friends, they make them for a
long time....I said also at Montreal that the first interest of the
British Empire was peace. We have all that we require. We have
coveted no man's territory, we are jealous or envious of no man's
glory. We have our own repute, our own interests, our vast possessions in every corner of the globe, under every sky and clime,
we have resources sufficient to occupy all the energy and skill of
all our peoples for generations and centuries to come. We envy
no one. We have a great inheritance, and we are content to
develop that. All we require for its development from others is
peace, and that, I believe, is in no danger at the present time.
Peace, I believe, is securely established, and I think Mr. Hoover
was quite right in saying the prospects of peace were better than
they had been for fifty years. Peace, I mean, between the great
civilized nations of the world. I do not mean what disturbances
may occur in barbarous parts of the world where the Russian
Bolsheviks come in contact with other nations; but as far as the
great civilized powers are concerned, I believe the foundations of
peace are stronger now than they have ever been in our lifetime.
But, gentlemen, we must be careful of one thing. Subversive
propaganda takes many different forms and disguises, and we
must be careful that the love of peace, the sincere resolve to
maintain peace, which is so universal through all the nations
which felt the wounds of the Great War, we must be careful that
that love of peace is not used as a cloak to press forward propos-

als which would weaken or injure the enduring strength of the British Empire. We must be careful that subversive movements do not effectually masquerade in the cause of pacificism and philanthropy. I dare say you have seen for yourselves how again and again certain classes of people go about to coax, cajole, cozen, and if they could, coerce the British Empire into giving up its rights, its interests and instruments of its vital security....When I was a schoolboy at Harrow I heard a lecture from a countryman of yours, I believe he came from this city, Sir George Parkin. He lectured on the subject of Empire Unity and Federation, and I sat, a little boy in an Eton jacket, and listened to his words. I remember that he said that at the Battle of Trafalgar, Nelson had set the signal flying "England expects that every man this day will do his duty." "Oh," he said, "if you take the steps that are necessary to bind together and hold together the great Empire to the Crown, and if at some future time danger and peril strikes at the heart and life of that Empire, then the signal will run, not along a line of battle ships but a line of nations." That is what Sir George Parkin said. I did not see him for 25 years or more and when I saw him it was at a banquet— not so large as this, indeed, but one of those great celebrations held to rejoice that victory had been won in the greatest of all wars, and that peace was now restored. And I went across the room to him and I said do you remember the words you spoke thirty years ago in your lecture, and he remembered that. All his dreams had come true, the dreams and hopes that no one would have dared even to breathe in many quarters before the war have been accomplished as actual facts. Miracles, as they would have been regarded by Victorian statesmen, have happened as the inevitable results of circumstances. The Empire has passed through the fire of war; the signal for help, the signal to arms was prepared along a line of nations which surround the world; and if ever again a peril loomed upon us we are confident it would be repeated again.

THE BIRTHPLACE OF SOUND
January, 1930
O.R. Harvey, Manager, Research Products Department, Northern Electric Company Ltd.

The Laboratories worked until 1925 on the development of talking motion pictures, and in 1925 they felt that they had a product which could be commercialized. They approached several large American producers and tried to interest them in the process, but they did not meet with a very cordial reception; and it is a peculiar thing that at that time the motion picture industry, as far as both producers and theatres were concerned, was perhaps at the lowest ebb that it ever has experienced since its inception. However, Warner Brothers, at that time one of the minor producers, might I say, were persuaded finally to take out a license and start into the production of talking motion pictures. They were probably a little afraid to have their name associated with the business, because they immediately formed a subsidiary known as the Vitaphone Corporation to handle that end of the business. A picture was made by John Barrymore, and it was shown in the Warner Brothers' theatre on Broadway on August 6th, 1926. The picture was only moderately successful. At the time the newspapers of the day carried comments from the various heads of the large producing organizations, and it is interesting now to look back and read those comments made by those men. I think without exception they all stated that the talking motion picture business was simply a novelty, something that would last a few months and then wear off.

INTERNATIONAL RELATIONS
Commonwealth and Empire
February, 1930
Dr. Frederick W. Norwood of City Temple, London

"Commonwealth" is the word we are learning to use instead of "Empire" and it is a great word....[It signifies] a true Motherland surrounded by her sons and daughters who are in the Empire, not because they are kept there but because they want to be there.

A LUNCHEON IN HONOUR OF THE RT. HON. SIR WILLIAM MULOCK, PC, KCMG, KC, MA, LLD, CHIEF JUSTICE OF ONTARIO

February, 1930
The Hon. N.W. Rowell, in tribute to The Rt. Hon. Sir William Mulock

Probably the best test of a man's character and worth is the position he holds in his own profession.

Sir William Mulock, in response to many such tributes.

Possessing true and tried friends no man is poor. Lacking them the richest are in penury.

SPECIAL LUNCHEON MEETING IN HONOUR OF HIS EXCELLENCY VISCOUNT WILLINGDON

March, 1930
His Excellency Viscount Willingdon, Governor General of Canada

What is to be the future of the British Empire? We all of us dream dreams; I suppose some of us see visions; but I have got a perfectly clear vision of what I believe the future of the British Empire will be. I can see in all parts of the world great countries grown up to their full strength, co-operating together closely, all loyal to our crown and King, co-operating in all matters of business and public life, administering their countries on the highest principles of justice, freedom and fair play, living in friendship with their neighbours, exercising an enormous influence to procure peace throughout the civilized world. That, to my mind, will be the inevitable future of the British Empire; that is what I in my humble way have worked for during my public life.

The Depression

In December, 1930, an address by a director of a statistical organization put into words what the average person was thinking, "As we meet here today, we are facing the situation which was unbelievable a year ago or so among the masses of people. They thought that a new era had dawned, and that a constantly mounting volume of business and great expansion in manufacturing facilities would have developed….[speculators] even invented new formulas for the expansion of credit which were to prevent our suffering from the insecurity that had existed before….with unbelievable success, consumers were taught to buy with money they did not have." The advice he gave was that "hard work in sales and cost-cutting efficiencies in production and distribution are the key-notes of your 1931 business policies. Your reward will come later in the year."

Echoing this, Graham Towers, then Chief Inspector, The Royal Bank of Canada, said that "during the latter years of the prosperous period we were told frequently that a new era had dawned for business, and that the suffering and disorganization which arose from the trade cycles of the past need no longer be expected. Towers could not offer an optimistic outlook. That same year a Professor of Commerce from Queens University opened his remarks explaining that to be invited to the Empire Club to talk about business conditions was to be invited to pick a topic such as "The atmosphere of gloom." There was much looking back at this point to find the reasons for the depression. He mentioned that one cause was that the world, while experiencing a great degree of nationalism, is, at the same time, an economic unit of one. And he added that other causes were an increasing volume of world production, a declining annual output of gold, a crisis in banking and credit. And the effects were being felt everywhere, particularly in agricultural areas.

The following year a speaker quoted Governor Norman of

the Bank of England as saying "Unless drastic measures are taken to save it, the capitalistic system throughout the civilized world will be wrecked within a year." So sure was he that he added, "I should like this prediction to be filed for future reference."

A sole optimistic voice was heard. In January, 1931, a minister of the federal government expressed his own optimism with "I expect that at the opening of the coming business season we will find Canada happier and more prosperous, and one of the first countries to recover from the business depression that is world-wide at present." That opinion, while well received, proved to be without a sound basis.

But in spite of all the gloom, it was still possible to have a good laugh at the expense of the depression. One speaker noted that Eddie Cantor had been invited to talk about economic conditions. This was difficult as he had just joined the Society for the Elimination of the Word "Depression" from Everyman's Vocabulary. He therefore began his remarks with "Gentlemen, this is not a depression but candor compels me to admit that it is the smallest boom I have seen in several years." And Stephen Leacock, professor of economics at McGill University and foremost Canadian humorist, noted that, while assessing the causes of the depression, some had decided that Mackenzie King was the cause. "Sir I am a stout Conservative," Leacock said, "but I do not believe that it is among the sins for which Mackenzie King will some day have to answer."

In the midst of the depression an event of great significance happened in Canada. In 1931, by Statute of Westminster in England, Canada's colonial status was ended. This prompted a British guest to the Club to say that recently an editor from the United States had suggested to him that Great Britain might settle its debt to the U.S., ongoing since the war, by selling them Canada. When the Brit demurred, the American went on to say, "Don't you own Canada?" The reply was "Are you quite sure we could deliver the title? I have the impression that Canada is owned by Canadians and nobody else whatsoever." (This prompted enthusiastic calls of "here, here" from the audience.)

War debts were still very much a contentious subject. A speaker noted that Germany, with a debt of 150 billions of dollars had no gold and only paper money which was of no use, unless the British who desired that kind of payment take it back to Germany and "sit there and drink German beer until it is all drunk up."

The world, and in particular the Empire, had its eye on India during these years and speakers, British and Indian, came to the Club to express a variety of views as to the solution to the current "discontent." In 1933 the Marquis of Lothian expressed what he said was the predominant opinion in England. His words showed how uncertain the British were in letting go altogether of control. "Doubtful as the future must be, the only thing to do is to proceed along the lines laid down by the Indian National Congress, to try to bring into being a Federation for All India in which Indian India, with its stable traditions, is balanced by Britain with its more democratic methods; in which real responsibility for their own affairs is entrusted to the vote of the Indian opinion....and that Great Britain should retain in its hands safeguards which, while they will only be called into effect if India should produce legislatures incapable of administering stable government, will yet be effective."

An Indian speaker brought to the Club's attention the changes in India that would preclude going back to pre-war status, one of which was the new role of women in the "civil disobedience" movement under Ghandi. There were about 5000 women sent to jail, "and they were women drawn from the highest of castes....women who formerly would not have been seen walking along the streets but who would have considered it a loss of dignity and lowering to their prestige if they were seen by male eyes. At the public meetings, thousands of women gathered together and they addressed the public meetings and were arrested by the law officers of the government and imprisoned."

Views of the term "Empire" were changing and the use of "Commonwealth" was more prevalent. This change was commented upon in 1933, with Daniel Webster quoted as epitomizing the old view of Empire, "It is a power which has dotted over the whole surface of the globe with her possessions and military posts; whose morning drum beat…circles the earth with one continuous and unbroken strain—the martial airs of England. How changed is our view today! Our theory today is not that of an Empire vested with force. We have an Empire resting on liberty and free associations, a family of free and equal sovereign states."

At the head of this Empire was a new king who came to the role after the abdication of his brother and who had never expected this responsibility to fall on his shoulders. The Hon. Charles Dunning, a Canadian who had represented our country at the coronation and the Imperial Conference, spoke in December, 1937 of his impressions. He spoke of the gathering of the Empire Parliamentary Association in Westminster Hall. "On that day there were gathered at tables similar to these down the length of the great hall, representatives from all of the Legislatures of the British Empire, and at the top of the historic stone steps a long head table, similar to this, and in the centre His Majesty, the King, flanked on either side by the Prime Ministers of the countries of the British Commonwealth of Nations. His Majesty, the King, facing one of the great ordeals of his life, in some respects an ordeal greater than the Coronation, for his duty that day was to do what had never been done before, to respond to the toast to his own health before a gathering of the parliamentarians of his Empire….There have been stories that our King suffers from disabilities which prejudice him in the performance of his duties. Rumours about his health. I can say without fear of contradiction from any one who has been close to His Majesty that physically His Majesty King George the Sixth is an athlete in very fine physical condition. Disability? Yes. From his youth up he has suffered from an impediment in his speech and one of the best evidences of the character of the man which I can give is the picture of him facing that ordeal before the most critical audience….He proceeded steadily from beginning to end. True, it was a fight, a steady, sustained fight, but the kind of fight that you could feel the speaker winning every second against the greatest odds."

The young king would show that strength of character sooner than any realized when, in World War II, he and his queen gave their country strength by example. And that coming war was the topic of many dissertations in the late 1930s at the Empire Club podium.

UNEMPLOYMENT
October, 1930
Harold B. Butler, CB, Deputy Director, International Labour
Office, League of Nations, Geneva

One can say without exaggeration—and probably it is an under-statement—that there are six and a half million men and women out of work in Europe....[and] five million persons out of work on this continent....I am sure it would not be an over-statement to say that perhaps fifteen millions of people are out of work in the world.

WOMEN 1830 AND 1930
November, 1930 (Ladies Day)
The Hon. Cairine M. Wilson, Canada's first lady Senator

Until your invitation was conveyed to me the day preceding my introduction into the Senate of Canada, I did not quite realize that from a position of obscurity I had suddenly emerged into prominence....History has shown many isolated instances of famous women, but these took no part in bringing forward their sisters....For thousands of years we have been obliged to accept a man-made estimate of our capabilities, and to rely for recognition upon his favour...This is now past, and those of us who have attained to a certain position must strive to show ourselves worthy....Dr. Gregory, with a certain irony in 1784 [gave his opinion] in his Legacy to his Daughters "If you happen to have any learning, keep it a profound secret"....In the United States in 1830...Margaret Fuller decidedly upset the conventions of the staid city of Boston by sitting down at a table in the Public Library to read a book....Teaching was practically the only employment open to women of the middle classes in the first half of the nineteenth century....It was only women with excep-tional powers who tried to surmount the difficulties of obtaining instruction....We, in Canada, have obtained the vote with so lit-tle difficulty that I fear we do not sometimes value it as we should....With many questions we have a more intimate acquaintance than men, and already women's influence has brought about much needed social reforms.

THE APPLE CART AND THE BRITISH EMPIRE
January, 1931

Maurice Colbourne, a famous actor, and close friend of George Bernard Shaw, addressed the Empire Club just two hours before he was scheduled to be on stage at the theatre in Shaw's *The Apple Cart*. In deference to the Empire Club traditions he entitled his speech "The Apple Cart and the British Empire." It was composed mainly of Shaw anecdotes. He told the story that Shaw, when it was suggested to him by a reporter that His Majesty the King was going to offer him a title, replied, "Well, I have not heard anything about it yet, but I tell you what I will do; if I can think of a title that is more famous than Bernard Shaw I will give the matter my serious consideration."

Applause
February, 1931
Rabbi Barnett R. Brickner

Rabbi Barnett R. Brickner, responding to enthusiastic applause from the audience as he rose to speak, said "Applause partakes of a religious character; that which is given a speaker on rising is an indication of faith; as the speaker continues his remarks, applause might be an indication of hope; and when he finishes and sits down applause is an indication of charity, and I wish to remind you that of all these cardinal virtues charity is the greatest."

THE CURRENT BUSINESS SITUATION
December, 1931
Professor W.C. Clark, Queens University

I have not the time to give a comprehensive analysis of the causes which have led to the present recession. However, to obtain a modicum of background, I would like to make brief reference to three or four special aspects of the depression which are important for an understanding of its nature and for the consideration of possible remedies. In the first place, we should be careful to note its world-wide character. Never before has the world witnessed a depression so comprehensive in its economic character and so extensive in its geographic scope. Every important aspect of the economic system, and every important country of the world have been affected. Moreover the process of influence has been cumulative. As each country came to be affected, it, in its own turn, exercised a depressing influence upon other countries, thus continually extending and intensifying the process of economic decline. President Hoover has recently summarized the measure of this international deterioration as follows: "Within two years there have been revolutions or acute social disorders in nineteen countries, embracing more than half the population of the world. Ten countries have been unable to meet their external obligations. In fourteen countries, embracing a quarter of the world's population, former monetary standards have been temporarily abandoned. In a number of countries there have been acute financial panics or compulsory restraints upon banking."

THE MANCHURIAN CRISIS
January, 1932
The Hon. Vincent Massey

Canada needs no argument to show that the situation in Manchuria is one to command her active interest. No disturbance as grave as this, and which affects in its immediate proximity one-third of the population of the world, can very well be isolated. As a matter of fact we have not forgotten the lesson which we learned in 1914 of what an obscure crime in a Balkan state can mean. We are therefore not unmindful of what events may flow from the destruction of a few metres of railway line four months ago at an unknown place in Manchuria—the Balkans of Asia. We may well be conscious of an added reason for concerning ourselves with this latter question. We belong to an international body whose duty it is to consider just such things, and the Council of the League of Nations represents the board of directors of a corporation of which we are shareholders and for whose actions we have a full share of responsibility. Again, it is for us, with the full obligation of nationhood, to arrive at an independent opinion as to whether the terms of the Treaty of Washington of 1922, which enjoins its signatories, amongst other things, "to respect the sovereignty, the independence and the territorial and administrative integrity of China," have been infringed.

MUSSOLINI AND THE NEW ITALY
February, 1932
Dr. William Sherwood Fox, BA, MA, PhD, LLD, FRSC

Primarily, Fascism is an organized attempt to realize once more in Italian politics the effective power formerly exercised by the heads of the old Roman Republic, and later of the Roman Empire. The symbol of power of the ancient authorities was the bundle of rods and axes borne by the lictors; from these bundles, or Fasces, comes the name Fascismo. Broadly speaking, the Fascists are the best men of the younger generation of Italians, and by the best I mean the best educated, the most self-sacrificing in their patriotism and the most industrious. The organization exists, on the one hand, to oppose and suppress Bolshevism, and, on the other, to effect in Italy that kind of social and economic revolution which, for example, the English-speaking peoples have gained by slower and more constitutional means. Certain over-enthusiastic Fascists declare Fascism to be a method of government applicable to any nation; personally, I do not believe it; 1 am strongly of the opinion that it should he regarded as Italian only, and its success estimated solely in its effect upon Italy....But we must not rate him [Mussolini] as a purely selfish nationalist, for in his endeavours to redeem his beloved Italy from anarchy and from economic and spiritual ruin at the same time he saved all of Western civilization from these very same calamities. There is no doubt that the one human being who is responsible for the stemming of the tide of Bolshevism in its westward flow is Mussolini. But, you will ask, should Fascism therefore not be invoked for the political and economic healing of all the Western nations? My emphatic reply is, "No," for in such a case as that we should each of us want to be a Mussolini.

THE NEW GERMANY
November, 1932
Professor Victor Lange, PhD

The temporary withdrawal of Germany from the disarmament conference, after years of patient but profoundly disappointing discussions at Geneva, meant nothing else but an appeal to the world to clearly indicate whether they want to go towards destruction and a repetition of 1914 or towards peace. There is no truth in the repeated newspaper assurance of Germany's will to rearm. Germany asks of the world, not only equality and political recognition—but what we young people want is something more difficult to give and something less easy to ask for—understanding.

UNEMPLOYMENT COMPENSATION IN WISCONSIN
December, 1932
Professor Harold M. Groves

The human wastage caused by unemployment is second only to that caused by war. We need some war-time courage in facing this problem. Charity is no solution of the unemployment problem; it is a necessary drug for a sick patient. But what we need most is some preventive medicine.

OUR INDIAN PARTNER
January, 1933
The Marquess of Lothian

Now, let me, in a few words, give you some idea of the extent and nature of the problem. India contains three hundred and fifty-two million people—as many as are in the whole of Europe, excluding European Russia. It falls into two natural divisions— British India which is that two-thirds to three-quarters of India which is directly governed by Great Britain, and Indian India which is governed by hereditary Indian princes of whom there are about a hundred and twenty-five important ones and five hundred minor ones....It is the greatest experiment, as I said at the beginning, to which any nation has ever set its hand—to bring into being a system of federal parliamentary government for three hundred and fifty million people, divided as the Indians are divided. There is, in my view, no other way but to move forward, resolutely and cautiously, in the hope that when you do appeal to man's better nature, when you do put on him or her real responsibilities, they rise to them and at the end of the thirty years, people will say that the political genius of this ancient race of which you are a part here has not faltered at the threshold of the greatest task put on them and in its wisdom it has guided India over the most difficult transition that has ever confronted a great people.

DISARMAMENT
January, 1933
The Hon. Maurice Dupre

I am convinced that without some form of disarmament the whole League system of outlawing war and peacefully settling disputes is in danger of collapse. I cannot conceive of the League of Nations surviving outbreaks in the Orient. I cannot conceive of it surviving failure to check that armament race which, as certain as night follows day, will result if the Geneva Conference collapses. We know the course of such a race. It is straight over the precipice and into the abyss of war. But would the European armament race, with all its disastrous consequences, involve us? Well, gentlemen, it is unnecessary to remind an Empire Club that we are a Dominion in the British Commonwealth of Nations. It is, I am sure, equally unnecessary to remind you that in the world of today there can be no longer isolation splendid or otherwise. The clashing rivalries and rumbling discontents of Europe may seem a long way off, but since 1914, we have known that a shot fired in a Polish corridor is heard across the Peace River and on Yonge and King Streets in Toronto. As Sir George Perley so finely put it last February in Geneva: "Bitter experience has taught us in Canada that under present conditions we live in a world of interdependent states and fifty thousand Canadians who will forever sleep in European soil are silent witnesses to that fact." So Canada must play its part in this great effort to reduce armaments as a step on the road to world peace.

THE RIDDLE OF THE DEPRESSION
February, 1933
Professor Stephen Leacock

When you ask the ordinary person what has caused the depression, you get a great number of answers. In the current press and in the current speech, you read and hear, perhaps, that it is caused by the gold standard, by the currency, by the collapse of the monetary system. I don't think so. Some people say that Mackenzie King did it. Sir, I am a stout Conservative, but I do not believe that it is among the sins for which Mackenzie King will some day have to answer. No single person, Liberal or Conservative, caused it. No currency, no tariffs caused it; not even national exclusiveness, the sin of our time, caused it. There is a peculiar flaw in the mechanism of the life we live; there is a peculiar defect in our wonderful apparatus of production; there is a peculiar power in our sudden inheritance of how to produce goods without a corresponding knowledge of how to organize society to use it. Sir, there would have been a depression if you had had world free trade; there would have been a depression if we had had no war; there would have been a depression if we had had a universal gold standard; and there would have been a depression even if we had had universal goodwill. Those things have not caused it.

MAN-MADE REMEDIES FOR A MAN-MADE DEPRESSION
February, 1933
Professor Gilbert Jackson

But what happened in 1928 and 1929, in the final boiling up of the speculative pot in Wall Street? There is no mystery as to what happened. After all, Wall Street is only the St. James Street of the United States—and the whole world has access to Wall Street when it wants. In 1928 and 1929 occurred the final frenzy which has destined to shake civilization. Men were growing fabulously rich on paper every day. Men were growing rich, not because they had contributed to the welfare and happiness of mankind, but because they had bought International Nickel (or Noranda, or Smelters, or General Motors, or United States Steel, or any one of a hundred other stocks). We decided to do likewise. The whole world decided to do likewise. There was such a flood of money from the channels of ordinary business into stock specu-lations, as the world had never seen, and, I hope, will not again see. From south, west and north, American money flowed to New York. From north and west, Canadian money flowed as fast. A great tide of European money flowed across the ocean to New York. Finally there was not enough money left in the ordinary channels of business to conduct the trade of the world; and the trade of the world broke down.

THE PUBLIC AND THE POLITICIANS
March, 1933
Grattan O'Leary

If there is one myth in this country greater than the myth of a strong silent man, it is the superstition that business men are invariably or necessarily successful in public life....One of the things wrong in Canada today is that we have too many business men interfering in government or trying to interfere to the detriment of the public weal....Well, I ask you...if you think, in the light of what has happened in the last few years, whether the business men of this country saw what was coming? If you think they did and don't want to become cynical, then I ask you never, never to go back and read the annual statements of our bankers and financial magnates—those pompous, pontifical, statements they gave us during the past ten years—if they were right in a single instance, I have been unable to discover it!....We heard that cry in Canada....Governments must not interfere with business....But when prosperity ceased...the rugged individualists became rugged "chissellers," they came to Ottawa like locusts to ask the Government to save them from their own folly with public money....In all the years I have been in Ottawa, I have never yet seen a deputation come to Parliament Hill, demanding government not to make a certain expenditure but I have seen parliament stormed, day after day, week after week, by people demanding social services, branch lines or railways, or some other expenditure. These are the things that you are paying for now....My main point is this: Constant abuse of politicians, constant attacks upon the efficiency and integrity of public men is having a bad effect in this country, resulting in destroying of public confidence in our representative constitution and instilling in the minds of our younger generation that public life and all politicians are corrupt.

Go to the Devil
October, 1933
A.J. Adams, Verger, Winchester Cathedral

William the First was asked to give wood for the building of the cathedral. His reply was, "You may have as much as you can cut in four days." The Bishops in those days had such power over their people that they conscripted four hundred men and in the four days given, they emptied William's hunting ground. They left one tree. That tree still stands today, the Gospel Oak. William was so angry at losing his forest that he pulled down thirty-two hamlets and seven churches on the other side of Winchester and he planted another forest and called it the New Forest. I am going to take this privilege of asking your President, Major Baxter, to accept a piece of wood from a sister tree of that Gospel Oak. The wood was given by William the First. (Gavel presented to Major Baxter.)

At Winchester College there is a 700-year-old historic building, St. Cross, that was originally built as a refuge for old men. In defiance of an old rule that no photographs were to be taken on Sunday an American visitor set up his tripod to take pictures. One of the elderly residents immediately protested and tried to stop the photographer.

The old man reported the incident to the master of St. Cross who was, by the way, a clergyman. The master asked the old man what had been said. "He was rude to me," said the old man.
"What did he say?"
"I don't like to repeat it, Sir," said the old man.
"Why not?," asked the clergyman.
"Because, Sir, you wouldn't like to hear it," was the reply.
"Well, what did he say?"
"He told me to go to the devil, Sir."
"He did! And what did you do?," enquired the master.
"I came to you, Sir."

THE FUTURE OF THE THEATRE
February, 1934
Raymond Massey, actor

In a moment I would like to make an attempt to answer the question as to whether the talking pictures or television will kill or even affect the theatre. In the first place, the theatre is the soul, the G.H.Q., the autocrat of the entertainment business. The moving picture even with dialogue and the ultimate inclusion of the third dimension is merely a reflection of primary theatrical effect which is in its pure form in the theatre. I will go so far as to say that no acting on the screen, however much the product of genius, can compare with a great flesh and blood perform- ance on the stage.

THE THEATRE
February, 1935
Dame Sybil Thorndike, CBE, actress

That is the function of the theatre, to interpret human beings to each other, to interpret human beings from A to Z. Audiences will impersonate themselves in the very actors that are playing and the whole crowd together will feel and respond en masse, and that has value, we believe, and we have been taught and told in the old saying of the Gospels where two or three are gathered together when there is an instinct for some fine thing, there is a spirit present which will lead men away from their personal selves and sink them, or rather raise them up into a larger self, the self of his community, the self of his country, the self of something larger than just his own little personality....Well, there is another part of us which is much more important than just the body which is only an outward expression of the inward thing and that is the most precious thing we have got, our imagi- nation. And it is to keep your imagination childlike that the the- atre exists. The theatre exists to keep us always surprised, always enquiring, always wanting to find some new aspect, always want- ing to see some new point of view, to keep our minds, our mentalities, flexible, not willing to be settled....Why can't we just go to the theatre when we feel like it and sit more or less dozily, or just as we like. Why do you make all this fuss about it? Because you will never get what you want from an art which has that valuing. You will never get from it anything that will be of real value unless effort is made, unless a real vigorous effort is made, and that is the main difference between the art of the theatre and the art of the cinema. The cinema has pandered to this devil of dullness. It has pandered to this thing which wants us to make no effort, which wants us to sit still.

COUNTRY DOCTOR IN NORTHERN ONTARIO
March, 1936

The speaker, Dr. Allan Roy Dafoe, OBE, had gained instant world fame in May 1934 as the family country doctor who attended the birth of the Dionne Quintuplets and had continued to be responsible for their care. This was the first such multiple birth where all the babies had survived and developed. Numerous jokes circulated about the prolific father....The Hon. Dr. Bruce, Lieutenant-Governor of Ontario, introducing Dr. Dafoe, told of Mr. Dionne calling at the new nursery to visit his babies. The nurse looked at him and said, "No, you mustn't come in; you have not been sterilized." The unhappy father walked away, murmuring "You tell me!"

THE GREATNESS OF THE GREAT LAKES
April, 1936
William Ganson Rose, Cleveland, Ohio

"The greatest cities of the future will not be cities of Europe, nor Asia, nor India, nor will they be cities located on the Atlantic or Pacific Oceans." So spoke in 1930, Dr. J. Paul Good, outstanding student of natural resources. Then he added, "The great cities of the future will be located on the Great Lakes." If the Great Lakes have as great an influence as this, we should become better acquainted with them and learn in what ways we can capitalize upon the many advantages they offer. Called "Great" because they constitute the largest body of fresh water in the world, their true greatness has a far broader significance. More than any other influence they have furthered the industrial and commercial development of the Dominion of Canada and the United States; their contribution to the ever higher standard of living of these countries is incalculable; their service to the territory bordering upon them has made this district the fastest growing industrial region in the world. The Great Lakes are indeed great!

THE SIGNIFICANCE OF VIMY
October, 1936
The Venerable Archdeacon F.G. Scott, CMG, DSO, DD, DCL, LLD

The speaker told a story about Mark Twain who was about to make a speech. The introducer went on so long that a fellow head table guest pulled on his coat tails to make him stop. Twain commenced his address…. "Mr. Chairman, I rise to move a vote of thanks to the chief speaker of the evening."

I just thought I would tell you some of the impressions that came to me at the Vimy unveiling ceremony. I feel that the unveiling of that monument and all that was connected with it was really something more than the simple display of a great memorial. It has a tremendous bearing on our whole national development. Today, I take you in thought, in order that we may realize what the monument at Vimy stands for. I take you in thought back, many of you, in your memory, to those bitter times at the end of 1916, when the Canadian Corps had returned north from the Somme, fighting which had ended in a very grievous disappointment because we had been told that the great offensive which was to be launched down at the Somme on July 1st, 1916 would probably put an end to the impasse in which both armies had found themselves. You remember the bitter fighting at the Somme. You remember the terrible attack made by the Germans on the French at Verdun. The year 1916 had closed leaving us a very anxious feeling. Then we Canadians were told that we should open the year with a very early campaign by an attack on Vimy Ridge, a height of ground which commanded an important section of the mining district of France where both the French and the British had once suffered very severe reverses....We look back upon that attack and are amazed at the performance. I remember I went up in the early hours of the day to Bray Hill and waited until five-thirty, the hour when the attack was to open. I looked down upon the great plain stretching out before me in the dim light of early dawn. Occasionally, a 'very-light' would go up and hover for a moment in the air or a shell would fall behind the lines. I thought what a tremendous thing it was for the Canadians to have that great task laid upon them. We had a nine mile front and on it, I think, 3,000 guns. In addition to our own artillery we had a great many guns that belonged to British units. It was a wonderful thing at that early hour to look across the plain and think of all that was involved. The attack was to be, we were told, the opening of a year which was to end the war and one was filled with enthusiasm mixed with anxiety. Well, I need not dwell upon that but the attack came off and our old 1st Division made, as General Byng told us afterward, every objective on the scheduled dot of the clock. It was really a great triumph.

A PLEA FOR THE CANADIAN NORTHLAND
November, 1936
Grey Owl

I had my cocoa and thought to myself about a time when I was travelling in the woods and had been two days and a half without food and I found in the snow the remains of a partridge which had been killed by an owl. He is a dainty eater, he will not eat intestines, he is not an epicure. I found a few feathers, the feet and the intestines, and I, a man, the leading creature of the world, was glad to play scavenger to an owl. I took the intestines, thawed them out and was mighty glad to eat them....I have my idea that we people need not be the hoboes and misfits we are at the present time. Civilization has made the Indian an outcast in his own country. That sounds like a paradox but it is a fact. Now you have beaten him, you have to keep him. That is a wrong state of affairs. You people are taxpayers, it is costing a lot of money to keep us in idleness and watch us disintegrate and slowly fade away. We have our place in the economic scheme of life in Canada and we want the same jobs we had before. We can do it. And it is worth trying one more experiment on that great job after the many failures you have already had. Put the Indian where he can do the most work and the most good for the country, a fifty-fifty proposition. You give us education, give us recognition, and we will look after your north country for you....I want you gentlemen to remember this one thing. I have been often asked what my work consists of. It begins to be rather ambiguous, I think. It is this: I want to arouse in Canadian people—excuse me speaking off my subject, I do that continually as thoughts come, I won't read a lecture—I want to arouse in the Canadian people a sense of responsibility, the great responsibility they have for that north country and its inhabitants, human and animal. I thank you.

Ed's note: In 1938, following his death, Grey Owl, famed conservationist and author, was revealed as British-born Archibald Belaney, not the son of a Scot and an Apache, the identity he had assumed.

CANADA IN WORLD HISTORY
December, 1936
Norman Wentworth DeWitt, BA, PhD, FRSC

We no longer have even in democratic countries a pure democracy. We have...pressure politics. For example at Washington you have the veterans' lobby, you have lobbies of financial men, you have lobbies of manufacturers, lobbies of the utilities, and all of these exert a pressure on the Government which is infinitely more urgent and more skillfully applied than the pressure that any constituency can exert upon the member who represents it.

EUROPE 1937: PROSPECT AND RETROSPECT
March, 1937
Harold MacMillan, MP

I have some personal relationships with Canada that made me
feel I was coming at least among friends. First, I have a long
business connection through the Macmillan Company of
Toronto, Canada, which is presided over by one of your former
Presidents, my friend, Mr. Eayrs. Secondly, I have lived here for a
year, in the year 1920 to '21, when I served a man, not only the
most generous of chiefs, but the most modest, genial and, I
think, devoted of the many Governor Generals who have served
Canada. Lastly, it was in the course of that year that I met my
wife and I have always attributed to the genial, rosy atmosphere
of optimism which pervades the great Dominion that a marriage
which has led to sixteen years of happiness, started in this country....I would like to say rearmament is not a policy in itself but
it is the inseparable condition, in my opinion, of any foreign
policy. Now, the unilateral disarmament, which is what we have
followed since the war, has proved a mistake from every point of
view. It has not led other nations to imitate us. It has merely led
them to think that England was down and out and whatever
policy you are going to follow I will say it seems to me you must
have a strong and powerful Empire in which England must play
the leading role as the foundation of such policy. The only policy
which would allow you to do without armament is the policy
which England will always respect as an opinion—I mean non-
resistance—(and I remind you that it was respected throughout
the last war as an individual opinion, of what we called the con-
scientious objector) but it will never be followed as a policy.
Therefore, rearmament is the foundation of and an inseparable
condition of any foreign policy a British Government can follow.

IS DEMOCRACY OUTWORN?
April, 1937
Arthur Eustace Morgan, MA, Principal and Vice-Chancellor, McGill University

One of the greatest dangers to democracy is its premature adoption. Unlike autocracy it cannot be imposed from above; it means nothing if it is not a natural growth from below.

FROM THE HEART OF THINGS
September, 1937
A. Beverley Baxter, Canadian-born journalist, author, Member of the British Parliament

We see the collapse of democracy in Europe and the rise of Hitler. Hitler didn't create the situation. The situation created Adolf Hitler.

THE HANDWRITING ON PARLIAMENT'S WALL
April, 1938
Norman MacLeod, Past President of the Parliamentary Press Gallery

Canadian democracy faces no greater problem today than the vanishing independence of the private Member of Parliament and the accompanying growth of party discipline within the Commons Chamber.

A Fitting Introduction
December, 1938
J.P. Pratt, KC, Empire Club President

I am sure that each one of us has at one time or another heard a chairman proudly and loudly declare that the guest speaker needs no introduction, and then proceed to occupy five or seven minutes of the speaker's time by telling who he is, what he is, and why. Today, it will be amply sufficient for this chairman to say that on behalf of the Empire Club we welcome for the first time as our guest speaker, the Hon. Mitchell F. Hepburn, Premier of the Province of Ontario. The Hon. Mr. Hepburn has chosen as his subject. "Present Day Problems." I have much pleasure in introducing the Hon. Mr Hepburn.

PRESENT DAY PROBLEMS
The Hon. Mitchell F. Hepburn, Ontario Premier

There has been a great deal said about national unity. I am just going to make this one observation with regard to my friend [Prime Minister] William Lyon Mackenzie King, and I want it made very clear here that when I drank the Toast to the King a few moments ago, it was to Our Majesty, the King. This gentleman at this moment is charging me with entering into a conspiracy to destroy Confederation. Now, I deny the allegation most emphatically. There isn't a more loyal Canadian in this great gathering than myself....I am not only a Canadian, I am an Imperialist, if you want to call me that....Mackenzie King said, "Not a five cent piece for relief for any province with a Tory Government"! Just imagine, my friends, that man talking today about anyone else breaking up Confederation, and talking about leading a party, based on the policy of national unity.

World War II and on to the Empire Club's 50th Anniversary in 1953

In the years leading up to 1939 there were some who saw the direction in which Hitler was moving and many who did not. For some Mussolini was a hero, "We must not rate him [Mussolini] as a purely selfish nationalist, for in his endeavour to redeem his beloved Italy from anarchy and from economic and spiritual ruin at the same time he saved all of Western civilization from these very calamities. There is no doubt that the one human being who is responsible for the stemming of the tide of Bolshevism in its westward flow is Mussolini."

"It is my belief that Hitlerism will not last through 1935 in its present form and under its present leaders. There are several strong forces in Germany today, jockeying for power."

And then one of the Empire Club's favourite speakers, Lieut. Colonel George A. Drew, brought his ideas to the podium in a powerful and direct way. His speech, in 1935, was titled "Germany Prepares for Conquest." He said, "In an amazingly short time Hitler has repudiated all the obligations of the Treaty of Versailles, has devolved one of the largest, if not the largest army in Europe, is building a powerful navy and has built up probably the most powerful air force in the world....I think it is quite correct to say that at no time in the history of the world has there been such a sudden transition affecting so many people as has occurred in Germany in less than two years....Germany is no longer the defeated power under the Treaty of Versailles. Germany today is a proud people; Germany is a proud nation seeking an opportunity to recover those things of which they believe they were improperly deprived."

And it was George Drew who came to the Club in March, 1939, in sombre mood, "I do not propose to make any attempt to entertain you. I do not propose to try to amuse you, or to make you laugh, for the occurrences of the last thirty-six hours of which I am going to speak must be closer to tears than laughter everywhere in the world…..Gentlemen, these are the Ides of March, and Hitler has marched into the Czech part of Czecho-Slovakia on the anniversary of his march into Austria a year ago…. There is about this date, however, something that may offer hope. You will remember that it was at the height of Caesar's power; when by unscrupulous use of Roman legions he had subjugated a vast territory that a soothsayer said to him: 'Beware the Ides of March.' While I hesitate to prophesy, I can express the hope that the Ides of March may be just as disastrous for this new and crueller Caesar, this man who has jettisoned international honour, this man who has disregarded everything that resembles international decency."

The following year Drew spoke of peace, even as war was beginning. Since it was barely twenty-five years since the world was first thrust into torment by Germany, he stated his view, which was also that of Joseph Chamberlain as spoken to the British House of Commons. It was a vow that this time the world must make such a peace that war be not the inevitable lot of every succeeding generation.

It became part of the preparation for what must be a long struggle, to analyse Hitler's goals and methods. Winston Churchill said "Hitler's plan is to make all of Europe one drab uniform and regimented Boche land. That is indeed Hitler's plan, because bigotry and utter servility to any dogmas and any creed knows no other method of survival than to suppress all that are not in agreement with it." He was a "colossal figure [that] towers over the Reich, in complete domination of the minds of all, pastors, capitalists, the proletariat, parents, children, youth, men of culture, those that are left, who go about with bowed heads and broken hearts." He "wanted the German nation to be a huge mass in complete instability, which he could, at will, hurl against any foe, unattached by any influences, moral, material, or even natural." And it was all set out in Mein Kampf. Hitler saw acquiescence with any of his demands as submissive weakness and lack of character, and knew that the more he extorted the more he could extort.

"The nations of Europe receded step by step before Nazi demands and menaces. They endeavoured to prevent a world cataclysm. Unfortunately they hastened it." Russia, in that way, having signed a Non-Aggression Pact with Germany, thought she had bought off the aggressor….But it was a dangerous price she paid.

Over the war years the Club heard addresses, inspirational, practical, and heartrending. Most, even in the early years, were confident of victory or at least spoke in that vein. Canada's Minister of Munitions and Supply, C.D. Howe, said in 1940 "I was never so sure as I am at this moment that Britain will be the ultimate victor." But there were sombre cautions, "There is no time to be lost in our race for armaments. Germany has been on a war footing for seven years, preparing for the present struggle. Her productive capacity was being geared to war throughout that period. She now has at her disposal all the great armament plants of Europe—Krupp, Schneider, Bofars and Skoda. For man-power she can draw on a population of one hundred and twenty million Germans and Italians, and in addition another eighty million conquered men and women who are being forced to work for the Nazis in order to exist. In other words Germany now controls the lives of two hundred million persons against who are ranged the eighty-six million of the British race. There is no time to be lost."

By January 1941 London was undergoing "death and stark terror, devastation and suffering." One recent visitor to London said "Before I left the British Isles, enemy air-raiders had exacted a heavy toll of life and property in their barbarous campaign of indiscriminate bombing. That wanton destruction is still going on. It is being pursued with all the savagery of an enemy we have learned from past experiences can always be relied upon to act according to the basest instincts of mankind." C.D. Howe had been there and recalled that one night he stood on the top floor of his hotel and, "I never expect to see a more terrifying or more spectacular sight. There were fires in all directions and it looked as though all

London must be burning. But by next morning a large part of London was doing business as usual."

War news was bleak. "Hitler holds all Europe from the walls of Moscow to the Pyrenees. He is master of fourteen formerly independent capitals. Including the vast area of Russia which he now controls and more than half of France, he rules over 300 million people….Despite her glorious resistance against the Italians and the belated, inevitably insufficient help we sent her, Greece was over-run….in Belgium in May last year we were beaten to the punch and fought a losing battle from the outset—we failed also to win the diplomatic struggle in the Balkans. Bulgaria and Rumania after Hungary, more or less unwillingly nevertheless finally threw in their lot with the Axis. Turkey is still an uncertain ally."

But such gloom was dispelled by a visit from a young Flying Officer in the Royal Air Force whose patriotic spirit was inspiring. He described his first flight over enemy territory. "The great moment for which we had been waiting arrived at last…Everything checked, we roared off into the darkness and, as we left the ground, I was overcome with the greatest feeling of relief I have ever experienced. The tension was broken and, in place of my feelings of anxiety, I felt a surge of pride in the knowledge that I was fortunate enough to be one of the first to get a crack at the enemy and experience the rare satisfaction that comes with the realization that you are doing something for your country….I and all my comrades thrilled to the same inner feeling that we were prepared without regrets to give everything we had for Britain and the Empire."

A secretary who had travelled with Churchill spoke about the great man. "The thing that strikes everyone who meets him for the first time is his overwhelming personality. It seems to fill any room he is in and to overflow it on all sides.…That 100-horsepower Churchillian mind can generate more ideas in a day than most people have in a lifetime." She recalled the time Churchill came to Toronto and addressed an enormous gathering at Maple Leaf Gardens…"Some of you here today may remember that in the middle of his speech at Maple Leaf Gardens the amplifying system broke down. Mr. Churchill didn't notice it until cries of 'Louder, louder,' began to echo from all parts of the enclosure. Now, here was a situation to unnerve many an experienced speaker. The thought of it makes me quail, but not Mr. Churchill. I can still see him advancing resolutely to the edge of the platform and raising his hands for quiet. Then he took the portable microphone which was attached to his lapel, held it aloft for everyone to see, and with a dramatic gesture flung it to the floor. In a loud resonant voice he thundered, 'Now that we have exhausted the resources of science we shall fall back on Mother Nature and do our best.' Then, just as though nothing had happened, he went on with his speech and held his audience spellbound to the end. I remember they gave him a great ovation—cries of 'Good old Winnie! You've done it again! Nothing downs you!'"

By 1943 there were proud words to hear at meetings. "Now, as we enter 1943, the scene is very different. The Germans and their partners-in-crime are tasting the bitter medicine which they thought so good for the rest of the world. In a New Year's message to his own people Hitler assured them that he never really wanted war. Certainly he never wanted this kind of war! The brilliant exploits of the British Eighth Army; the dramatic occupation of the North African seaports by forces from the United States....the tremendous hammer blows of the mighty Russian army along the whole battle line from the Baltic to the distant Caucasus; the American naval successes in the Pacific, the ever heroic fortitude of the Chinese resistance to Japan; and the constant pounding of Germany and Italy by ever-increasing numbers of aircraft in which so many of our own young Canadians are flying with sublime courage and incomparable skill…"

In January 1944 a British journalist, Percy James Philip, was able to remind the Club members that, "In the first speech I made to this Club on November 21st 1940 I began with the statement, 'I am sure that we can win this war.' It was rather a bold claim to make at that moment for France had been beaten, neither the Soviet Union nor the United States showed any intention of fighting and we were alone at war with Germany....I think I may amend my prediction of three years ago that 'We can win this war,' to make it read 'We can win the war against Nazi Germany this year.'"

When the war ended there were problems amidst the euphoria. In a speech titled "The Last Canadian Battle and the Surrender of the German Army," Lieut-General Charles Foulkes talked of the many problems encountered in Holland alone. "The Germans had laid 2,000,000 mines in Holland, and these mines were laid all along the Coastal belt and along the rivers. I decided that those who laid them must pick them up. So the German engineers, some 4,000 of them, were given the task of picking up their mines...."There were problems in the cities. George Drew, now premier of Ontario, spoke of Berlin, "That shattered city is symbolic today of the tremendous problems with which the victorious powers are confronted. In a city where four and a half million people lived before the war there are still three million people living in all that indescribable wreckage," some are "living in what are merely caves in the rubble itself." And in Britain, trying to rebuild, there were floods and unprecedented snows, "The loss of four and a quarter million sheep, more than three million cows, and the lost production of many thousands of acres of Britain's richest lands....constitutes a major calamity."

There were concerns about the United Nations Organization. Major Rt. Hon. Anthony Eden stressed the importance of giving "the United Nations Organization constructive tasks for peace to carry through and not merely to put before it controversies as they arise. We have got to marshal the forces that make constructively for peace, wherever they may be, and they are immensely powerful, and however deep the disappointment may occasionally be we must not lose heart. It is only by maintaining faith in our determination to win the peace as we won the war that we can be true to those who from your country and countless others went and returned not."

The Marshall Plan was being debated in the U.S. Congress. An American author noted that "The price of democracy is high, and the world must wait until nearly every Congressman has achieved the most obscure form of immortality known to man—a few pages in the Congressional Record." "But," he noted, "America will not fail mankind." In referring to the fact that he was speaking on the day of the wedding of Princess Elizabeth to Prince Philip he said that "the bride, in all her sincerity and charm, has already won the hearts of all true men and women." He predicted a glorious new Elizabethan age.

And now, speeches that should have had as their subjects re-building and confidence were laced with new worries. In October, 1948, after enumerating the great heritage and glorious future before us in Canada, a lawyer and parliamentarian jolted his audience with, "We stand a chance to lose it all. Canada and the Anglo-Saxon world of today are faced with the possible destruction of all freedom. Why? We have just fought a great war to defeat a conspiracy of evil men to achieve world conquest; but we now face a still more formidable conspiracy by the gangster members of the Kremlin assisted by tens of thousands of traitors in our own country. The Kremlin is the terroristic dictatorship of a small Communist Party over the masses of the people….All other parties have been suppressed in blood." This fear of Communism would become the predominant topic for many years to come.

In 1951, Lester Pearson, then Secretary of State for External Affairs, spoke of Canada's foreign policy in a world where Communism was the threat. Summing up our stature in the world he said, "The formulation of foreign policy has special difficulties for a country like Canada which has enough responsibility and power in the world to prevent its isolation from the consequences of international decisions, but not enough to ensure that its voice will be effective in making those decisions….the present situation of war without warfare may continue for years. This will confront us with just about the most difficult political and economic problem that has ever faced a democratic society…." As for relations with the United States, "There will be difficulties and frictions. These, however, will be easier to settle if the United States realizes that while we are most anxious to work with her and support her in the leadership she is giving to the free world, we are not willing to be merely an echo of somebody else's voice." Relations with the United States on the level of tariffs and trade were always an issue, but it was surprising to note that an American businessman titled his talk "Lets Free Trade," and that in the process of his arguments quoted C.D. Howe, "Our two main objectives from this time forward are: first, to bring about a further expansion of trade; and second, to get rid of the restrictions that prevent the free world from making the most effective use of the resources available to it."

There were, however, other subjects to consider. The Aircraft Industry in Canada was one. "One of the oldest firms in Canada is the DeHaviland Aircraft Company of Canada Ltd. just north of Toronto at Downsview. This plant, since the war, has designed and built two entirely new types of aircraft….Canadair in Montreal is producing the well-known 'North Star' airliner….The Third of three large aircraft plants in Canada is our own company, Avro Canada at Malton." (The Avro Arrow, a supersonic jet developed in 1949, would be the source of a controversial cancellation in 1959.)

Commenting on a perennial subject, the dullness of Canadians, a novelist quoted numerous remarks made by Canadians about themselves, including "stodgy," with "no independent intellectual identity," and even "spiritually constipated." "I can't understand," said the speaker, "as I glance around me, how you all look so happy. It leaves me wondering why you don't all emulate the lemmings of Norway and swarm down to the Bay and jump in." "But," he added, "it leaves me puzzled that so poor a place as Canada could produce an Osler and a Banting and a Graham Bell and a Vincent Massey, could give birth to a Roberts and a Carman and a Lampman."

As the decade was ending, the advent of television was duly debated. With regard to all the disadvantages which he enumerated, the controller of Television for the BBC concluded with amazing foresight, "Now, having said I do not regard television as a short cut to happiness, I do say I look forward to the day, which I hope will be soon, when television comes to Canada, and I would ask only one thing of you, that having taught your family how to tune the set properly and how to focus it, you also teach and instruct your own family how to turn the set off again."

BRITAIN FACES GERMANY
December, 1938
Willson Woodside, traveller, journalist

The only way we can ever stop the aggression of the Fascist powers is to be willing to fight, if necessary. Appeasing Germany has only served to prove to the Germans that it is strength that counts....We should also keep in front of us when we listen to Hitler's promises, this saying which he has uttered over and over again, "What is right is what is good for Germany"....Harold Nicolson, well-known British diplomat and writer, explains the fundamental difference in the British and the German view of diplomatic negotiations. The Briton looks upon them as little more than a business deal. He wants the parties to sit down on either side of a table and come to some satisfactory compromise, each yielding a little, and then agree that this being the best possible solution, they will keep to it. The German regards this as little better than horse-swapping. To him it is a demeaning process. To him diplomacy is something much more glorious, a form of warfare, and he brings to it the technique of warfare, attacks and camouflage and flanking manoeuvres, and strategic retreats if necessary to more solid positions. What he is pursuing is really some abstract goal, Triumph-Power. He looks upon every concession demanded of him as an insult and on every concession which you show yourself willing to make as a proof of your weakness.

CAN WE ACHIEVE CANADIAN UNITY?
January, 1939
Jean Charles Harvey, Quebec journalist

There will always be people who care more for disunion and disagreement than for peace and good understanding....When I come to discuss with you means of cementing Canadian unity, I come with no illusions. I know, as well as anybody, that there will always be friction between the members of the Canadian family, and that the most we can hope to do is to erect a few shock-absorbers at key spots in the nation.

THE IDES OF MARCH
March, 1939
George A. Drew, KC, MPP, Leader of the Opposition, Ontario

I do not propose to make any attempt to entertain you. I do not propose to try to amuse you, or to make you laugh, for the occurrences of the last thirty-six hours of which I am going to speak must be closer to tears than laughter everywhere in the world. I do not propose to make any pretence at humour, because, although it is the custom of the British to smile in the face of tragedy, the thoughts of every one of us should not only be directed toward the tragedy that is taking place, but toward the future and all that it implies for us. The title I chose when I was asked to be your guest is indicative of the sudden change that has taken place in a comparatively few days. When I chose the title, "Britain Wins the Second Round," it was perhaps rather like leaving a game with 20 seconds to go, and then finding you had missed the final result. I based my second choice of title on an article by an extremely able commentator on foreign affairs. It is very hard to realize that the article appeared only last week, for it starts with these words: "There will be no Ides of March"....I say, without any reservation at all, that yesterday was one of the turning points in the world's history. Until yesterday morning people could argue that we found in the Nazi programme and in Mein Kampf a clear statement of the German desire to have incorporated in one nation all people of German speech and race, and the return of the colonies they lost in the war, but that they had no intention of going beyond that. Now we know that there is no limit to the extent of German expansion except the limit of German desire, and you and I must consider what the impact of that may be upon ourselves. A cruel Sadist is at the head of an increasingly powerful nation, but when we recognize that we should not forget, it would be very unwise to forget, that Hitler and Nazism are not yet representative of Germany as a whole, and I do not believe they ever will be. We cannot forget these people have given to the world music, literature, art and philosophy, and I cannot believe that the spirit is dead which created this contribution to mankind. And when you think of Germany, when you think of the physical Germany, what comes to your mind is the thought of the tidy attractive homes in the cities and in the country. What comes to your mind is a recollection of the real country, the beautiful scenery of Bavaria, the simple wholesome family life of a people who, unfortunately for the moment are living under this accursed Nazi doctrine.

LONDON TO PARIS TO ROME
April, 1939
Gregory Clark, journalist

True, Italy is filled with police. Every cop has two assistant cops. The streets of Rome, especially, but also in most of the other cities, are full of soldiers, well-dressed, smart, self-conscious soldiers, with that look both Hitler and Mussolini deem to be part of the faith, a self-conscious, stony expression....I saw in the same restaurant a long table, full of thirty Fascist Black Shirts, in their uniform of black shirt and gray trousers, entertaining about twelve members of the German Nazi Party in their bright brown uniforms and red swastikas. The dark Italians and the bright blonde Germans were all laughing heartily together but the Germans, fresh down from Germany, were casting curious, haughty and cold eyes around the restaurant at all us rag tag and bobtail. Before I left an official said to me, "Of course these Germans think they are God." Gentlemen, it isn't biological....The office wired me in Rome to try and see the Duke of Windsor....I made the promise which I kept. I will not tell you how keen and renewed he is, how gone all the old nervous, harassed mannerisms, how incredibly beautiful she is, with a beauty that led her to so strange and fabled a life. I will not even tell about their lovely little house, nor of how he asked of so many things in Canada, and how we laughed about nabobs and snobs—all the things you could talk about to even plumbers and newspapermen and Dukes.

THE PART WE PLAY
November, 1939
The Hon. Iva Campbell Fallis, Senator

Someone has said that any woman who attempts to combine home duties with a public career needs the skill of a tight-rope walker, the endurance of a marathon swimmer, the faith of a revolutionist and the fatalism of an explorer. I am not saying for a moment that my colleague [Senator Wilson, the first woman in Canada to be made a Senator] or I possess these qualifications, but I can assure you that there are times when we feel the need of them all.

RETROSPECT AND PROPHECY
Freedom
December, 1939
The Rt. Hon. R.B. Bennett, PC, KC, LLD, DCL, Prime Minister, 1930–35

I shall never forget that Sunday morning when Mr. Chamberlain made the declaration of war. There are many people who say, "Why should we fight for Poland? What interest have we in Poland?" Poland is but an incident. The issue…is the challenge to a Christian civilization and the defence of Poland and of our own civilization happily coincide.…Freedom is something that men and nations little realize until they have lost it, and liberty we in Canada enjoy to such an extent that sometimes it degenerates into license.…There can be no real liberty without restraint.

A QUARTER CENTURY OF COMMUNICATIONS DEVELOPMENT
February, 1940
Dr. J.O. Perrine, U.S. telephone executive on the 25th anniversary of the first transcontinental phone call from New York to San Francisco

The question these days before the communication business is not so much what can we do technically, but what can we do that the people want, will use and will use for the good of society.

THE CHALLENGE OF DEMOCRACY
February, 1940
The Hon. D.G. McKenzie

A man cannot be a good citizen, he cannot be free and independent and a strength to the state without a livelihood, without a home, without some property, or business or occupation, or some other interest to give him concern for the welfare and good order of the community.

DICTATORS AND DEMOCRATS
Hitler
March, 1940
Rosita Forbes, FRGS, explorer, writer, and lecturer, quoting from an interview with Hitler in 1939 and sessions with Mussolini and Stalin

I asked Hitler in July if he were quite sure that Russia would come in as his ally. As early as July he said, "The terms of the Russian-German Pact may not be quite settled, but I am convinced the two great totalitarian states of Central Europe and the North will fight together." That did not surprise me because as early as March last year my German friends had been quoting to me actual terms of the Russo-German Pact. If you had studied the newspapers you would have realized that for a whole year Hitler had been saying nothing against the Communists. I don't believe Hitler's loathing for Communism has changed. I think that is still one of the strongest points in our favour. He once said, "My last war will be against the Soviet. There is nothing good in Russia. To say there is anything good in Communism is treachery to humanity." I think quite possibly he believes that. I am sure his Generals refused to fight on two fronts and persuaded him at least a year ago into this alliance with Russia....[Hitler said] "If a man does not agree with me he might as well take his own life because he is of no more service to Germany"....It seems to me also when I have heard this song, "O, Canada, the true North, strong and free," sung over and over again at mass meetings right across your Continent and back again, at which I have had the privilege of speaking, it has seemed just then that you are fighting with a blazing faith of a free people who will not in your minds admit that any other nation should be by force less free than you are yourselves, and that has comforted me, personally—just me, Rosita Forbes—because I have thought, even if England goes down, our so little, so vulnerable island, if she went down—of course, after the manner of the Royal Navy, firing gun for gun while men are alive to work them—if we did go down, I think the Empire would be safe in your charge, and whatever you like to say about it politically in your papers, I believe our Allies, with your help, would be sure of eventual victory, whatever happens to us in England.

ESSENCE OF THE EMPIRE CLUB
April, 1940
Dr. F.A. Gaby, retiring Club President

The traditions of the British democracy are the very fibre of our nation and the greatest of all democracies is the British Empire. It is the purpose of this Club to maintain these traditions by bringing to you the latest thoughts of the day and by bringing men capable of delivering same.

THE PRESENT CHALLENGE TO CANADA
June, 1940
The Hon. Norman McLeod Rogers, MA, BLitt, BCL, Minister of Defence

The seriousness of the situation does not warrant the expression of optimistic platitudes. It is better to face grim realities with courage and resolution. But never let us lose for a moment our supreme confidence in final victory.

From the text prepared for delivery to a joint meeting of the Empire Club and the Canadian Club. While the meeting was in session, the Royal Canadian Air Force bomber, especially chartered to bring Mr. Rogers to Toronto for his speaking engagement, crashed nine miles east of Bowmanville. All persons on board including N.M. Rogers were lost. The tragedy was unknown to the meeting. The address was read by Colonel James Mess.

THE BLITZKRIEG IN FLANDERS
August, 1940
Gregory Clark, *The Toronto Daily Star*

Only last spring I stood right here before some of you, fresh from France, and I told you about the Maginot Line. I told you no human power could penetrate it. I was right but there was a human power than went around it. After telling you of the might of the French Army and the readiness of the British Army and the Maginot Line, I went back again to France and arrived two days after Holland and Belgium had been invaded. I was exactly in time to see that Might brushed away as though it were dust.

CANADA AT WAR

September, 1940

The Hon. C.D. Howe, BSc, MEIC, Minister of Munitions and Supply

As we enter the second year of the war we may well look back at the year just past and review the progress that has been made toward our war objective. It has been a discouraging year, a year that has seen the armed forces of Germany meet with success after spectacular success. Britain has seen her Allies one by one give up the struggle and become subject to her enemy. Yet, as I stand here today, I was never so sure as I am at this moment that Britain will be the ultimate victor. I am sure that everyone within the sound of my voice shares that opinion....One year ago we had forty-five hundred troops available for service overseas or elsewhere. Today the Canadian Active Service Force numbers over one hundred and fifty-five thousand. A year ago there were no troops outside of Canada. Now, the Canadian Active Service Force is in England, Iceland, Newfoundland, and in the Caribbean, and over one hundred thousand in Canada are available for duty anywhere. Besides this, some sixty thousand volunteers will be training this summer in our militia camps. This winter in addition to the militia training at local headquarters, there will be, each month at the militia training centres, another thirty thousand. This means that until further contingents of the Canadian Active Service Force go overseas there will be on service and in training camps or headquarters about two hundred thousand men in this country....One year ago our Navy had seventeen hundred officers and men; now it has nearly ten thousand. A year ago the Royal Canadian Air Force had a personnel of four thousand men; now its personnel is twenty-five thousand, exclusive of the Air Training Programme. Three squadrons of the Royal Canadian Air Force are operating in the United Kingdom today and another squadron of the Royal Air Force is composed wholly of Canadians. You may read of their exploits in the account of many an air battle over England. Canada has been assigned the task of training a large proportion of the pilots that will defend Britain in future years and our Air Training Plan is well ahead of the schedules laid down for it when the programme was undertaken.

WINGED WARFARE OVER BRITAIN
November, 1940
Air Marshal William A. Bishop, VC, DSO (with Bar), MC, DFC

On my trips through the countryside which I tried first of all by motor car, I saw many things that were amusing in their cheerfulness. Here is a country at war—any section or part of which may be blown to bits at any moment—but yet, on the main roadway, referring of course to their national effort, they put up huge billboard signs saying, "GO TO IT!" Of course, as a result everybody is driving too fast. Another sign which expresses best of all the pure British humour was, "BE LIKE DAD, KEEP MUM." I also saw in a newspaper the headline, "IF YOUR HOUSE GOES GIVE THE POST OFFICE YOUR NEW ADDRESS." It is going to take a long time to beat a nation that, in a moment when their enemies claim they are beaten to their knees, paint signs like that on their billboards....During my visit over there I was called to Downing Street for a chat with Mr. Churchill, whom I knew very well in less troublesome times. Suffice it to say that I found him exactly as one pictures him when listening to his inspiring broadcasts— strong, fearless and determined—the stern, courageous, unflinching leader of his people—nay more, the leader of all there is left of freedom in the world today. Great crises in England have produced great men. The threat of Napoleon gave her Pitt. The menace of Hitlerism gave us Winston Churchill. I also had the honour of a three-quarter-hour audience with the King and I feel that it was as a compliment to our Service that he received me wearing the uniform of Marshal of the Royal Air Force. Let me say here that every person that I met in England is full of the most profound admiration for both Their Majesties. Their work has been tireless. They are a constant inspiration to their people. The anger at the bombing of Buckingham Palace is tremendous.

"BRITAIN"
January, 1941
His Excellency The Rt. Hon. The Earl of Athlone, KG, GCB, GCMG, GCVO, DSO, ADC, Governor General of Canada

Experience....has bred in us a certain dislike of the doctrinaire and distrust of undiluted logic. "Resign yourself," says Andre Maurois, "to giving your logic a rest when you stay in England." He might have chosen as an excellent but extreme example the epitaph which actually adorns a grave in an English churchyard:

> Here lies John Bun
> Who was shot by a gun
> His name was not Bun but Wood
> But Wood would not rhyme with gun
> And Bun would.

There you have the fine flower of illogicality, an opportunism with an honest purpose and entire frankness of motive.

Optimism at the Age of Ninety
1941

Sir William Mulock (1844–1944) former Cabinet Minister and Chief Justice of Ontario was a head table guest at age 97. In response to a warm welcome he said "It is not my fault I am still on this earth. It is true I have entered upon another year of life, but I am not going to say what sort of a career I shall carry on when I start my second century."

INFLATION AND WAR FINANCE
February, 1941
F. Cyril James, BCom, MA, PhD, Principal, McGill University

Inflation is not a nauseous poison that frightens those who look on it; it is a seductive drug which, like opium, destroys its victims more effectively because it offers initial pleasure and inspires a taste for ever larger doses.

THERE ARE NO CIVILIANS IN LONDON
February, 1941
Mrs. Marcus Dimsdale, UK Ministry of Information

Well, in England it used to be, when I was young, "Is that a job for a woman?" Now it is "Is there a woman to do this job?"

CANADA AT THE CROSSROADS
March, 1941
Lieutenant-Colonel George A. Drew, KC, MLA, Leader of the Opposition, Ontario

We have been warned in Canada of the danger of complacency about which we should be much more concerned than we have been in the past. We have recognized the increasing difficulty of efficient government in a country where the conflict of authority between the Federal and Provincial Governments has created a complete impasse in many fields of legislation. We know, or should know, that we are the most over-governed nation in the whole world. I say that without reservation of any kind. We know, or should know, that we have more Cabinet Ministers and Members of Parliament per capita than any other democratic nation in the world.

In June, 1942, the Hon. Mr. Justice Norman Birkett, whose subject was "Britain and Canada—Brothers in Arms," introduced the subject of speakers with the tale of a distinguished but verbose alumnus who spoke in lavish praise of Harvard University. Taking each letter of the word he orated at length on H for Honour, A for Ambition, R for revolution, V for Victory, and so on. The speech was interminable and, as the exhausted meeting dispersed one listener exclaimed "Thank God this is not the Massachusetts Institute of Technology."

CANADIAN AGRICULTURE IN THE WAR EFFORT
War Rations
December, 1943
The Hon. Mitchell F. Hepburn, MPP, Ontario Premier,
1934–1942

Now, that reminds me of a little story [there were many]. It seems there was a very estimable lady walking up and down the street looking for a well-stocked butcher shop. Finally she saw a store in which there appeared to be meat for sale and she went and asked the butcher if she could buy a roast of meat. [After she had bought a twenty pound roast, twenty pounds of round steak and a large order of chops] the lady said, "Now will you just deliver all this to my home, please?" and [the butcher] said, "That is physically impossible; that I cannot do," and the lady said, "Well, that is strange, I see your butcher wagon out in front of your door," and the butcher said, "Yes, that is true, but you have just bought my horse."

THE FIFTH YEAR AND THE FUTURE
January, 1944
Percy J. Philip, Ottawa correspondent of the *New York Times*

Thirty years of watching the ways of governments and men have taught me that the worst guides of all are often the most clamorous ones; the narrow nationalists, the doctrinaires, the moralists, the fanatical idealists, the easy optimists, the preachers of peace by disarmament, or isolation, of prosperity without toil, of social security without obligation, of life without effort. These were the people who by their weakness gave Hitler his illusion of power and opportunity. They have not been conspicuous in the days of danger, but they are getting busy again.

WHAT IS TO BECOME OF THE BRITISH PROTECTORATES?
March, 1944
Leading aircraftsman, David Yalden-Thomson

Despite benefits of colonial order and efficiency, Ghandi of India expressed demands for independence as follows: "If the alternative to British rule is chaos, I prefer chaos"....Let us look at the history of the British Empire over the last 150 years....There are two distinct lines of policy. One follows the line of self-government in quick time, instances are Canada and the other Dominions. In these instances self-government was given before lasting bitterness had been aroused. Look on the other hand at what happened when independence was withheld in Ireland and Egypt! They received independence or won it by force of arms. But our reluctance, our procrastination for reasons good or bad, left behind a legacy of hatred which may never be quite forgotten.

WAR AIMS AS SEEN FROM GREAT BRITAIN
May, 1944
The Most Rev. and Rt. Hon. Cyril Foster Garbett, Archbishop of York

I am quite certain, though I am a lover of peace…by my profession and by conviction, I am quite certain that in an imperfect world you can not have peace unless force is used or force is ready to repress the aggressor. Within the nation, behind the laws there is force to be used if necessary—our police forces exist for that purpose—and the more certain the action of that force the less likely is it that the law will be broken. And the same is true of the international world.

EMPIRE CLUB BROADCASTS
Annual Meeting, April, 1944
W. Eason Humphreys, Club President

Broadcasting has enlarged the scope of the influence of your Club and I am told that our air audience can be anything up to 800,000 listeners, depending, of course, on the attractiveness of the speaker and his subject.

AS THE ALLIES FACE THE FUTURE
November, 1944
Col. Willard Chevalier, New York

During the past couple of years we have developed what amounts to almost a new major industry. I refer to the activity popularly known as "Post-War Planning"....Anxious though our business men may be to revert to civilian production and anxious though our civilian population to obtain more goods and new goods and better goods...if these aspirations are permitted to interfere with our war production we shall but postpone the day of final victory and thereby add to the toll of sorrow that is the heritage of war.

EUROPE—A SEARCH FOR IDEAS
Decadence
March, 1945
James Smith-Ross, author, editor, traveller

Is it true that great wealth brings decadence?...No....What causes decadence is wealth among the few and poverty among the many. Neither great wealth, nor great intellect, nor great spiritual qualities bring decadence in their train. It is an extremity in any one of these three that causes trouble....If a nation is strong only, but hasn't developed its mental or its spiritual side, it will fail; or, if it is very religious but hasn't looked after its strength or its wisdom, it will fail.

THE LAST CANADIAN BATTLE AND THE SURRENDER OF THE GERMAN ARMY
October, 1945
Lieut.-General Charles Foulkes, CB, CBE, DSO, Chief of The General Staff in Canada

No soldier has been found wanting: they have all gone through hardship, suffering, and above everything lived a generally unnatural life. They have been away from their relatives and friends for five years....What I want to appeal to you now for is to be long-suffering, to be tolerant toward these men. You want to remember that it was Crerar, Simmonds, myself and many others who, for the past five years have been teaching these men to be tough, to be blood-thirsty, grafting, vicious, to kill in cold blood, to scheme and deceive the enemy, and you cannot change that over night by an Order-in-Council. I hope the majority of these men will settle down; I am sure they will. But there will be break-ups in family relations, there will be untoward incidents which none of us will condone. But I do appeal to you to be patient, to be tolerant and helpful, remembering it was these men who risked, and some of them lost, their lives in order that you and I can be here today.

THE NEED FOR CANADIAN MILITARY PREPARATION
Principle, not Expediency
April, 1946
General H.D.G. Crerar, CH, CB, DSO, Commander, Canadian Army

It is high time that as citizens we Canadians thought more deeply in terms of the next generation and much less importantly in terms of the next election. Expediency represents neither principle nor policy in a man, or in a nation.

FREE MEN OR AUTOMATS
April, 1946
Jean Charles Harvey, Quebec journalist

Democracy is neither capitalism, nor corporatism, nor fascism, nor communism. Democracy alone proclaims the right of each to a share of happiness....The whole story can be summed up in two words, reason and love. There will be no future in society, no progress, not even the maintenance of our present good estate, without a free exercise of individual reason; there will be no security for the weak without the great love which comes from Christian morality. Everything else is but vanity.

AN ADDRESS BY MAJOR RT. HON. ANTHONY EDEN
June, 1946
Major Rt. Hon. Anthony Eden, PC, MC, JP, BL

As in these days I have been in your great cities and flown over your beautiful and fertile countryside, again and again. I have thought you in Canada have indeed a great country, a land of promise and of unrivalled opportunity, and I have thought too in these days of another occasion on the Clyde, now nearly six and a half years ago when with my friend, Vincent Massey, we watched the sun slowly breaking through the gray skies and lighting up one of the largest armadas that ever sailed into that great river. That armada carried the first contingent of your Forces to Britain, and there are men here, I know, who from that day until a few weeks past or a few months past have been away from home, playing their part in this titanic struggle. I looked over the ships that were there—ships like the *Empress of Britain,* the pride of your Merchant Marine, which now, unhappily, suffered in the contest, and I remember too the troops that were there. Your own 48th Highlanders—and I remember that as Mr. Massey and I stood there on the deck of the *Warspite,* we had a feeling that here indeed was a partnership in a common struggle.

May I say to this gathering how proud I am that Vincent Massey should be with us on this occasion. I think it is his first public appearance in Toronto since he ceased to be your High Commissioner in London, and I think it is fitting that I, to whom it fell to do so much work with him, should tell you that there is no man in either of our lands who has made a fuller, a more sincere contribution to understanding between our two countries than has Vincent Massey.

DO WE FACE IDEOLOGICAL CONQUEST?
October, 1946
Major Stuart Armour, DSO, Croix de Guerre

This ideological warfare which is even now taking place within our own boundaries is warfare of the most ruthless character. It is carried on by fanatical and ruthless men and women; with no weapons or stratagems outlawed by any feeling of chivalry or good sportsmanship....Nor should we be under any apprehension as to the objective of this undercover offensive. It is nothing short of the total elimination of the middle class—an objective laid down quite explicitly as early as 1848 in the Communist Manifesto of Karl Marx and Frederick Engels....Briefly the Communist Manifesto further says that Communism supports every revolutionary movement against the existing social and political order of things. It represents the enemy in every case to be the private ownership of property.

DOMINION PROVINCIAL RELATIONS
The Cost of Unemployment
November, 1946
The Hon. Thomas D. Pattullo, KC, LLD, past Premier, British Columbia

It is true that to put people to work does, for the moment, cost more in dollars and cents than to feed and shelter them in idleness, but, not to keep people employed is a costly business, both in money and morale.

YOUR UNIVERSITY AND CANADA'S FINEST GENERATION

January, 1947

Dr. Sidney Earle Smith, KC, MA, LLD, DCL, President, University of Toronto

I must confess that I have, these days, a degree of allergy to speaking, particularly when I recall a definition of university presidents as "pillars of brass by day and bags of gas by night." For your comfort and, perhaps, for my solace, I remind ourselves that this is the luncheon period. Within the past three years, I was introduced to a luncheon audience by a chairman who, after describing certain aspects of my career, stated that he had heard a declaration, in which he concurred, that if all the aftermeal speeches were laid end to end, they should be left there. Last autumn, I heard Mr. L. W. Brockington state in an address to students in the Ajax Division of the University that there are in Canada more speeches to the square meal than in any other country....The students in the University who were too young to enlist during the war have a rare opportunity to work and to play alongside these veterans. They can learn from the veterans the ideas and ideals that are the very stuff of nationhood for which the men and women of the Armed Forces were ready to give of their very lives....Since Armistice Day, 1918, the world has been given the lesson that nations can be remade with astonishing rapidity, and indeed with astonishing completeness. Hitler and Mussolini recreated, within a few years, their countries for evil purposes. From my confidence and my faith in the generation of whom I have been speaking, I can envisage them with wise leadership building in their time a greater and a finer Canada. Herein is the task of your University. As Field Marshal, the Viscount Montgomery of Alamein stated in his Convocation Address to the University on August 31st, 1946, we must "train our youth to give their best to the country in peace, as they did in war. We must pour into those who must win the peace, the spirit that won the war."

THE WAR ACCOMPLISHMENTS OF BRITISH FILMS

May, 1947

J. Arthur Rank, film magnate, United Kingdom

In spite of a feeling of nervousness, I welcome this opportunity to speak to you. I understand that over the wireless I am addressing a much larger audience than I see before me. I have always had in mind that if an opportunity such as this should ever present itself to me, I would pay a sincere tribute to all Canadian soldiers, and especially to those whom I saw at the second battle of Ypres early in 1915. In the first gas attack, when troops were fleeing, I saw those Canadian soldiers of the First Division go in and hold the line and but for their bravery the history of the first Great War might have been very different. I welcome this opportunity of being able to refer to the wonderful courage shown by you men on that occasion and express to you the admiration I shall always have for the Canadian people....The record of the British Film Industry has been a very varied and difficult one. Prior to the war of 1914–18, the pioneers of the industry were leading in this field, but owing to and during the war, Hollywood took the lead and after the peace Britain never really recovered her lost ground. Just prior to 1939 we were making a great effort to compete with the strong and well established Hollywood companies, then along came the second Great War and that put a stop to all our hopes and ambitions. Just before the last Great War, the American producers had what was practically a monopoly of the world's screens. It is of interest to mention here that toward the end of 1940, or to be more explicit, the late summer of that year, there were only about two pictures produced in Great Britain, and it looked as if history was going to repeat itself, and as was the case in 1914, the production of British films would be out altogether. However, we had a little bit of luck on our side. The Government was very anxious that the morale of the people should be maintained by entertainment through the cinema, and, moreover, the authorities were of the opinion that certain of their wartime policies could be put over to the general public by the same means, and furthermore that training films should be made, not only for the service but also for industry; and so we had our opportunity which we were quick to seize.

THE PRIME MINISTER REPORTS
June, 1947
Colonel The Hon. George A. Drew, VD, KC, LLD

If the lesson we said we had learned in 1939 is still correct, then the hope for peace depends upon the firmness with which all the democracies tell Russia this year, by November, or when the Foreign Secretaries meet again, that the people of the world, of the free world, do believe in the principles laid down in the Atlantic Charter, and subscribed to by Russia as well as the free democracies, and that those free nations do want to assert, just as strongly as Russia, the right of Russia to determine their own course within their own bounds, but that they are also insistent that Russia shall not impose by force its form of government upon any other nation against its will.

THE CANADIAN ECONOMY AND ITS INTERNATIONAL ASPECTS
March, 1948
Robert Patterson Jellett, President, The Royal Trust Company, Montreal

One naturally hopes for a great decrease in pubic expenditure now that we have a kind of peace or at least a cold war instead of a very hot one....We have had some relief in taxation and may hope for more but we can never get back to anything like a pre-war basis....No government having embarked on schemes of social benefits to a large portion of the population is ever likely to face a serious downward adjustment of such benefits....
An inept metaphor is often amusing. I asked one of our representatives in Parliament why his party didn't come out for the

removal of the ban on the importation, manufacture and sale of margarine. He replied that "Margarine was too hot a potato!"

FREE ENTERPRISE
April, 1948
C. Bruce Hill, MC (and Bar), President, Canadian Chamber of Commerce

There are too many, and there are probably some in this room, who give lip service to free enterprise and rush to Ottawa the next day and say, "Let us have a law." Gentlemen, you cannot ask the other man to be regulated for your benefit without expecting that he is going to ask also for a little regulation.... The greatest fallacy of all time fallacies [Socialism] places equality rather than production as a means of raising the standard of living.... If you took every income in the Dominion of Canada over $5,000 and distributed it, what would you have? Nothing. Yet sixty years ago we produced $100 per capita and you know what the standard of living was. Now, we produce $400. Gentlemen, there is the answer—Production.

THE THREAT TO WORLD FREEDOM
Control by Bluff
October, 1948
Arthur Graeme Slaght, KC

A few days ago I read an interview which the Lion Tamer at the Maple Leaf Gardens Circus gave to the press. He said that his control over the beasts was entirely bluff and that he had to keep them from finding out it was bluff, or he would be destroyed. Vishinsky—I think on the same day this appeared—in effect warned the Paris delegates that Russia had the atomic bomb. No one believed him. And on behalf of the British Lion—Ernest Bevin pulled no punches! Foreign Secretary Ernest Bevin of Great Britain answered Vishinsky in unmistakable language, and told the United Nations Assembly in impassioned tones that only Russia will be to blame if the black fury of atomic warfare descends on mankind.... So Vishinsky, the Lion Tamer, did not fool the lions.

CANADA FINDS HER VOICE
April, 1949
Arthur Stringer, author, traveller

You know, I'm at last beginning to understand why the beaver is our national emblem. I thought once, it was due to the industriousness of what had been designated merely an amplified rat. But I was wrong there, for outside its industry the beaver has one peculiar and distinguishing trait. That peculiarity stems from the conviction that its home isn't habitable until it has been well dammed. And recent events in this fair land of ours persuade me that the Canadian isn't happy in his home until he sees it well damned....And now that I'm too old to set bad examples I can at least give some good advice. That advice would be to tell you to be more aggressively Canadian, to be more passionately proud of our great nation and not to overlook those men who are translating its greatness into literature.

THE ROLE OF THE OPPOSITION IN PARLIAMENT
October, 1949
John G. Diefenbaker, KC, MP

I am fully aware that parliamentary majorities are not prone to acknowledge the necessity of the Opposition. One political writer has expressed it. "The Government tends to regard the Opposition as a brake on a car going uphill whereas the Opposition thinks the car is going downhill."

THE PRESENT CONDITION OF ENGLAND
Modern War
October, 1949
Douglas Jerrold, author and publisher, London, England

If military operations went badly, the Atom Bomb might have to be used to save Europe from a fate worse than death, but it could not possibly save Europe from death: the destruction which would be imposed by the use of that weapon would make impossible the economic recovery of Europe for many generations....The whole of history is one long lesson of the fatal and irrevocable consequences of not being prepared militarily.

FREEDOM'S CROWNING HOUR
April, 1950
The Hon. George A. Drew, KC, LLD, MP, National Leader, Progressive Conservative Party

Defence of freedom starts at home. We must stop playing with Communism as if it were some ordinary political doctrine....Freedom was never intended to provide the means by which freedom could be destroyed....Every member of the Communist Party in Canada, as elsewhere, is a servant of the Kremlin....Every one of them is a traitor to Canada.

SPORTSMEN, INDEED?
April, 1950
Gregory Clark, writer, humourist, orator

A sportsman is one who will not show his own father where the best fishing holes are and will deliberately show him the wrong ones.

MOBILIZING OUR IDEAS AND IDEALS
Freedom to...
February, 1951
Donald Kirk David, AB, MBA, LLD, Dean, Graduate School of Business Administration, Harvard

We want a positive kind of freedom; freedom for the individual to do things—freedom to rather than freedom from. In my opinion the "freedom from want" and "freedom from fear" slogans are not basically consistent with our goals....It is that the traditional role of our governments is to act as a referee—to see that no individual, in his own freedom to, unfairly interferes with another's freedom.

TALKING SHOP
March, 1951
Donald Gordon, CMG, LLD, Chairman and President, Canadian National Railways

There is no activity more vital than railways to the security, prosperity and progress of the Canadian people.

A GLANCE AT THE FUTURE
March, 1951
Thomas B. Costain, historian and novelist

Don't grow too fast! Don't grow too much. Don't grow so fast that the Canadian type will be lost in a melting pot. Don't grow so much that it will be possible for the incoming rush of alien people, with their own ideological conceptions, their isms and their ways of life, to submerge the native stock, don't grow so much that it will be possible for the traditions and ideals of Canadianism to be swallowed up in political patterns under which you would not willingly live.

CANADIAN FOREIGN POLICY IN A TWO POWER WORLD
April, 1951
The Hon. Lester B. Pearson, OBE, MA, LLD, MP, Secretary of State for External Affairs

The formulation of foreign policy has special difficulties for a country like Canada, which has enough responsibility and power in the world to prevent its isolation from the consequences of international decisions, but not enough to ensure that its voice will be effective in making those decisions....On the other hand, and many think that this is the more probable development, the present situation of war without warfare may continue for years. This will confront us with just about the most difficult political and economic problem that has ever faced a democratic society. It is unprecedented and so we have little to go on as we try to work our way through the jungle of the difficulties and dangers of what the London "Economist" calls "three-quarters peace." Certainly we have to become collectively strong in a military sense to meet the shock of a sudden attack; or, and this is more important, to make such an attack unlikely by convincing anyone who contemplates aggression that he has no hope for victory. At the same time, we have to be careful in this country, and in other countries, not to divert to and organize our resources for military defence in such a way or to such an extent that we sap and weaken our economic and social strength and morale.

ESSENTIAL ELECTRICITY
October, 1951
Robert Saunders, Chairman, Hydro-Electric Power Commission of Ontario

There is no commodity as vital to our economy, our production, or employment—yes, our defence—as is electricity at low cost, available wherever and whenever it is needed.

THE UNITED NATIONS TODAY AND TOMORROW
October, 1951
Arnold Heeney, Under Secretary for External Affairs

The United Nations is not an entity in itself. It is the sum total of the wills of its members and the combined contribution they are willing to make.

CANADIAN LABOUR IN 1951
November, 1951
The Hon. Milton Gregg, Minister of Labour

The labourer of 1900 earned in a week about what a similar work now is paid in one day. There was no limit on hours of work; no minimum wage requirements. He was virtually held responsible for the consequences to himself of any accidents on the job....The position of labour at the start of the century was one of hardship and insecurity.

TODAY AND TOMORROW IN BRITAIN
January, 1952
Lady Megan Lloyd George, daughter of Prime Minister Lloyd George, former Deputy Leader of the British Liberal Party, Lady Member with the longest years of service in the House

Lady Megan Lloyd George told the story of Shackleton, the famous explorer, who called on Liberal prime minister David Lloyd George for advice and help in soliciting corporate support for an Arctic expedition. The prime minister was enthusiastic but warned that he might not be popular in business circles. Nevertheless he suggested the name of a leading industrialist. Later he heard that Shackleton had received a warm reception and had been offered $20,000, provided he took Lloyd George on the venture—and $30,000 if he returned without him.

CANADA'S CENTURY IF...
January, 1952
W.F. Holding, Immediate Past President, Canadian Manufacturers Association

What we fail too often to realize is that manufacturing has taken over as the principal source of national income. It was recently reported that one-third of Canada's national income is now earned in manufacturing industries. Manufacturing now provides employment for 26% of Canada's labour force as compared with 20% employed in agricultural pursuits.

POWER AND RESPONSIBILITY
January, 1952
Arthur Hays Sulzberger, President, *New York Times*

It would be rather disarming, for example—and might even be good politics—if the President of the United States had managed to say somewhere in his State of the Union message that all our tribulations were not made in Russia, that maybe at least a few of them had been caused by our own miscalculations, and even one or two of them by our own foolishness....It is my conviction that Soviet tyranny is the greatest menace of our time....[But] our constant criticism...does not persuade them and...if we concentrate on criticizing them, there is a real danger that we will not pay enough attention to criticizing ourselves.

THE BRITISH COMMONWEALTH TODAY
Poverty and Democracy
March, 1952
John G. Diefenbaker, MP, Lake Centre, Saskatchewan

Over the years I have endeavoured to find a reason to explain why it is economists on occasion can be wrong, and I was very much impressed the other day in reading that the American Association of Economists, 2000 strong, met in the City of Boston for the purpose of discussing the subject "INFLATION, ITS RESULTS AND ITS CURE." When they arrived there they found that the fee for this year had been raised from $2 to $5 for membership in their own organization....We talk about "H" bombs and weapons. The great Hweapon that is used by Communism today is hunger. Only the other day Mr. Paul Hoffman, the great American business man turned world philanthropist, made this statement: Communism would never have over-run China if the United States had gone into China with a rural reconstruction programme, and had spent one billion dollars in 1945. Action then would have saved thousands of lives and billions of treasure. In other words, you can not, and you never can secure the support of people who are poverty-stricken and fearful by the promise of any democratic principle.

FORTY YEARS IN THE BRITISH HOUSE OF COMMONS
June, 1952
Lord Campion of Bowes, GCB, former Clerk, House of Commons

Not long ago a Minister who was explaining an estimate to the House, made a mistake in his figures, which involved a small enough printing correction—he added a nought and made twenty million into two hundred million. One or two Members questioned this and when he sat down he realized he had made a 'bloomer.' So he went up to the office of the editor of Hansard and asked to make the correction. The editor objected that he could not correct an error of substance. However the Minister persisted. At last the editor said casually, 'You play golf don't you?' 'Yes, I do' said the Minister, 'but what's that got to do with it?' 'Well, you ought to know then that there's a rule against trying to improve the lie.'

CANADA IN 1953
March, 1953
The Rt. Hon. Louis S. St. Laurent, PC, QC, Prime Minister of Canada

Two possible obstacles to the almost unlimited development of Canada are outside our own borders. The greatest of all is the danger of another war, and next to that is the risk of a contraction of world trade, on which we depend so largely for many of the necessities of life and for the income with which to purchase those necessities. Action by other nations as well as by ourselves is required to meet those dangers. We cannot, of course, direct the conduct of other nations. But I suggest that our weight in world affairs and the influence we can exert is greater than our numbers would indicate. Are we really making the best use of that influence to promote peace and to foster international trade? We have established our outer lines of defence in Korea and West Germany, but we dare not concentrate all our military strength in those places. The promotion and safeguarding of peace begin at home. We have to do our part to provide for the territorial defence of our homeland and the continent in which we live. We know that modern science has opened up our north-land to potential danger of attack. We also know we could not bar a northern invader alone. We realize that the defence of this continent is a joint operation with the United States and that is why both countries have carried forward into the post-war world their co-operation in continental defence.

Fifty Years On

In 1953 the Empire Club celebrated its 50th anniversary and, on June 1, the coronation of Queen Elizabeth II. On that occasion an ancient toast was made:

> "Here's a health unto Her Majesty
> Confusion to her enemies.
> To him who will not drink her health
> I wish him neither wit nor wealth,
> Nor yet a rope to hang himself."

To any member who had heard the addresses in 1903–4, there would have been thoughts of déjà vu. Canada's relationship with Great Britain and the Empire was now reflected in speeches on the subject of the Commonwealth. Author, Nicholas Monsarrat, praised the accomplishments of Commonwealth countries, including the fact that on Coronation Day itself Mount Everest was first climbed, and by a New Zealander. He said that the Commonwealth had showed the world its greatest achievement, the "science of living together in peace." Another speaker called the Commonwealth "something which is unique in the whole course of history, something which is living and virile and vital." The young Queen was praised for her attitude to the Commonwealth countries and for "moving amongst them with such grace and understanding." The words of Sir John A. Macdonald were recalled as being a prophetic insight into the way in which the Commonwealth would develop, "The colonies are now in a transition state. Gradually a different colonial system is being developed—and it will become year after year, less a case of dependence on our part, and of overruling protection on the part of the other country, and more a case of health and cordial alliance." For the next two decades this topic always commanded attention. Through the 1950s and 1960s there were some 35 addresses on Empire and Commonwealth, including "The British Commonwealth in a

Bewildered World," "Bonds of Commonwealth Life," even "What Good is the Commonwealth?"

There were, as well, interesting Canadian issues of great importance raised in the anniversary year—emerging issues such as the "The Impact of the Jet on Aviation." The chairman of BOAC said, "Your fathers and mine might well have thought us insane had we told them that one day I should fly to you from Britain in a matter of hours." In 1953 George Hees, Minister of Transport, talked about air traffic in superlatives, as in the previous ten years domestic passenger traffic had sky-rocketed from one million to five million passengers per year. The president of the Bell Telephone Company spoke of advances that would have been considered science fiction a short time ago, announcing that already most long distance calls in Canada are dialled with the help of an operator straight through to the distant telephone.... "And soon you, our customers, will be dialling your own long distance calls, without regard to provincial or international boundaries." There were perennial problems in the country's unifying sym-bol, the railroad. Donald Gordon said, "Revenue simply must exceed expense or misery follows." The Club took pride in lauding medical research done by Canadians, and applauded Dr. Charles Best, discoverer of insulin, as he spoke with pride of the new Charles H. Best Institute on College Street in Toronto. Dr. Wilder Penfield, international famed neurosurgeon, spoke to the Club, but as an author. As a speaker he was teamed with a relatively unknown author, Pierre Berton, who had just writ-ten *I Married the Klondike*.

And then there was that perennial topic, Canadian /U.S. rela-tions. There were speakers from both sides of the undefended border. In an address titled "Let's Be Friends" the chairman of Kimberly-Clark noted that we were fast friends in spite of Canada's unhappiness with the 'New Look' in the U.S. defence program. George Romney, president of American Motors, in welcoming our diversity, quoted the story from a parliamen-tary session when one member, speaking on women's right to vote, said "After all, there are very slight differences between men and women," whereupon his opponent jumped up to proclaim, "Long live the differences." The Editor-In-Chief and Publisher of the *New York Tribune*, explaining that sometimes Americans take Canada for granted, said "Neglect is the sincerest form of flattery." He compared this situation with that of Latin Americans who say that the U.S. only pays attention to them when they have revolutions. He praised the joint project, the St. Lawrence Seaway, calling it "One of the most massive works in the history of mankind." The Seaway was the subject of an address by the Hon. Lionel Chevrier, Chairman, who said, "Look at the map of North America and you will see that the Great-Lakes-St. Lawrence Seaway is almost in the centre of the continent." When one realizes that more yearly tonnage passes through the locks at the Sault in the upper lakes region than through the Panama and Suez canals together, one gets some idea of the traffic likely to go through when the project is completed."

One crucial issue in Canada was the potential abolition of the death penalty. A debate took place between Arthur Maloney, who maintained that capital punishment was not a deterrent, and Joseph Sedgwick, who took the other side. Mr. Maloney injected some "gallows humour" into the argument with the story of the condemned prisoner mounting the gallows to his execution. As he climbed the thirteen steps he reached the last one which gave way beneath him. He grabbed the railing when he was inches above the trap door and turned to the Governor in anger to say, "This damned thing ain't safe!"

In tackling another issue of great importance to Canadians, Douglas Ambridge took on those who criticized Canada's forestry laws. According to these extremists, disaster was inevitable because the trees in Canada were mostly infected with disease and were doomed as surely "as if 75% of the population were affected by tuberculosis where there could be no segregation and where all were huddled together, coughing and expectorating over one another." Ambridge meticulously detailed the measures that were in place to prevent over-cutting, noting that "the drain on the forests caused by all industry is less than the annual yield." On the vital topic of atomic energy, Canada's role in the development of peaceful uses at the Chalk River Nuclear Laboratories was praised. "We, in Canada, may be justly proud of the contribution our scientists and engineers are making to the peaceful application of Atomic Energy....Never before have such possibilities been offered to mankind to improve his health, happiness and intellectual satisfaction as those now available from the future developments in Atomic Energy." From INCO a speaker said with optimism "Canada is now going through one of the great stages of its metal development; new mineral deposits are being found in all parts of the country. Many of these are deposits of metals for which the market is at present very limited."

Amidst all this optimism Billy Graham addressed the Club in an emotional and strongly worded plea. He described the age (mid-century) as one of "frustration," "nervous tension," of "selfishness" and "fear," and said, "You find lying, cheating, bigotry, greed, hatred, and immorality where ever you go." He quoted intellectuals who were saying that "We are now at the end of history, and we know it." Leaving a sober audience behind him, he charged them to look to a religious revival.

There were international issues to discuss in the 50s. In the Suez crisis Napier Moore, editorial director of *Maclean-Hunter*, said that "Much more than shipping tools are involved in Nasser's grab of the Suez Canal and always behind it is the shadow of Russia, the Kremlin's object being, as you know, the foothold in the Mediterranean and domination of the Middle East." Moore's speech was titled "Dulles Ditchwater" because, he said, "When the Suez crisis broke, the British press, which was supporting the government's policy of a firm, quick action, came out very strongly for such action. Then came Mr. Dulles, U.S. Secretary of State, with his restraining hand, and the subsequent conferences and talks, and talks, with the result that the British press coined the phrase that the Suez Canal had become Dulles' Ditchwater."

The Middle East would be a topic for the rest of the century and beyond. Brigadier Claude Dewhurst, who had worked in intelligence posts there for many years began by saying that "The Middle East really has been Great Britain's baby." He heaped credit after credit on the mother country for helping Syria and Lebanon to independence, founding the borders of Iraq and discovering oil there, defending Persia, carving out Israel and Palestine, "so that the Jews throughout the world owe to Great Britain's inspiration the fact that Israel exists." Now in full flight he praised Great Britain's success in Jordan, for putting the king there, and in Saudi Arabia, backing the great dams on the Nile, laying down railways and defending the Suez Canal, and keeping the Soviets out of the Middle East. And then, with all this behind her, Britain withdrew, "mostly in her own time, leaving good governments behind." He stated that "Great Britain does not like Nasser," who he called the "Blue-eyed boy of the Americans." That same year another speaker pointed out some practical concerns, noting that there were heightening tensions between Israel and the Arab world and that there were also real problems of security in the Middle East.

There was time amid these pressing issues to celebrate with Tom Patterson the huge success of Stratford, as the permanent theatre was now being built. Patterson called it Canada's Big League Theatre, praising the employment it gave, the boost to the tourist business, the opportunity to showcase the country's great talent, the sense of unity with the French-Canadian actors, and the prestige which created opportunity to do experimental things. He revealed what Tyrone Guthrie had written to Alex Guinness, extolling the project as a chance to strengthen ties with Canada, as the country was being wooed by the United States. "If we British are as stupid, as tactless and as apathetic about this as we look like being it is just going to be George III and the Boston Tea Party all over again." That year Torontonians enjoyed a cultural treat when the Metropolitan Opera came to town. Rudolph Bing spoke of performing in Maple Leaf Gardens. "When people ask me what I think of opera in Maple Leaf Gardens I reply we only hope ice hockey will look as well in the Metropolitan Opera House." He added, however, giving Toronto a pat on the head, "quite seriously we would never have believed that our performances would have ever been so successful in the Gardens....Your equipment is by all odds the best." Canada was now embarking on a remarkable step forward in support of the country's artists, the formation of the Canada Council. The Hon. Brooke Claxton, Chairman, spoke of its potential "the future of our country, in every field, but particularly in this, depends on people."

A foretaste of conflicts to come was given in an address by Sir Robert Watson-Watt in 1959. Sir Robert, a Canadian, "led the team which perfected the science of radio location—now universally known as Radar. It was this machinery of radio detection and control which revolutionized air warfare in the Battle of Britain." In words significant still in 2003 the speaker said, talking of the dangers of the nuclear age, "The diligent reader may even have learned that the Big Bad Bomb may be surpassed in demonic destructivity by the Poor Person's Poison....biological weapons of destruction. [There is] a toxic substance of which a total quantity of eight ounces, appropriately distributed, could kill off every human being on the planet, and this is only one item in the biochemists' Chamber of Horrors."

At the end of the 1950s Larry Henderson addressed the challenge of the one country on everyone's mind—Russia. The dramatic visit of Chairman Khrushchev to the United States and his visits to other countries had focused attention on his personality and the power of the country he led. "Within the past few weeks, we have watched Premier Khrushchev's remarkable progress across Asia, scattering largess wherever he went. In India he left nearly three hundred million dollars in credits, in Indonesia another two hundred million or more, even a hundred million in tiny Afghanistan. All this, in addition to another two hundred million a month ago to Egypt for the purpose of completing the Aswan Dam—not to mention the hundred million Mr. Mikoyan advanced about the same time to Cuba, on this continent."

There were harsh words when the U.S. rocket, the U-2, landed in the Soviet Union and harsh words were now stock in trade in the Cold War. Blair Fraser, editor of *Maclean's*, said, "The way to make gains in the Cold War now in 1960 and 1961 is to forget it, to stop talking about the Cold War, to stop trying to recruit so-called allies in this so-called conflict. Let us keep ourselves as strong as we must. Let us disarm as quickly as we can. Meanwhile, let us not go through this amphitheatre of conflict as if harsh words were a substitute for strength. Harsh words from both sides, I am now convinced, are doing nothing but alienating not only the uncommitted but some of the committed too."

Disarmament was the subject as the 1960s continued. General Burns, Permanent Mission of Canada to the United Nations, spoke of the Berlin crisis and the set-back to disarmament negotiations. "As everyone knows, the NATO powers and Warsaw Pact powers are confronting each other in Berlin and along the Iron Curtain. We know very well that the Russian attempt to alter the present situation in favour of the Communist bloc by the permanent division of Germany....has been such a threat to vital Western policies that the possibility of war is foreseen."

There was a new word on the Canadian scene—Medicare. It was causing considerable debate which reached the podium of the Club. In 1962 the president of the Ontario Medical Association spoke strongly against it, saying, "I would suggest to you that history shows that trying to control, or run, or centrally plan medical care can and usually does harm it." The president of the Canadian Medical Association echoed this position. "Canadian doctors recognize and support the need for government aid in making possible high-quality medical services for a proportion of our population. They believe that this can best be provided for by the provision of a voluntary plan, available to all Canadians."

As the 60s progressed thought turned to Canada's 100th birthday and Canadian unity, with the fear of separatism at the fore, as it would be for the rest of the century. Prime Minister Lester Pearson said, "There must be a determination to understand the real nature of Canada and the forces eroding that nature; to recognize the peril of serious internal divisions....to realize the opportunities of national strength through unity and the fatal weakness of division and discord." Peter Nesbitt Thomson, CEO of Power Corporation of Canada, and an English-speaking Quebecker noted that, fashionable as it was to blame English Canada for Quebec's problems, there was in the history of the French a background that led to the present situation. The French had been the explorers, the English developed agriculture and industry. He blamed the educational system of the French as "the most inhibiting factor in French-Canadian life," a position that would be hotly debated by others. The French prepared themselves for politics, Peter Thomson said, and for the professions and the priesthood, the English for commence and industry. Then Guy Favreau, Minister of Justice, said that French Canada finds itself in a position of near economic subservience to Canada's English-speaking majority. "Her people feel deeply that the time has come—indeed that it is their duty—to bring about economic liberation, and its corresponding social equality."

During the late 1960s Canadian unity was on the minds of many speakers. In 1964 the Hon. Leon Balcer spoke of the repatriation of the Constitution, challenging his audience with the proposition that Canada was probably the only major independent country in the world which had to depend on the Parliament of another country, not only for the power to amend the Constitution, but in fact to carry out the most insignificant amendment." While applauding repatriation, he saw the pitfalls, "We will have the power in Canada to amend our Constitution, but this Constitution will have to be amended and brought up to date by a long series of federal-provincial meetings. We are running a great risk of government by federal-provincial Conferences."

The great event of the 1960s was anticipated when, in 1964, plans were in the making for Expo '67. It was called an opportunity for unity. "We as a nation have been plagued with self-doubts for too long. The 1967 World Exhibition in Canada is an opportunity to bestir our imaginations and exercise our pride in our country." As a Canadian effort, it would bring pride to "all people, whether they live in Heart's Content, Newfoundland, or in Kitimat, British Columbia." Pride in Canada was echoed in many speeches with ringing pronouncements such as "The courage, dedication, vision and work of the Confederating Fathers, as well as the pioneers who joined hands with them, or who have followed in their wake, is our great heritage. Even the great poet, John Milton, was brought into the Confederation debate with his words, apparently written about Canada, "Providence being their Guide they builded better than they knew."

The 1960s ended as the century began, with the subject of Canadian-American relations, this time from the president of the Xerox Corporation, who tackled Canadians on their frequently expressed deep and resentful concern about excessive American investment in Canada. He quoted a great Canadian, Robert Stanfield, who said "I believe Canadians owe more to themselves than distrust, resentment, suspicion and antagonism in their relations with the United States. Instead they owe themselves a pride of great accomplishment, achieved by their own hard work and by offering freedom and stability to those who have had the faith and incentive to invest in this nation's future."

FIFTIETH ANNIVERSARY
November, 1953
A.E.M. Inwood, President, The Empire Club

The Empire Club was founded on November 18th, 1903 by a group of far-sighted gentlemen of Toronto headed by Lieut. Col. James Mason, having in mind an organization such as we know it today with the objective of furthering the interests of Canada and the Empire or the Commonwealth, as it is now known. Fifty years later The Empire Club of Canada, due chiefly to our past presidents, is known around the world and has the reputation of being the most effective forum in Canada. One of the reasons for this is that the Empire Club was founded upon the same ideals and with the same high interests as the British Commonwealth of Nations, which is also stronger and more closely knit than ever before and it is still the most important United Nations on Earth!

MR. MACKENZIE KING AND THE DEVELOPMENT OF THE COMMONWEALTH OF NATIONS
December, 1953
The Hon. John Whitney Pickersgill, PC, MP, Secretary of State of Canada

From 1922 on, I believe Mr. Mackenzie King had a greater influence on the development of the Commonwealth than any other public man in any part of the Commonwealth....He saw clearly, and earlier than most public men, that the only way the Commonwealth could be preserved and strengthened was by a relationship not only of complete equality but also of complete autonomy between its members—in spirit as well as in letters.

AN ADDRESS BY DAG HAMMARSKJOLD
February, 1954
Dag Hammarskjold, Secretary-General of the United Nations

Need I tell you what great personal admiration and affection I have for the man who was President of the General Assembly of the United Nations when I started my work there—your Secretary of State for External Affairs, Lester B. Pearson. I am sure it will not be news to you to hear that this admiration and affection are shared by many, many others—foreign ministers and other representatives of countries large and small, and officials of the Secretariat high and low—who have worked with him. His term as President of the Seventh Session of the General Assembly was not the first occasion, nor, I am sure, will it be the last, upon which he has exerted a significant influence on the side of that positive and constructive approach to world problems which is epitomized in the United Nations Charter....An example of how the United Nations exerts its influence toward the just and peaceful solution of a dangerous problem is in Palestine. This problem has been with the United Nations since 1947. Aside from those issues directly related to the Cold War, it is at once one of the most difficult and the most challenging of all, because the claims on both sides are so strong and so extremely difficult to reconcile. The problem is still far from ultimate solution and the danger of a breakdown in the armistice continues to be a cause for concern to the Member Governments in the Security Council and to me as Secretary-General.

WHAT MAKES A GOOD SCHOOL?
Human Relations in a Nutshell
March, 1954
Dr. C.C. Goldring, Director of Education, Board of Education of the City of Toronto

Periodically one hears statements such as the following: "Children now love luxury. They have bad manners, contempt for authority. They show disrespect for elders, and love chatter in place of exercise. Children are now tyrants, not the servants of their households."

That, gentlemen, was written by Socrates about 2400 years ago….

In human relations the five most important words are: "I am proud of you."

The four most important words are: "What is your opinion?"

The three most important are: "If you please."

The two most important: "Thank you."

The smallest word: "I"

The home that exemplifies the spirit implied in that quotation is a good home for children.

OUR SON'S HERITAGE
April, 1954
The Hon. Gaspard Fauteux, Lieutenant-Governor, Province of Quebec

If we are to become a united nation we must develop an esprit-de-corps among Canadians, old and young, French and English or whatever their origins are. We must learn to drop the racial origin tag on our official documents; when a man or woman is a Canadian citizen, he or she is a Canadian—period.

OPENING MEETING, SEASON 1954–55
October, 1954
The Rev. Canon V.J. Pike, CB, CBE, MA, Chaplain to the Queen

I love the words of an anonymous writer, and I leave them with you…they describe success. "He has achieved success who has lived well, laughed often and loved much, who has gained the respect of intelligent men and the love of little children, who has done his part, who has filled his niche and who has left this world a better place than he found it."

RAILWAY HIGHLIGHTS
Passenger Pessimism
November, 1954
Donald Gordon, Chairman, President, Canadian National
Railways

To put the matter bluntly, human freight is a losing proposition
all over North America. It is particularly unprofitable in Canada,
which leads the world in its number of miles of track per capita
and where an increasing preponderance of inter-city personal
travel is by automobile or bus.

OUR PARLIAMENT, ITS ORGANIZATION AND
WORK
January, 1955
J.B. McGeachy, Editor, *The Globe and Mail*, Toronto

A long time ago Sir Wilfrid Laurier, with a Quebec senatorial
appointment to make, could not decide between the merits of
two claimants. They were so nearly equal in vigour, wisdom and
party service that Sir Wilfrid was unable to make up his mind.
To solve the problem he named Monsieur Hyppolite
Montplaisir, a deserving gentleman of 80, on the assumption
that when, in due course, this Nestor among legislators had been
gathered to his fathers, the close contest would have settled itself
in one way or another. Many years later, gentlemen, M.
Montplaisir died at the age of 103. Sir Wilfrid and the two rivals,
by this time, had long ago gone to their rest. A Senate seat is a
great aid to longevity.

NEW CHALLENGES OF NORTH AMERICA'S
FASTEST DECADE
March, 1955
Ralph Jarron Cordiner, President, General Electric Co.

The real opportunity to create more employment is not by
resisting mobility, not by resisting progress in technology but

rather by putting more and more effort and attention upon research and advanced engineering development.

THE PEACETIME APPLICATIONS OF ATOMIC ENERGY
April, 1955
David Arnold Keys, Scientific Advisor to the President, Atomic Energy of Canada Ltd

No scientific discovery has created such devastating possibilities and at the same time offered vast opportunities for the benefit of mankind as that of the controlled release of atomic energy by nuclear fission. A fission of a pound of nuclear fuel releases as much heat as obtained from burning 2,700,000 pounds of coal, 360,000 gallons of gasoline or about 30 million cubic feet of natural gas.

PEACE, FREEDOM, SOCIAL JUSTICE—INVISIBLE VALUES
October, 1955
Dr. Walter P. Reuther, U.S. Labour leader and President of the United Automobile Workers (U.A.W.) and President of the Congress of Industrial Organizations (C.I.O.)

We have the challenge of proving that man can have both bread and freedom. That to get food in his stomach man need not put his soul in chains.

IS THERE AN ANSWER?
Ecclesiastical Protocol
October, 1955
Dr. Billy Graham, evangelist

I am reminded of an incident that happened to the archbishop of Canterbury some years ago. He was scheduled to visit an orphanage. In preparing for the occasion, the head of the orphanage gathered all the children together and said, "Now when the archbishop comes, there is a certain protocol you must observe. The Archbishop of Canterbury is always addressed as either 'My Lord' or 'Your Grace'....So the archbishop came. When he stopped in front of one small boy, he asked, 'Son, how old are you?' The little boy, frightened, looked up and answered 'My God, I am ten.'"

THE HUMAN FACTOR—A PERSONAL STORY
November, 1955
Commander Edward Whitehead, President of Schweppes (U.S.A.) and the General Manager of Schweppes (Overseas)

Winston Churchill is supposed to have told a certain General that he thought there was room for some improvement in his communications—particularly between officers and men. "I've always taken the view, Sir, that familiarity breeds contempt," replied the General. "Without a certain amount of familiarity," said Churchill, "it would be difficult to breed anything at all."

YOU AND YOUR DOCTOR
January, 1956
Dr. T. Clarence Routley, CBE, MD, LLD, President, British Medical Association, President, Canadian Medical Association

Health in the full meaning of the word is one of life's most priceless possessions. Your doctor should be one of your very best friends. In him you confide your innermost thoughts and sooner or later you place your life in his hands. He is not unmindful of the trust which he shares with you. He, like all other citizens, requires money to live, but his greatest joy and satisfaction comes from the realization that he is privileged in a high degree to save his fellow man.

THE FINANCING OF ECONOMIC GROWTH IN CANADA

February, 1956

James Elliott Coyne, Governor of the Bank of Canada

After ten years of depression and six of war, we have seen on this continent during the past ten years a renewal of the phenomenon of overall growth of the civilian economy. Perhaps it is not too much to say that we now take both the desirability and the fact of continuing growth for granted and when we think of Canada's economic prospects; we think of them in terms of growth, of how much and what kind of growth....For Canada as a whole, economic growth has developed on three bases—population, productivity and investment. Our total population is growing more rapidly than most other western countries, both by natural increase and by immigration, and so is the size of our working force. Output per man-hour is also growing in most industries, and so is the total national product. Conceivably the increase in productivity could be converted into more leisure rather than a greater production of goods and services, but that has not been done to any marked degree, so that production per head of population and the material standard of living have risen substantially over the past ten years. The third factor in our rate of growth has been the high proportion of total product that is devoted to capital expenditures for new construction and for machinery and equipment. The rate of such new investment is higher in Canada than in most other countries, higher than in the United States, for example, and higher than our own level of annual savings could sustain. It is probable that our rate of saving out of gross national product is also higher than the United States, but not so much higher as in the case of investment. At all events, investment has for several years exceeded saving in Canada; the deficiency has been made up from the outside world, and particularly from the United States, where saving exceeds domestic investment.

DEFENCE AND THE NORTH
April, 1956
The Hon. Ralph Osborne Campney, QC, MP, Minister of National Defence

In the last ten years our population has increased by nearly one-third and now stands just short of 16 million. Of this increase, some one and a quarter million people are new Canadians who, since 1945, have come to this country as immigrants. At least one out of every four of these new Canadians has made his start here in greater Toronto. The past decade, too, has witnessed the greatest period of industrial expansion, prosperity and general well-being in the history of our country. Canada's gross national product has risen from less than $12 billion in 1945 to more than $26 billion last year, and throughout that period we have consistently been one of the top trading nations of the world....as we look hopefully forward we think we see Canada ending the twentieth century as one of the world's major powers.

SO IT'S DULLES DITCHWATER
October, 1956
H. Napier Moore, former Editorial Director of Maclean-Hunter Publishing Co. Ltd.

I do want to say how pleasing and happy it is to be back at the Empire Club, because in these days, even in England, and in other parts of the world, the word "Empire" has almost achieved the connotation of a naughty word....I should, I suppose, explain the title of this address today—how it came about. When the Suez crisis broke, the British press, which was supporting the government's policy of a firm, quick action, came out very strongly indeed for such action. Then came Mr. Dulles with his restraining hand, and the subsequent conferences and talks, and talks, with the result that the British press coined the phrase that the Suez Canal had become "Dulles Ditchwater"....[A Britisher] after making a round of the pubs, being a little wobbly, got on a bus. He hadn't been there very long when a lady got on and immediately he jumped up and gave her his seat and spent the rest of the journey swinging on a strap. [As he got off he asked the conductor if he was impressed that] the "days of chivalry are not over." And the conductor said, "Well, I was wondering why you did it because there were only the two of you on the bus."

CANADA'S BIG LEAGUE THEATRE
November, 1956
Tom Patterson, Director of Planning, Stratford Shakespearean Festival

Theatre as with all the arts, can provide an opportunity for the 20th Century citizen to relax his body and obtain the food that is needed every bit as much as bread—the food that feeds the mind. Now let's look at theatre from a national point of view— and here again, we have some very practical values. First of all, it gives employment to a large number of Canadians and this number is considerably larger than the layman suspects. As well as the actors, there are stage hands, musicians, wardrobe and property people, designers, ushers, publicity people and many others. It sometimes comes as a shock to people when they are told that the payroll in Stratford at the height of the season con-sists of from 150 to 200 people. Then there is the tourist busi-ness—again using Stratford as an example—we have had char-tered buses from as far away as Texas. Special trains from Detroit, Quebec City, and the weekly tours sponsored by the Toronto *Telegram*. In its four years—or a total of 35 perform-ance weeks—Stratford has played to about half a million peo-ple—of which about 20% or 100,000 have been foreign visitors. Calculating the expenditure of each person at the very low amount of $25, think what this has meant in extra money in the country. Another value to the country—non-material perhaps, but nevertheless important—the success of the Festival has given Canadians a sense of pride in something of which heretofore we have felt rather ashamed. We had to go to New York or London to see the best in the arts. Now, we can see the best right here. And this sense of pride, in the community and the country, is very important to the development of a well-balanced population. Last year, the Festival made another contribution to Canadian life when it invited French-Canadian actors to participate. This move has been hailed as one which has done more to promote better understanding between the two major racial groups of Canada than anything else since Confederation. To quote the *Financial Post*: "Here is an example of the real mingling and intertwining of the country's two cultures.…No country but Canada is able, or has even tried before, to present Henry V just this way."

THE CONTRIBUTION OF CREATIVE CHEMISTRY TO THE HUMANITIES
February, 1957
Sir Miles Thomas, DFC, Chairman, Monsanto Chemicals, London, England

Moral progress is of no real significance to the vast under-privileged majority of mankind until certain basic material needs are met. A saint may embrace poverty, but national poverty will not breed a race of saints. It is the destiny of science to create the material climate which will nurture moral progress. The arts may point the way to paradise on earth, but it is science, and not the least the science of creative chemistry, which provides the means of getting there.…Nothing is so likely to capture the headlines of the press as an air crash, nothing less likely to receive well-merited publicity than a million miles of safe flying.

BRITAIN TODAY AND TOMORROW
February, 1957
Sir Saville Garner, KCMG, High Commissioner for the United Kingdom, Ottawa

Britain is an industrial country and must export or die. We live by world trade and must have the means to manufacture for sale abroad in order to pay for our imports. In the industrial revolution we were well endowed by nature since we had rich quantities of coal and iron. But we do not have in our islands all the natural resources for modern industrial production.

THE ROLE OF THE OPPOSITION IN PARLIAMENT
March, 1957
Stanley Howard Knowles, BA, BD, MP, C.C.F. National Vice-Chairman

Any opposition worth its salt must check the government, and it must prod the government. It must also address itself to its main task, which is to replace the government....No one will deny that our system works best when there is a change of government at reasonable intervals. Most of us have the feeling that the interval between changes in this country is becoming a bit longer than is reasonable.

ONTARIO'S ECONOMIC PROSPECTS IN 1957
April, 1957
The Hon. Leslie M. Frost, QC, LLD, DCL, Premier of Ontario

Since 1946 a million and a half people have been added to our population—an increase of one third. In less than a decade we have added to our population a number greater than the present population of the whole of British Columbia, or any other Canadian province with the exception of Quebec.

ONE MILLION DOLLARS FOR WHAT?
October, 1957
The Hon. Brooke Claxton, PC, DCM, QC, BCL, LLD, Chairman, The Canada Council

So, to meet the challenging needs and the opportunities of the country as we see them ahead, the Canada Council is there. It will be best judged by what it accomplishes. I believe that the best things it will do will be to assist people, individuals, to make a better use of their own capacities by taking them abroad or to

159

another teaching institution in Canada, by giving them a year within which to learn how to work, how to teach, how to study, how to paint better than they would otherwise do, because the future of our country in every field, but particularly in this, depends on people.

CANADIAN WOMEN AS CITIZENS
December, 1957
The Hon. Ellen L. Fairclough, Secretary of State for Canada

Despite the work of Emily Murphy and her confreres, there have only been six women appointed to the Senate of Canada, and now there are five sitting in the chamber. Since 1921 when they were first eligible for election to the House of Commons, there have just been nine women elected, and in this present Parliament there are only two. We do not show up very well in this regard in relation to European countries, but it is my opinion that one of the difficulties is in the size of the territory which is represented. No doubt some of the hesitation on the part of women to offer themselves for election to legislatures and to the House of Commons is the distance which they must necessarily travel in many cases to discharge their duties. There have never been any women in any of the legislatures east of the Province of Ontario and there has only been one in Ontario. But when we look at the municipal level of government, we find a different picture and I think that this bears out my contention that distance presents one of the main difficulties. It is very hard to arrive at the exact number of women who are serving on municipal councils and school boards, because the information is not available for some of the rural areas, but judging from the number who are recorded, I believe that a reasonable estimate is that there are approximately 1200 women at the present time serving in elective posts at the municipal level across Canada. When you consider in addition to that the number who serve at the non-elective level on hospital boards and local boards of one kind or another, the number must indeed be impressive.

REPORT OF ANOTHER JOURNEY
Compulsory Service
June, 1958
John White Hughes Bassett, Chairman and Publisher, *The Telegram,* **Toronto**

Preparedness is the first responsibility of citizenship.…I have advocated compulsory military service for most of my adult life because I have always believed that this is the best possible way in a country like Canada to build in our young people a sense of responsibility combined with the idea that they must give something to their country as well as take.…By mixing young Canadians from varied backgrounds and different geographical parts of the country in a common life of service under discipline, we could build a nation and a national consciousness more quickly than any other way.

TORONTO SHOULD HAVE THE BEST
The Eye of the Beholder
October, 1958
E.P. Taylor, CMG, **President of Argus Corporation, Chairman of the Executive Committee, Massey-Ferguson, Member of the Canada Council, President, The Art Galley of Toronto**

A man with a piercing eye and a shrinking wife on his arm, delivered himself of art judgements with the quick decision of a big business man. "Ho, Ho!" he exclaimed, blocking the traffic in front of Tom Thomson's *The West Wind,* "so that's the wonderful marvellous picture they're all taking about. Well I don't like it. I can't see anything in it." "Perhaps," suggested his wife softly, "we could see it better if we were further from it." "That's where I'm going to keep," he replied, "well away from it" and he stalked by the other Thomson pictures as if they were insults to his intelligence.…Today *The West Wind* has come to be the most popular picture in the Canadian Section of the Art Gallery, both in sale of reprints and in response to popularity polls.

GOOD NEIGHBOURS
Obedience to the Unenforcable
November, 1958
Charles E. Wilson, former United States Secretary of Defence,
Past President General Motors

Mere obedience to law does not measure the greatness of a
nation. It can easily be obtained by a strong executive and most
easily of all from a timorous people. Nor is the license of behaviour, which so often accompanies the absence of law, and which
is miscalled liberty, a proof of greatness. The true test is the
extent to which the individuals composing the nation can be
trusted to obey self-imposed law....[to] recognize the duty of
obedience to the unenforceable.

GOVERNMENT AND PRIVATE ENTERPRISE
February, 1959
The Hon. Robert H. Winters, President of Rio Tinto Mining
Company and former Minister of Public Works

With all these considerations in mind, I believe that Canada
should always be in the forefront of the world wide effort to
reduce barriers to trade and we cannot be in that position unless
we practise what we preach. Some risks are involved in such a
policy and I am not in favour of indiscriminate cutting of tariffs.
Every case must be carefully considered on its merits and there
may, on occasion, be justification for some upward adjustments
in individual cases. There should, in my opinion, be no doubts
of the direction in which we are moving. If our free institutions
are to survive, there must be fewer barriers to trade throughout
the free world. From the particular Canadian point of view we
should be part of that collective approach not only because we
are part of the free world, but because it is in our own selfish
interest to gain increased access to foreign markets. I conclude
by re-asserting my belief that greater freedom of trade is a necessary ingredient of our national welfare and that it will become
increasingly so in the years ahead.

CANADA'S ARTISTIC BOOM
The Myth of Art in a Garret
February, 1959
Celia Franca, Artistic Director, National Ballet of Canada

We have all heard the theory that great art can only be achieved by depriving the artist of all but the bare necessities of life so that his attention will not be distracted from the "creative process." Most artists disagree with this theory and believe that certain great composers and painters of the past pulled through despite appalling circumstances and not because of them....I can see no reason to be ashamed that the arts cannot pay their way on gate receipts. We do not ask that our universities, our libraries, our hospitals meet their expenses out of earnings. Surely it is also important that we have first rate music, painting and ballet. In the enjoyment of these arts we find ideas for the mind, and refreshment for the spirit, which makes our country a more pleasant and interesting place in which to live.

WHAT SHOULD BE DONE WITH THE CANADIAN SENATE?
March, 1959
The Hon. Arthur Roebuck, QC, Senator

The Civil Service largely controls the Executive, and the Executive controls the Commons, and, were it not for the Senate, between the two of them they would control Parliament....The Government House Leader and the Speaker are the only members of the Senate who continue to owe preferment to the Government of the day... All other members, once summoned, hold office for life, with nothing further to hope for and nothing to fear, with no masters but conscience and their loyalty to their country....It is not the role of the Senate to obstruct the elected Government of the day in the carrying out of its policies. Our function is to assist rather then hinder what is done in the Commons, always reserving the right to delay or reject what is plainly evil.

B.T. Richardson, Editor, *The Telegram*, Toronto and President of the Canadian Club of Toronto

The Senate has had few more ardent defenders than the honourable Senator from Toronto-Trinity....[It is] the duty of the Senate, to give, as Sir John A. Macdonald put it, a sober second thought to public matters. In its silent and somewhat glum way, that is what the Senate has been doing all these years, mainly to its own satisfaction but to the satisfaction of hardly anyone else. Senator Roebuck has amply demonstrated, on other occasions as well as this, that he possesses a sensitive grasp of the fact that the Senate is not popular with the public in Canada, that it is in need of reform, and that he shares some of the imaginative and creative ideas that are in circulation on the subject of what should be done about the Senate....It is an honour to be appointed to the Senate. It is an honour that should be borne with a sense of dedication to public service...not as a substitute for some order of chivalry.

NATO STRATEGY
May, 1959
General Lauris Norstad, Supreme Commander, Allied Powers, Europe

I want to speak to you about the North Atlantic Treaty Organization, to tell you briefly where we stand and to suggest to you the basis or the background of what might be called our military thinking. In speaking of NATO today, I do so in the special context created by the fact that we are just now celebrating the Tenth Anniversary of the Alliance. These have been ten eventful years, and years in which NATO has more than fulfilled the highest hopes of its founders. Let us recall for just a moment the world scene in 1947, 1948 and 1949. Let us look particularly at Europe and the area of the Atlantic Community. Among the events which compelled our countries to come together was the loss of Czechoslovakia behind the Iron Curtain, and the Soviet efforts to make a pawn of the courageous people of Berlin by their brutal attempt to deny to these people, by blockade, the bare necessities of life. In those years as I travelled through Europe I was impressed, as I am sure many of you were, by the general apathy, the lack of interest and activity and, in fact, the despair written on the faces of most of the people. There was little hope for tomorrow. If there was thought of tomorrow, there was fear of what the day would bring. We are all familiar with the change, the truly miraculous improvement, that has taken place in the past ten years. Today, the shops are filled with goods and people, the factories are working at full speed; construction is taking place everywhere and, most important, hope and confidence are written on the faces of almost every man, woman and child. Some of this change must be credited to the passage of time. Some of it may by accounted for by the fact that in these ten critical years, Europe has been coming out of the disaster and destruction of a great war. But these are passive factors which cannot fully explain the miracle of change. A positive factor has been the North Atlantic Treaty Organization and the strength, perhaps more moral than military, that has sprung from this tangible evidence of the desire and the determination of free people to face the threat against them, to remain free.

THE OIL INDUSTRY—WHERE DO WE GO FROM HERE?
October, 1959
E.D. Brockett Jr., President, the British American Oil Company Limited

[When] Kettering [of General Motors]....was told to double his research staff and complete a research project in half the scheduled time, he asked his boss, "How much faster do you think an egg would hatch if you put two hens on it?"....The penetration of markets for Canada's surplus gas is a matter of extreme urgency, for producers must soon begin to realize a reasonable return on their investment in this phase of business. If they do not, they must be forced to cut back on the exploration necessary to the orderly development of the industry in Canada. It is essential that prompt action be taken by the National Energy Board and the Canadian Government to approve pending applications for export before markets that are available today are lost to other sources of supply.

THE DEVELOPMENT OF MEN
March, 1960
Moorhead Wright, Manager Operations, General Electric Management Research and Development Institute

Managing is a separate and distinct kind of work which is emerging as another profession....We must estimate, from sensitive observation of his work, whether he has demonstrated the desire and capabilities that fit a man for the profession of managing. This is a safeguard against the very common mistake of saying, "We need a Manager of Engineering. We'll look around and pick our best engineer and put him in this spot." If we followed this line of reasoning in, say, baseball, Ted Williams would be manager of the Red Sox....many times the outstanding individual performer is made a manager and we lose the good individual performance and get a mediocre manager.

THE IMPACT OF AIR TRANSPORT ON WORLD AFFAIRS
March, 1960
Sir Gerard D'Erlanger, CBE, Chairman of BOAC (now British Airways)

During his visit to London, in a broadcast, President Eisenhower made this statement which I believe to be significant and fundamental: "I like to believe that people in the long run are going to do more to promote peace than are Governments. I think people want peace so much that one of these days Governments had better get out of the way and let them have it"....We at home have recently been informed that the best we can hope for under present circumstances is four minutes warning of our impending doom, and I don't suppose you over here have many more minutes coming to you. Now, people can only promote peace by getting to know each other....We are not all alike and there is no use pretending otherwise, but at least by contact, conversation and at first hand we can get to a point of understanding and respect which no amount of printed material can achieve, and this again is where air transportation is revolutionizing the scene.

SOME ASPECTS OF THE PUBLIC SERVICE
April, 1960
The Hon. S.H.S. Hughes, QC, Chairman, Civil Service Commission of Canada

There is a most useful and salutary tradition which is part of our parliamentary institutions and which protects the civil servant from criticism in Parliament of his actions and his advice. Here, the head of the department, a Minister of the Crown, takes all responsibility for the activities of his staff, and is the only legitimate object for attack....Without it, governments would only get from their professional advisers the type of advice which they wanted to hear and to support in the House of Commons. The independent, unprejudiced position of the Civil Service, upon which the security of the State so largely depends under our democratic system, would be fatally compromised.

GAINS AND LOSSES IN THE COLD WAR
October, 1960
Blair Fraser, Editor, *Maclean's Magazine*

Let us begin with the personality of Mr. Khrushchev and his alleged susceptibility to uncontrolled, childish, kindergarten temper tantrums. I don't suppose it needs to be recalled that this interpretation is a little implausible on its face. Mr. Khrushchev spent many years working very closely directly under a mad tyrant whom, as we now know, he hated with every fibre of his being. He was able to conceal this hatred not only well enough to survive but survive at the very top of the Soviet hierarchy and, first of all, to win an engagement—a duel to the death, literally—with the most powerful and well armed scoundrel then surviving in the whole world, Beria. And finally he emerged to his present position, as the established, if not unchallenged, director of the Communist half of the world.

SOME ASPECTS OF MY PROFESSION
January, 1961
The Hon. Mr. Justice Samuel Freedman, Judge of the Court of Appeal, Manitoba

I recall the statement of a lady who said, "Don't talk to me about lawyers. I have had so much trouble with my husband's estate that sometimes I wish he hadn't died."

PROBLEMS OF NATIONAL MATURITY
February, 1961
His Excellency Major-General Georges P. Vanier, Governor-General of Canada

One of the greatest needs of the moment is for a more active and widespread Civic Spirit. We must take pride in our communities and refuse to tolerate injustice and inefficiency within them. Edmund Burke once remarked: "All that is necessary for the triumph of evil is that good men do nothing." And one of the leaders in Canadian industry asked, only the other day: "Are enough Canadian corporations and business men accepting their responsibility and grasping their opportunity to participate in public affairs? Are there enough Canadians whose sense of responsibility will lead them to share in the democratic process?" For democracy is a challenge to all. Active democrats must have faith that their fellow-citizens love and seek the common good. It is up to us not to disillusion them. We must prove our zeal for the common good, which is above individual interests, by standing firm for justice and truth even at the cost of personal sacrifices. If we can spread this attitude we shall find that the law will be obeyed because it is seen to involve the common good. It will be kept even when it could safely be broken for the sake of private gain.

THE FUTURE OF CANADIAN TELEVISION
February, 1961
Joel W. Aldred, President, Baton Aldred Rogers Broadcasting Ltd.

Colour is the great new dimension in telecasting....In 1960, approximately 150,000 colour sets were sold in the United States, bringing the total in use since production started six years ago to approximately 650,000. It is estimated that within our own viewing area there are approximately 1,800 to 2,000 colour sets.

HOW INTERNATIONAL IS SCIENCE?
The Meighen Speeches. Unrevised, Unrepentant
February, 1961
Dr. John Tuzo Wilson, OBE, Professor of Geophysics University of Toronto

Perhaps I might tell you a story about Mr.[Arthur] Meighen....When his book of speeches was published, it was entitled *Unrevised and Unrepentant*. His granddaughter was asked what she thought of it. She was a very bright young lady and she said she thought it was "Unrevised, unrepentant and uninteresting."

ONTARIO'S NUMBER ONE HEALTH PROBLEM
March, 1961
The Hon. Matthew B. Dymond, MD, CM, Minister of Health, Ontario

Cancer and Heart Disease vie with each other for the position of Number One Killer in Canada. There is, however, a very real and great difference between Number One Killer and Number One Health Problem. On all counts mental disorders constitute the

Number One Health Problem in Canada....For every hospital bed occupied by the physically ill...including all the diverse physical diseases and handicaps which afflict mankind, we have a bed occupied by one suffering from mental disorder....Thirty three of every 1,000 babies born will be mentally retarded in some degree....2.5 of each 33 will probably require institutional care for their entire lives.

INDIA—TODAY AND TOMORROW
March, 1961
Ambassador Braj Kumar Nehru, Commissioner General for Economic Affairs, India

The per capita income in India today is about $70 per annum; that of Canada is $2,050 per annum. It may help you to imagine how the average Indian is compelled to live if you were to attempt to limit your weekly expenditure on food, housing, clothing, transportation, medical relief, schooling, and everything else, to a dollar and a quarter.

ATLANTIC TRADE COMMUNITY, FOUNDATION OF THE FREE WORLD
Peaceful Coexistence
April, 1961
The Hon. Lester B. Pearson, Leader of the Liberal Party in Canada, and Leader of Her Majesty's Loyal Opposition

Let us not fool ourselves. When the Communist leaders talk about peaceful coexistence, they do not mean friendly cooperation with our form of society. As James Reston of the *New York Times* wrote during Mr. Khrushchev's visit to U.S.A., when the Soviet leader was making friendly noises, "Khrushchev did not take back his threat to 'bury us;' he merely promised not to kill us first." Capitalism would be buried alive, overwhelmed by the 'superiority' of Communism, as feudalism was overwhelmed by Capitalism.

THE WORLD AROUND US

February, 1962
His Excellency, Livingston T. Merchant, U.S. Ambassador to Canada

It is perhaps harder for North Americans than for Europeans, or even Asians for that matter, fully to appreciate the significance of the changes which have occurred in the lifetime of those in this room. Two broad oceans gave both Canadians and the people of the United States, for long decades, a sense of fundamental security and detachment from a world which from time to time seemed dangerously disordered. I think Canada's close ties with Britain—the bonds of Empire and then the Commonwealth—and Canada's participation from the very outset in two World Wars probably gave to you in this country an earlier and better perspective and less of an inclination to build a foreign policy on isolation. We in my country, however, have come a long way in the last twenty years as we learned in Donne's words that "No man is an island, entire of itself." And then, to underline the interdependence of all men, the poet goes on to say: "...therefore, never send to know for whom the bell tolls; it tolls for thee." We accept interdependence today. We accept it not in substitution for independence but in the knowledge that only by an acknowledgment of interdependence can any country, which desires to remain free, insure, in fact, its own independence. I am certainly safe in saying that changes in the world around us have been great and have in turn enforced changes not only in our attitudes and outlook but in our national policies. Nevertheless, the rate of change in science, in war-making potential, in economic relationships and institutions, in the number of new nations, in the break-up of great empires and the rise of new ones—less benevolent than the old empires, if I may permit myself an understatement—compel us, as I said a moment ago, to step back and look at the world environment in which we live if we, as individuals and countries, are to understand the dangers and the opportunities that lie ahead....President Kennedy recently said that all the elements in the foreign policy of the United States lead to a single goal—the goal of a peaceful world of free and independent states. I think Canadians likewise would agree that all the elements in Canadian foreign policy are similarly designed to lead to that same goal. The President went on to say: "This is our guide for the present and our vision for the future—a free community of nations, independent but interdependent, uniting North and South, East and West, in one great family of man, outgrowing and transcending the hates and fears that rend our age."

THE BATTLE LINES OF THE 1914–18 WAR REVISITED
March, 1962
The Hon. Lt. Col. J. Keiller Mackay, Lieutenant-Governor of the Province of Ontario

In the Town of Ypres the Great Cloth Hall and stately Cathedral, as well as every other building, were razed to the ground. Here stands the majestic Menin Gate Memorial bearing the names of 55,000 killed in the Salient who have no known graves, over 10,000 of whom are Canadians. Within a few kilometres of Ypres over 1,000,000 died. In this area alone there are 137 military cemeteries. On the evening of May 2nd last year, along with my wife and two sons who accompanied me on this high and inspiring pilgrimage, I presented under the silent majesty of the Menin Gate to the Burgermaster of Ypres and to the Chairman of the Last Post Fund, on behalf of Colonel E. C. Lancaster of St. Catharines, two silver trumpets. This presentation was made in the presence of a vast concourse of the people of Ypres and military representatives from Great Britain, France and Canada. When at nightfall four trumpeters sounded the Last Post the solemn grandeur of the moment, the rushing waves of sentiment and the flowing tide of stirring memories almost overwhelmed me. Once again I saw the forces of Great Britain, of the Dominions and of Belgium, yea and gallant France, hurl themselves with invincible valour on the advancing or retreating foe. Once again I saw the blood of France, Belgium, the British stream on the same field. In those myriad graves their bodies were deposited. The rain and the dew now fall from heaven upon their union in the tomb and the green corn of spring has broken forty-six times from their commingled dust. Yea, every hill and valley that invests that long line from Soissons to the North Sea is sacred as a battleground of Canada, consecrated by those who fought and doubly consecrated and hallowed by those who fell; rich with memories of brave and heroic youth, speaking an eloquent witness to the matchless valour of their hearts, the deathless glory of their arms and the indissoluable union and imperishable brotherhood of all people.

THE CHALLENGE OF TODAY'S AFFLUENT SOCIETY
Medicare
October, 1962
The Rt. Rev. Dr. J.R. Mutchmor, Moderator of The United Church of Canada

The development of the welfare society has brought a new word into a sharp focus. This word is "Medicare." More than the people of Saskatchewan are going to become excited about it in the very near future. It is a current index word of the Welfare Society.

FACING FACTS IN LABOUR RELATIONS
November, 1962
H. Carl Goldenberg, OBE, QC, federal mediator

I have entitled my talk "Facing Facts in Labour Relations" because I have found that a refusal to face facts by one side or the other or by both sides is a major cause of misunderstanding between labour and management. The public, in turn, not knowing the facts, often tends to reach unfair and unwarranted conclusions on industrial disputes. People are inclined to judge a dispute in terms of "right" and "wrong"; the fact is that generally neither side is wholly right or wholly wrong....Normal everyday behaviour does not constitute news. The fact that 99 percent of employed workers in an area may be at their work every day is not reported in the press. But when a group, however small, goes on strike—That is News!

THE LAW IS YOUR BUSINESS
November, 1962
Deputy Commissioner George B. McClellan, Royal Canadian Mounted Police

It has been reckoned that during the Pre-Christmas season this last year, Canadians stole some 3% of all goods that moved out of retail stores in the month of December.

THE WINDS OF CHANGE IN THE NEW NATIONS
January, 1963
Roy Thomson, Chairman, Thomson Newspapers Ltd.

It is with this purpose in mind that I recently announced the setting up of the Thomson Foundation. With the complete consent of members of my family, who are my heirs and partners in my various businesses, it is the intention to place in this Foundation securities to a value of some $15 million. This will be available to assist in the development of mass media in these new nations. The purposes of the Foundation are many and the ways they will operate to advance these purposes are manifold....In conclusion, let me make myself quite clear on one point. If the Thomson Organization goes into the newly-emergent countries of Africa, Asia and the Caribbean in order to promote newspapers, magazines and television stations, this is because we feel we have a technical job to do. We do not regard it as our function to use these media in order to interfere in their social or political affairs. This is not our business, any more than it is the business of an engineer who builds a hydroelectricity plant, what food is cooked with the electricity he provides.

THE CHALLENGE OF 1963
January, 1963
Claude Jodoin, President, Canadian Labour Congress

Mr. David Grenier, financial editor of *The Telegram* in this city, recently made reference to the effects of automation in one of his columns. He used these words. "Let's not kid ourselves about automation: It can hurt—and hurt bad." And then he went on to cite two myths…Myth One: That workers displaced through automation can find jobs elsewhere. Myth Two: That the automation industry itself creates enough jobs to offset lower demand for production workers. I can't say we always agree with the editorial views of the Toronto *Telegram*—it can hardly be considered a paper leaning to the left; but I must say I share Mr. Grenier's views.

CANADA'S ECONOMIC POSITION
Government and Business
February, 1963
The Rt. Hon. John G. Diefenbaker, Prime Minister of Canada

A politician, in an argument with a surgeon and an engineer, expressed himself very well.…They were arguing the question as to which was the oldest profession. The Surgeon said, "Of course, it is the medical profession. The operation on Adam's rib created woman." The Engineer said: "We came in before you. Who created order out of chaos?" But the politician said: "I win. Who created chaos?"….Some of you in business say: "Oh, if you could only run government the way you run business." Well, it would be interesting. What would you do in business, if every decision that you made, every expenditure that you indulged in had to go before a daily meeting of the shareholders, beginning at two-thirty each day and lasting until ten p.m.; where you are required to answer some questions more or less relevant to the business, some not; where…you would be required to place the estimates of every department of your business before the shareholders in detail; you would allow them to debate and discuss a single department for days. That is democracy.

PERSONAL RESPONSIBILITY AND INTERDEPENDENCE
Communism and the Church
August, 1963
The Most Rev. and Rt. Hon. Arthur Michael Ramsey, MA, DD, Archbishop of Canterbury

The Soviet Government has a kind of two-fold policy towards the Orthodox Church, the historic church of the country. On the one hand, the State allows freedom for worship in a number of churches which are allowed to be open for worship by a State license....On the other hand there is intense pressure and, indeed, persecution upon the Christian church. No sort of church activities are allowed outside the church building itself. No meetings, no schools, no clubs, no gathering of members of the church beyond a certain number...and all the time intense anti-God propaganda goes on in schools, in colleges, on the radio and in many other ways as well....It would take the most immense courage for a young man or woman in a school or university in Russia to declare themselves to be a Christian.

A NATIONAL PURPOSE
October, 1963
The Rt. Hon. Lester B. Pearson, Prime Minister of Canada

I do not think that a national purpose can be set down in glowing phrases. It is expressed in the spirit in which we deal with particular problems. It is the purpose, and the determination to make Canada "a union not of parchment, but of men's hearts and minds."

THE WORK OF THE CENTRAL BANK
October, 1963
Louis Rasminsky, Governor, The Bank of Canada

Nearly a century ago, Walter Bagehot, the English banker and journalist, said "Money will not manage itself," and the essential task of the central bank is to manage the nation's money. This task is obviously a public responsibility. The central bank is therefore, in all countries, a part of the general apparatus of government. But most countries, including Canada, have established their central banks on a basis which removes them from the ordinary machinery of government and endows them with a degree of independence, and thus of responsibility, which is not to be found in a government department. Presumably this reflects the view that the interests of the community will, over a period of time, be best served by arrangements of this character. But since monetary policy is an instrument of public policy, and since it is conducted by the central bank under a statute passed by Parliament, it is clear that the Government must also feel responsibility for the policy which is followed. In the nature of things, the responsibility for day-to-day operations lies with the Bank of Canada, but the Government, in the person of the Minister of Finance, is kept fully informed about the policies being followed by the Bank, and the Government has the opportunity and the responsibility to form its own views as to the appropriateness of the Bank's policies. If the Government should find the Bank's policies unacceptable, it must make its views known and this would naturally give rise to efforts to reach a common view as to the policies that should be followed. If this should not prove possible, then in the final analysis, in a democratic society, the views of the Government must prevail on this as on other matters. But this fact would not relieve the Governor of his own responsibility. The public is entitled to assume, as long as the Governor remains at his post, that the monetary policy followed is one for which he is prepared to take responsibility. This is the principle of joint responsibility for monetary policy as I see it. I think this principle is now well understood and widely approved in Canada and that it is working well at the present time.

CENTENNIAL BUSINESS IS YOUR BUSINESS
Canada. No Better Place
October, 1963
George C. Metcalf, President, George Weston Limited, Director of the National Centennial Administration

Canada—nowhere in the world a better place to live. We have a boundless wealth of natural resources, bounteous harvests—enough to feed the world. Truly a nation supremely blessed....The world knows us as a young, dynamic, prosperous nation, willing to tackle anything, and thrill to the unknown. A nation growing in grandeur, measured for the mantle of greatness...exhilarating and free, exploding with opportunity—wide open to the genius and activity of free men.

WHAT IS WRONG WITH PARLIAMENT?
Insuring Separation
November, 1963
Peter C. Newman, National Affairs Editor, *Maclean's Magazine*, author of *Renegade in Power: The Diefenbaker Years*

The...element currently baffling the professional politicians in Ottawa is how to deal with separatism in Quebec. I was in Quebec City recently, and noticed that a local general insurance agent was advertising his services, in *Le Droit* by using the slogan "WE INSURE EVERYTHING EXCEPT CONFEDERATION."

CANADA'S DEFENCE
Homage to the Speaker of the House
November, 1963
The Hon. Paul T. Hellyer, PC, MP, Minister of National Defence

Often we do things unthinkingly by habit, without any reference
to the rationale on which they were originally begun. If you have
visited the House of Commons and watched members bowing
to the Speaker, you would assume that the reason was based on a
deep respect for the high office of the first commoner. No doubt
this is a conscious factor for some, but the origin, I am told, is
far removed. In the old Westminster, the Chapel of St. Edward
was directly behind the Speaker's Chair. Members, on entering
the Chamber, paid homage to the Cross. The ritual has continued long after its original meaning has been almost forgotten.

DIAMOND JUBILEE DINNER
February, 1964
The Rt. Hon. Sir Alec Douglas-Home, Prime Minister of Great
Britain and Northern Ireland

I remember at the beginning of the war being in a sergeants'
mess in Glasgow with a lot of Scotsmen around, throwing their
weight around, and there was a corporal of the Irish Fusiliers
there and he could stand it no longer. He went up to a sergeant
in the Argyles and he shook his hand in his face and he said,
"The heart of an Irishman beats as loyally under the tunic of an
Irish Fusilier as ever it did under the kilt Of a Highlander."
Confused anatomy, but the meaning is clear. Under what better
circumstances could I come to talk to The Empire Club of
Canada than coming fresh from conversations that I have had
with the Prime Minister of Canada, one who has always played
such a creative part in international affairs. I don't think I shall
be revealing any secrets when I say that one of the subjects we
touched on was Anglo-Canadian trade, and I said to him that I
hoped Canada in the future would buy more from Great Britain
than she is at present, at which he looked faintly surprised but

readily agreed that our trade ministers should meet and talk. Very good—this is splendid. I must warn both Ministers I hold the whip hand because if Britain wants to earn dollars from Canada, I warn you, I shall send the Beatles to Toronto—and they will bring back, I think, either Canadian dollars or Ontario silver or whatever it may be.

DIFFICULTIES OF THE UNITED NATIONS IN MAINTAINING PEACE

April, 1964

The Hon. Paul Martin, PC, MP, Secretary of State for External Affairs

The Cyprus situation raised such a demand yet, when the call came for the United Nations to establish a peace force in Cyprus, the response from member governments was on the whole disappointing. Canada was among the first countries to be approached for assistance. We were the first country to commit itself definitely to provide troops. Other nations joined us in this move and I pay warm tribute to Sweden, Finland and Ireland whose contingents are to serve with Canadians in the Cyprus operation. I make special mention of the United Kingdom, which is continuing under the United Nations flag to contribute substantially to the cause of peace in that troubled island....The method of financing the Cyprus force is significant because, once again, it brings into sharp focus the fundamental issues raised in relation to the financing of these peace-keeping operations. This audience will be aware that for the past few years the United Nations has been teetering on the brink of bankruptcy, because of the heavy burdens assumed in the Middle East and the Congo, but more significantly because a number of member states—including two Great Powers—with full capacity to pay have failed to pay their share of the financial costs. Others have been slow in paying, even when reductions were granted to take into account their relative incapacity to pay. This is a deplorable situation for an organization established primarily to maintain peace and security. It is especially urgent in view of the growing demands for peace keeping operations, which have demonstrated their worth. It is moving toward a climax this year because a number of states, including the Soviet bloc, now have accumulated arrears of payment which make them vulnerable to Article 19 of the Charter. It provides for the loss of vote in the General Assembly when arrears amount to two full years. When it next meets, the General Assembly will have to deal with this critical situation, which has far-reaching political and financial implications, unless steps have been taken in the meantime by those in default to liquidate their arrears. As a consistent and firm supporter of the United Nations, Canada believes that all member states should willingly accept their share of the financial burdens of peace keeping, just as they all share in the benefits which flow from continuing peace and stability. Our policy in this regard is straightforward. We have responded promptly to requests for military assistance in all theatres of United Nations peace-keeping. We have paid our assessments in full. We have made voluntary contributions on an ad hoc basis to keep the operations afloat. We have made and supported proposals designed to afford an opportunity for negotiated settlement of the financing arrangements.

CANADA—A NATION OR A SATELLITE
April, 1964
The Hon. Thomas Douglas, MP, Leader, New Democratic Party

How often have we sung "O Canada, we stand on guard for thee," apparently unaware that more and more of Canada has fallen into foreign hands, not by conquest or armed might but by the steady acquisition of our industries and resources by American corporations. Increasingly we are like a man who started out by renting some of the rooms in his attic to his neighbour and now finds that he has rented one room after another until he and his family are living in the basement.

MINING IN AN UNDERDEVELOPED COUNTRY, AFRICA
April, 1964
Sir Ronald L. Prain, OBE, Chairman, Rhodesian Selection Trust Group

Two thirds of the world's population is poor, and the poor are multiplying twice as fast as the rich. Two thirds of the world's population has an average income in cash or in kind of $100 a year; for the other third it is $1000.

CANADIAN UNITY
October, 1964
The Rt. Hon. Lester B. Pearson, PC, OBE, MA, LLD, Prime Minister of Canada

I am prompted on this occasion to make a few observations about the recent visit with which, because of my office, I was closely associated—a visit which gave me, as I am sure it gave millions of Canadians, the greatest pleasure and a feeling of privilege for having the Queen in Canada. A visit which was initiated some two years ago, when it was thought fitting and indeed it was fitting to invite the Queen and her consort to come to Canada to take part in the celebration of events which I believe were worthy of the Royal Presence, the two Conferences of 1864, a hundred years ago, in Charlottetown and in Quebec City, which led to our Confederation. The invitations were extended at a time when conditions were a little easier in one part of the country to be visited, than they have been in recent months. And because of unhappy developments in recent months I, as the head of the government, was under some worry and anxiety and indeed, pressure—whether to put this off and advise that it should be cancelled or not. The pressure came from a few extremists in one part of Canada. And I believe, the more so now that the visit is over, that the purpose of their crude pressures, and I was subjected to them—the very purpose of this pressure was to get the government to cancel the visit.

And that would have been a great triumph for them, if it had been cancelled, and would have given them a prestige and authority in their own area which they didn't deserve and shouldn't have. These threats were made the more significant and, I believe, the more dangerous by the publicity that they received, some of which, I think, was excessive and exaggerated and was just what they wanted. And we read, all of us, phrases such as "subjecting Her Majesty to awful risks," "slighting the danger," "Is Quebec to be another Dallas?" All that kind of thing which was bound to stir up public opinion, which was what they wanted—the extremists. And I reaffirm that to cancel the visit in the face of threats of that kind would have been their triumph and our humiliation.

MOST FREQUENT SPEAKERS AND TOPICS
1964

A sixty year list of Empire Club speeches recorded that the most frequent guest speaker was the Hon. George A. Drew who addressed 15 meetings between 1933 and 1954. By far the most frequently addressed subject on one aspect or another was "the Empire and the Commonwealth" which was the topic for 115 speeches.

THE UNITED STATES AND CANADA—COMMON AIMS AND COMMON RESPONSIBILITIES
March, 1965
The Hon. George H. Ball, Under Secretary of State of The United States

By agreeing to eliminate tariff and other barriers to automotive trade we avoided economic warfare....The [recent] handling of the automotive problem is a good example of how two nations can live together rationally on a single continent. In its simplest terms the central problem that we face together...is how we can preserve the distinct values of two separate national identities while still employing the resources of this vast continent in the most efficient manner. This is not, I submit to you, a problem that should outrun the imagination of highly ingenious peoples. After all, in the life of any nation there are many areas where the strict application of economic laws is traditionally tempered to preserve social values. This is almost the universal experience of nations with regard to agriculture and natural resources....Our governments are constantly consulting as to how to find a balance between common economic logic on the one hand and each nation's social and political objectives on the other.

AN AMERICAN VIEW OF BRITAIN
March, 1965
Douglas Fairbanks, KBE, DSc, Chairman, Fairbanks
International, actor, diplomat

There has always been much to praise about Britain, much to deplore, much to criticize, much to inspire, much to pity, much to laugh at, much to irritate. But it would be a poorer world...were she to fall back into the shadows of history.

RESEARCH IN THE UNITED KINGDOM
March, 1965
Lord Rothschild, GM, SCD, FRS, Chairman of Shell Research

The unknown and the tantalizing stimulate me most. Will fuel cells be used in the next ten years on a large scale for the generation of electricity? Will insecticides completely specific to particular insect pests be developed? Will you go on using a motor mower on your lawn or will you spray it with a harmless growth regulant twice a year? Finding the answers to these questions does not imply the expenditure of vast sums of money; it requires the creation of environments in which good scientists, of whom there are not too many, can work happily and successfully. Huge teams with gold-plated equipment will not provide answers any more than the monkeys on the typewriters produce a sonnet by Shakespeare.

ROYAL VISIT DINNER
June, 1965
Her Majesty Queen Elizabeth, The Queen Mother

I think that I fell in love with Canada when the King and I came here in 1939. And each time I come back my feeling of affection seems to grow. So, it is a great pleasure for me to be once again in Toronto, where this evening, as on all previous occasions, I have been so much moved by the warmth of your welcome. I am happy that this visit affords me the opportunity of dining not only with the officers of my Regiment but also with the members of both the Royal Canadian Military Institute and The Empire Club of Canada. These three institutions are firm bulwarks in a changing world preserving and perpetuating those traditions which have contributed so much to the greatness of Canada. The unity of the Commonwealth finds expression in such enduring organizations with their common attachment to the principles of peace and freedom. To The Empire Club of Canada I extend my gratitude for the honour you do my Regiment tonight. Your name reminds us of the unique service of the British Commonwealth in linking and harmonizing the Old World and the New. Your constant efforts for a united Canada have proclaimed for over sixty years the ideals of faith, responsible nationhood and loyalty to your Sovereign.

STEEL
October, 1965
Vincent William Thomas Scully, CMG, FCA, President, The Steel Company of Canada

Steel is, of course, the most precious of metals. Without it the world would have seen few of the great advances in science and technology that have characterized the 100 years that have elapsed since steelmaking on a large scale began....Our people, our natural resources, our rapidly expanding educational facilities, and by no means least the security we enjoy (whether we like it or not) by sharing this North American continent with a friendly, powerful and generous neighbour—these are assets beyond price. So long as we preserve and foster them, Canada's prospects will be limitless.

INDIA AND PAKISTAN
November, 1965
Escott Reid, Principal of Glendon College, York University

When I left India in 1957 I was worried by what seemed to me to be Nehru's failure to realize sufficiently that "his most important task in international policy was to get a settlement with Pakistan on all the deep and difficult issues which divide the two countries, and, that to get this settlement, he should be prepared to use all his powers of leadership to persuade India to accept the necessarily unpalatable compromises." I emphasize the words, "the deep and difficult issues which divide the two countries." The issues which divide India and Pakistan are not simple issues capable of easy solutions. They are extremely difficult issues, issues which are rooted deep in the long history of the Indian subcontinent. Hinduism is separated from Islam by a wide gulf. There are proud memories of imperial Mogul grandeur. There is the resentment on the Indian side that India had to be partitioned 20 years ago on the basis of religion. There is the suspicion on the other side that India has never really accepted the existence of Pakistan as a separate nation. India has been governed by men who made the revolution against the British. These men have tended to look down on the former army officers and civil servants who have been governing Pakistan.

LAW REFORM—THE BUSINESSMAN'S RESPONSIBILITY
February, 1966
John L. Biddell, President, Clarkson Company

Let's face it; government—any government—is going to move powerfully slow in the area of commercial law reform. Anything done in this area usually has comparatively little vote-getting power and it is much easier to ignore the problem and hope it will go away than to take responsibility for initiating measures which could just turn out to be a mistake. I am firmly of the opinion that the responsibility for initiating action in the field of commercial law reform must be seized by members of the business community. Government is bound to procrastinate as long as possible.

VIETNAM TODAY
Dealing with Communism
February, 1966
Gen. Maxwell D. Taylor, Special Consultant on Diplomatic and Military Affairs to the President of The United States

I would remind you that it is hard to negotiate with Communists even when you are in a reasonable position of strength. It's disastrous to sit around a table with them when you appear timid and clearly want to go home....As I analyze the holding strategy, it is not a true alternative in the sense that it is another way by which we might reach our end objective, a South Vietnam that has the right and the possibility of choosing its own future. I am convinced that to follow the passive line will in the long run compromise our objective and end in something far short of what we have been striving for since 1954.

EDUCATION—A CANADIAN PRIORITY AND A PROVINCIAL RESPONSIBILITY
March, 1966
The Hon. William G. Davis, Minister of Education, Ontario

I strongly endorse this view that our shrewdest and most profitable investment rests in the education of our people.

LAW AND SURVIVAL
An End to Wars
March, 1966
Mr. Justice W.O. Douglas, Associate Justice, Supreme Court of
The United States

If we are to survive, there must be an end to wars. For most people it may be inconceivable to think of a world without war,
because war has written some of the largest, most stirring chap-
ters in our history. Wars get caught up with national pride,
national enthusiasm, feelings of loyalty, deep passions, and are
propelled by almost uncontrollable forces. Yet people at one time
thought it was man's destiny to live in a slave-ridden world. That
was the view on this continent, even 100 years ago. But slavery
has pretty well been abolished and in time, if we survive, war
will be too.

A NEW LOOK AT FOREIGN AID
April, 1966
The Hon. S.J. Randall, Minister of Economics and
Development, Ontario

It has been said 'One thing money cannot buy—poverty!' My
friends, I have visited countries in many parts of the world,
where our foreign-aid money is buying poverty. Why? Because it
is placed in the hands of those who spend it foolishly to build
monuments...to their vanities and colossal stupidity.

THE CHOICE—EXCELLENCE OR MEDIOCRITY IN
HEALTH CARE
October, 1966
Dr. J.F. Mustard, Professor of Pathology, McMaster University

For the brilliant young medical graduates who could become the
staff members needed by our medical schools, the lure of the
United States is very strong. Not because they want to leave
Canada, but simply because opportunities for study and research

are greater in that country. Canada graduates nine hundred new doctors each year—and promptly loses as many as two hundred of them permanently to the United States. They go—and it's usually the best ones who go—because adequate financing provides a productive research environment in the States. The U.S. spends about $6.50 per capita of public funds on medical research each year. Canada spends $1.05! The Federal Government has already committed itself to spend $500 million on health training facilities, including medical schools, and comparable or greater amounts are to be made available by Provincial Governments. But these schools must be staffed. Canadians cannot afford to accept the status of an "underdeveloped" nation as far as research goes, living on the fruits of American and European genius. Moreover, if Canada is to capitalize on research ideas she must have adequate numbers of people actively engaged in the research process. The failure to plant, nurture and harvest sufficient numbers of properly trained and critically minded individuals in this country in the past has left us in the position where we are already having or soon will have difficulty in incorporating new discoveries made in other countries into our current medical practices, with the result that the standard of health care will gradually fall below the best practice in the more favoured countries.

VIETNAM—A REPORTER'S VIEW
February, 1967
Peter Jennings, ABC TV newscaster

In 1965 there were few who imagined that within a year and a half, 500,000 of their sons would be fighting and dying for a commitment which they themselves could neither understand nor explain to those around them. Now after five years of continuous escalation the realization that this war exists and is a major one is finally hitting home. With that realization has come for a majority of Americans the two intangibles which form the country's mood today…frustration and confusion. With these two symptoms has grown a longer and more compelling list of questions about American foreign policy in Southeast Asia. I don't mean to imply for a moment that this questioning or lack of faith in U.S. policy has gained the upper hand, for that is far from true, but I do suggest that support is seriously wavering and that those all-out supporters of government action have a position today which is far less defensible than it was eighteen months ago.

A LOOK INTO THE FINANCIAL CRYSTAL BALL
April, 1967
Allyn Taylor, President and General Manager, Canada Trust Co., The Huron and Erie Mortgage Corporation

More and more voices are being raised in this country against the soaring cost of government, of which a huge part is attributable to social progress. I am not against social progress. If I were, I would have little company. But I do firmly believe that we must not, dare not, bleed our economy to death by trying to attain the utopian welfare state overnight....Let me relate a story having to do with the shape of things to come. It's about the proverbial old lady on a sightseeing bus in New York City. The bus stops in the course of its tour in front of the Metropolitan Museum on 5th Avenue. The old lady from her seat in the bus looks up at an inscription carved into the stone over the entrance area. It reads "The Past is Prologue to the Future." She...asks the driver what it means....He's never been asked the question before. However, typical of his breed, he's not easily stuck. He...says "Lady, that means you ain't seen nothin' yet!"

THE ROLE OF SELF-REGULATION IN THE SECURITIES BUSINESS
April, 1967
J.R. Kimber, QC, President, The Toronto Stock Exchange

I submit that in Canada the philosophy was resolved in 1935 when the Royal Commission on Price Spreads stated that legisla-

190

tion should not be designed to eliminate the individual's "inalienable right to make a fool of himself," but to prevent others from making a fool of him.

ASIA TODAY
May, 1967
The Hon. Richard M. Nixon, former Vice-President of The United States of America

After that very gracious and generous introduction and your warm reception, I can only conclude that I ran for president of the wrong organization.

[Mr. Nixon had lost the Presidential election of 1960 by a margin of less than one tenth of one percent of the popular vote. Previously he had served eight years as Vice-President; in 1969 he was elected President of the United States]

...On an occasion like this, the speaker from the United States has a formula which is sure-fire for an audience. Inevitably, almost invariably, the speaker ends ups with a speech that goes somewhat like this: A discussion of those great traditions we have in common; the common law, the English language, the representative system of government. A discussion of those great conflicts in which we have been comrades in arms, World War I, World War II. A reference always to the greatest, longest, border in all the world which is not guarded by either side....I am going to depart from that formula tonight, not because it isn't more pleasant to refer to those things on which we agree; but because this is a special kind of organization with a very special name, The Empire Club.

[Mr. Nixon, then out of political office, proceeded to state forcefully the case supporting the action of his country in resisting Communist aggression in Asia, particularly Vietnam].

THE UNSINKABLE COMMONWEALTH
July, 1967
Earl Mountbatten of Burma

Mr. Churchill, as he then was, and President Roosevelt were extremely good friends. They rather enjoyed pulling each others' legs. Our Prime Minister sent me over to Washington in June 1942 to explain to the President that it would not be feasible for the Allies to carry out a successful invasion of France before the spring of 1944. This was of course very unwelcome news to the Americans who were keen to open a second front right away, but we offered as a compromise solution that there should be a landing in North Africa in 1943. While staying in the White House I heard of a joke which the President was preparing to perpetrate on Mr. Churchill. He had come across one of those middle-aged crusading women one so often meets in the States. This lady's particular crusade was that the British should quit India. Knowing that Mr. Churchill was violently opposed to this idea the President thought it would be amusing to arrange a leg haul. I understand that this took place after I had left. The lady was asked to a small luncheon just with the President, the Prime Minister and perhaps half a dozen of the staff. Everyone except Mr. Churchill was in the know. After the first course our crusading lady could not contain herself any longer and attacked him by saying: "Mr. Prime Minister, what do you intend to do about those wretched Indians?" Winston was taken aback for a moment and then looked at her and said: "Madam, to which Indians do you refer? Do you by chance refer to the second greatest nation on earth which under benign and beneficent British rule have multiplied and prospered exceedingly; or do you by chance refer to the unfortunate Indians of the North American Continent which under the present Administration have become practically extinct?"...On one occasion when I was staying with President Eisenhower at the White house he was complaining about the bad relationship between India and the United States. I suggested to the President that he should pay a personal visit to India when I was sure he would have a very good reception. He told me that the Secretary of State, Mr. Foster Dulles, had advised against this as he said he would have a bad reception. I promised him that he would not only get a good reception but I would arrange a special invitation for him to be issued by the Prime Minister, Mr. Nehru. Eisenhower accepted my suggestion. He received the invitation and went to India and as everybody knows the visit was a great success. President Eisenhower wrote to me from Delhi to tell me of the success of his visit and then added something to this effect: "This morning I received an honorary degree from Delhi University. In the little robing room there was a large marble slab and in letters of gold it proclaimed that you had proposed to Edwina in this office on 14th February 1922. This was, of course, a great astonishment to me; what made it even more curious was that I was wearing a pair of socks you had given me for Christmas!" In fact, of course, Delhi University had been the temporary Viceregal Lodge while the big Viceroy's House was being built at Delhi and in 1922 when I was on the Prince of Wales' staff we stayed in the temporary Viceregal Lodge. It was here that I proposed to my wife who was on a visit to the Viceroy....I recently visited Paris and had the honour of receiving a gold medal from the Society pour L'Encouragement de l'Invention et la Recherche. This gave me the opportunity of an informal discussion with some of the French scientists and I asked them if they suffered in France from the same brain drain that we were suffering from in the United Kingdom where the United States appear to be enticing away most of our best scientific research workers offering them higher pay to work in the United States. One of the French scientists replied as follows: "Non, monsieur, et cela pour trois raisons: Notre langue, Notre cuisine, Nos femmes."

FOCUS ON INDIA
Look Before You Leap
October, 1967
General J.N. Chaudhuri, High Commissioner for India

We are well aware that an increase in food production by itself is not enough unless measures are taken to control the growth of population. India's population today stands at 495 million and it has been increasing at 2.4% a year. Thus the annual increase comes to 12 million. An increase in life expectancy of about 20 years has also added to the population crisis. A network of 22,000 family planning centres has been set up all over the country staffed by medical personnel whose services are free. During the last two years 2.2 million males have undergone Vasectomy. For women the intra-uterine contraceptive device popularly known as the "loop" has been found suitable to Indian conditions and a factory in Kampur is making 30,000 loops a day. I have always said India's motto for the present should be "Loop before you leap."

THE NEXT HUNDRED YEARS
November, 1967
Eric Kierans, President, Quebec Liberal Association

What is bothering Canadians, young Canadians, French Canadians, English Canadians, new Canadians, is that we don't want Canada to be a mediocre nation. We react against mediocrity as youngsters do; against the junior satellite status nobody wants; and for this reason, most of them ask for something different, that their Canadian role in the future will be a peace-making role, because we are not going to contribute very much with one per cent nuclear power, if you assume the Americans and Russians have a one hundred per cent destruction of the world in their power. I think we, if we want to make a distinct contribution in this country, then we should decide exactly what our interests are and follow them out independently. We don't want to be, and the Canada of tomorrow cannot be, a mediocre country.

CANADA'S NEW STATUS
November, 1967
The Rt. Hon. D. Roland Michener, Governor General of Canada

In recent years we have all been conscious that Canada has many friends and practically no enemies. Our record as a middle power, independent and influential but not decisive in world affairs, our freedom from the much echoed taint of imperialism, our role in peacekeeping operations under the United Nations, our devotion to the just settlement of international differences, and our substantial aid to developing countries, have combined to win us friendship and respect.

WHY NOT APPLY TOMORROW'S DISCIPLINES TODAY?
Self-Interest
January, 1968
George Gathercole, Chairman, Hydro Electric Power Commission, Ontario

In a democratic society, where opinions, wants and needs vary greatly and individual freedom and independence are so much prized, it is not always easy to persuade an individual that there can be a higher interest than his own.

BRITAIN TODAY
January, 1968
The Rt. Hon. Harold Macmillan, Prime Minister of Great Britain, 1957–63

In conveying the invitation, the organizer was clearly apprehensive. For I received an urgent—almost tearful—warning that my remarks should not extend to more than twenty-five minutes or half an hour as the very maximum. No doubt he thought, like other people, that old men talk too long. Nevertheless, you must remember that they do not have long to talk....Just as a good driver of a car applies sometimes the accelerator and sometimes a touch of the brake, so a government should be able to steer the economy of our country. Of course it must be prudent, not arrogant; cold sober, not drunk with power. Nor should it apply the brake and the accelerator at the same time. Not only is that a somewhat bizarre method, but it is bound to lead to a smash— as it has.

TAX REFORM
March, 1968
Kenneth Carter, Chairman, Royal Commission on Taxation

Taxation is primarily a means of transferring purchasing power from the citizens to the government....There may well be some economic ends in business growth that taxation can serve best. However, it is my view that taxation has been over-used for such purposes in the past. I can see no difference to a taxpayer in exacting from him the full amount of taxes on parity with other taxpayers and then bonusing him with government funds for economic or social purposes....But I can see vast differences to government. Tax abatements slip by in government accounts with very little public concern.... [Yet] if these amounts, or if similar amounts, were paid out in subsidies they would be apparent and subject to annual review....Tax abatements can only benefit profitable tax-payers, whereas to assist or direct economic growth it is frequently desirable to provide help before profits result. Whether we abate taxes or pay subsidies, there should be public and frequent review of the benefits received against the taxes conceded or payments made.

CANADIAN-AMERICAN RELATIONS
April, 1968
Knowlton Nash, CBC Washington correspondent

It is interesting to note on this question of the war cost that in the days of Julius Caesar, it used to cost 75 cents to kill an enemy soldier. In World War Two, the cost rose to $50,000 for every enemy dead. In Vietnam, I was told the cost now is running about one million dollars for each Viet Cong or North Vietnamese killed. But not only is it costing American money, but of course American lives as well. Ten thousand Americans were killed last year and likely at least that many will be killed this year in Vietnam....In our economic relations with the United States we Canadians act as a kind of mixture of fools and angels—we rush in and fear to tread at the same time....We can and must control our future...or at least steer it in the right direction. It's been said that God invented man because he was disappointed in the monkey. I hope we don't disappoint him again.

THIS WORLD AND THE MIND OF MAN
Science and Religion
January, 1969
Dr. Wilder Penfield, OM, pioneer in neurosurgery

It was indeed a surprise, at Christmas time, to hear one of those three admirable American astronauts, in outer space, read from the Bible the story of creation—and fitting too. What a story! And what an audience! Science does not contradict, nor does it throw any light on religion. Religion has to do with the things of the spirit. Science has to do with the brain, the body and the material universe....It is my impression that there are at least as many who believe in God, and make some personal use of the belief among the men of science as among non-scientists....The acceleration of change in human society is, in large part, the end result of scientific innovation which sometimes, but not always, deserves to be called advance. In the amazing expansion of our scientific knowledge, there has been no proven contradiction of spiritual values, no valid opposition between science, on the one hand, and the basic concepts of morality in human society and man's belief in the spirit of man or God, on the other.

CAN CANADA HAVE AN INDEPENDENT FOREIGN POLICY?
The New Left
January, 1969
Maxwell Cohen, Dean of Law, McGill University

Recently I was reflecting on the difference between academic life and public life, and I came to the innocent conclusion that in public life the knives come at you from the front....The whole theory of the New Left, which is occupying so much of our time, I think was beautifully epitomized in a phrase of that remarkable longshoreman philosopher Eric Hoffer the other night, when he said that whatever may have been the contribution of Louis the Fourteenth to the cliches of western thought—one of them being 'Apres moi le deluge'—the motto of the New Left seems to be 'Apres le deluge moi!'

THE NEW LOOK IN U.S. POLICY
Power Neurosis
February, 1969
Frank Church, U.S. Senator from Idaho

For all their immense physical power, the two dominant nations in the world, the United States and the Soviet Union, suffer from a neurotic sense of insecurity, although neither regards itself as being in imminent danger of attack by the other. At tremendous cost their nuclear armories keep them at bay and, barring some unexpected technological break-through on one side or the other, the delicate equilibrium will hold, leaving the two rivals in a state of chronic but low grade anxiety over the danger of attack by the other. It is a costly, irrational and desperately dangerous way of keeping the peace but it is all we have shown ourselves capable of so far.

THE COMING REVOLUTION IN TELECOMMUNICATIONS
Spend and Tax
March, 1969
R.C. Scrivener, President, Bell Telephone Company of Canada

We are now trying to cope with the aftermath of the great governmental spenders, spending unrelated to our ability to pay, the result, a frightening taste of inflation. Inflation robs all of us by destroying the value of our investments, our savings, our insurance, our pensions, our wages and salaries....Spend, spend, spend, tax, tax, tax is not an acceptable philosophy....I'm on the side of those who believe that balancing income and out-go has merit.

D-DAY DINNER—COMMEMORATING THE 25TH ANNIVERSARY OF D-DAY
The Cinderella Service
June, 1969
Major General Sir Francis de Guingand, KBE, CB, DSO, Chief of Staff, 8th Army, 1942–44

[The Empire Club held a dinner on the 25th Anniversary of D-Day. Field Marshall Montgomery was prevented by ill health from attending but he sent a message to be conveyed in person by his war time Chief of Staff Major General Sir Francis de Guingand. On the subject of his replacing the Field Marshall the Major General said].

There was a great lunch party in some town in Germany, and the admiral was asked, and the general commanding the troops was asked, and the chief airman was asked. At the end of the lunch the admiral got up ...[and] said how pleased he was to see the three services represented, particularly the 'Cinderella' of the services, the Royal Air Force, by a flight lieutenant, because the Air Marshall had got the flu and sent his ADC instead. And then the General got up and made the same sort of speech. And he said precisely the same thing, how pleased he was to see the 'Cinderella' of the three services there....the flight lieutenant stood up to make his reply and started off by saying 'I would like to remind you gentlemen that Cinderella had two bloody ugly sisters.'

POLICY MAKING IN NATIONAL POLITICS
Work for Your Party
October, 1969
The Hon. Robert Stanfield, PC, QC, LLD, MP, Leader of the Opposition and National Leader of the Progressive Conservative Party

The point I want to make is one that I think you may want to remember, especially those of you who exercise your democratic right not to support a political party. It is well for you to remember the system could not operate without those who do support a political party. The active support for a party often involves more than the token sacrifice of time or money and, if your neighbours, friends, employees or employers make an effort, for the most part largely anonymous to the public in the sense they play it quiet (I don't mean a secret, but a quiet, role in their party), they deserve at least as much honour as those who take part in any other worthwhile cause. I am not attempting for a moment to downgrade the importance of the independent voter, but I do think we should from time to time pay tribute to those who in their own way make their contribution to the political party of their choice.

CANADA'S STAKE IN ARMS CONTROL AND DISARMAMENT
November, 1969
George Ignatieff, Ambassador of Canada to the Conference of the Committee on Disarmament, Geneva

The answer to the achievement of national security clearly cannot be found through a competitive application of military technology alone. National security being primarily a political problem, the solution lies primarily through political means. Hence the importance of arms control negotiations, coupled with efforts to moderate the confrontations between the great powers. But we have to admit frankly that arms control and disarmament has so far had only limited success. Today the bombs that were used at Hiroshima and Nagasaki are to current models, as Lindbergh's "Spirit of St. Louis" is to the modern jet plane. We are faced today with the intercontinental ballistic missile with multiple warheads, underground missile silos, submarines that can shoot missiles without surfacing, the hydrogen bomb, chemical and biological weapons, to name only some of the items in the arsenals of the two powers which have become so highly developed that thousands of years of civilization could be destroyed in a matter of minutes....But let us have no illusions that to bring the nuclear arms race under international control is an easy matter. Even under the Charter of the United Nations, the nation state is sovereign, and nation states tend to take the position of being a "law unto themselves."

HELPING THE MENTALLY RETARDED
November, 1969
Mrs. Joseph P. Kennedy, mother of President Kennedy

In the Canadian government, on the contrary, however, although the civil service rule regarding the written test has been lifted, and technically retarded people could work in the government, there has been little rapport between the government and this group. And so I should like to call this to your attention, in the hopes that you can facilitate their entry into government service. Some of you may feel that other employees in your offices or your companies may object if retarded workers are brought in to perform the same tasks which they do. We have found, however, that employees have taken an almost paternal interest in the retarded worker, and do all they can to help him adjust on the job. The retarded do not become emotional or temperamental.

They are not mentally ill, but simply have a limited intelligence and a limited ability to learn. They are very stable.

The 70s and 80s

Throughout the decades of the 1970s and 1980s the most frequent subjects for addresses to the Club were national unity, Quebec, and the constitution. These issues dominated the agenda leading up to the Quebec referendum of 1980 and patriation of the constitution. Opinions clashed. The premise that Quebec had been held down by an obsolete educational system led by the clergy was challenged with the argument that while "most of America was busy conquering, settling and organizing, French-Canadians had their hands full simply ensuring their survival," and now "the Quebec of today is looking for the best ways to apply her own definition of her own identity." Bilingualism, key to the Trudeau government's policy, was supported by a French federal minister who asked the question, "Is bilingualism acceptable as a political concept? That is easy to answer. I say Canada cannot exist without it." Of a distinctly different opinion was Claude Ryan, publisher of *Le Devoir*, a frequent speaker. In 1973 he said, "We have also seen in the last few months that the language policies of the Trudeau government have not been too successful. In English Canada they aroused a feeling of uneasiness and even exacerbation in those circles to whom they more immediately applied. In Quebec they were greeted with marked scepticism and indifference not only by the separatists but by many moderates, who never believed that they could provide the key to a lasting solution of our problems."

Patriation of the constitution was on all political minds. The Hon. James Richardson spoke to the Club just after resigning from the federal cabinet where he was serving as Minister of National Defence. His difference of opinion with his government was regarding patriation of the constitution, which, he argued, was purely symbolic. His problem was with the amending formula in which he saw troubling possibilities—language rights and changes to the make–up of the Supreme Court of Canada.

Separatism was a distinct possibility and Senator Eugene Forsey voiced the opinion that "I hope we shall go on doing our best to make this whole country one where French Canadians feel it's just as much their country as it is ours. …Canada is their homeland." Approaching the referendum, one speaker said, "Rivalry between French and English has done as much for this country as wheat. And I wouldn't want to see all of it ground down." Speaking for Ontario, Premier Davis said "There are many in Quebec who believe that they can vote 'yes,' not because they are in favour of sovereignty association, but because they would like to see a negotiation process move forward.…For those in English-speaking Canada who are committed to constitutional change, to better meet the needs of our communities, provinces, and language groups, a 'yes' vote by the people of Quebec would be a terrible setback and a major frustration." And after the "no" vote prevailed, Claude Ryan, at the podium for the fourth time, said that the decision had been rendered on the basis of the country and the attachments Quebeckers have to Canada rather than on concepts of federalism. On the contrary, said Jacques Parizeau, "I feel profoundly that the outcome is inevitable, that independence cannot be shaken off once a small taste of it has been had."

Then as the decade ended the Hon. Lucien Bouchard came to the podium as Minister of the Environment in the federal government. He spoke on the topic "The Meech Lake Accord." He likened the turmoil it was causing to the debate on the Canadian flag—one that saw a lot of uproar at the time, which died quickly away. He predicted that the same would be the case with the Meech Lake Accord which, he said, "Provides us with the best possible way to turn a page and open a new chapter of cooperation and economic development." Three months later Lucien Bouchard had changed his colours, resigned from Cabinet and become part of the Bloc Quebecois.

For whatever reasons, national disunity, Cold-War fears,

recession, the FLQ crisis, fear of American domination, there seemed to be a trend to look at Canada in the 1970s and see negatives. Author and historian Donald Creighton on the one hand saw the horrifying measures that separatists used in their struggle for liberation—kidnapping, extortion and murder—and on the other the dangers of North American continentalism and domination. He said we differed from our neighbours to the south with our belief in "peace, order and good government," rather than "life liberty and the pursuit of happiness." He saw Canada "selling its birthright, like Esau, for a little 'red pottage'" in terms of American materialism. Another speaker asked if Canadians were simply "Americans on Snowshoes." And answered his own question with "I believe Canadians are simply rather unconfident, democracy-seeking, French-English speaking, usually polite, parsimonious, but newly ambitious members of the human race—on snowshoes." Canadian/U.S. relations, that ever-compelling topic, continued to be covered in depth with some rather dramatic outbursts, "Some people suggest that the Americans have raped us. But this is obviously slanderous, for there is no rape where there is invitation and consent," or "American conquest is based on American strength, the Canadian surrender is based on Canadian weakness." And "It took us one hundred years to create our own distinctive flag but if we don't have the intestinal fortitude to wave it once in a while that flag may outlast the country."

Such 70's negative rhetoric was attacked by political columnist and broadcaster, Ron Collister, who said, "I have been away from Canada for two years. The changes have shocked me—not only in the area of separatism and economic rot and linguistic bitterness. But also in the Canadian view of the United States. In some ways, I feel I am not returning home. I am landing on an unknown planet. I am appalled by the anti-Americanism, the paranoia, the senseless nationalism, the distorted view of the United States." Thomas Enders, United States Ambassador to Canada said, "I have also heard a good deal about Canadian economic nationalism, but just because we have separate identities doesn't mean that we can't work together."

By the mid-1980s Free Trade was the hot topic. In 1987/88 there were five addresses on that contentious subject, including one by Ambassador Clayton Yeutter, United States Trade Representative and another by Ambassador Simon Reisman, Chief Trade Negotiator for Canada.

Certain appearances were thrilling—that of Captain James A, Lovell Jr., Commander of Apollo XIII; Mrs. Indira Gandhi, Prime Minister of India; Sir Edmund Hillary KBE conqueror of Mount Everest; Dr. Marc Garneau, OC, first Canadian Astronaut, John Polanyi, 1986 Nobel Prize Winner, and Audrey Hepburn, actress and Special Ambassador to UNICEF. Some subjects excited the spirit of adventure—development on the Polar Sea, Dr. Joseph ManInnis' description of diving under the North Pole, visions of a white whale sanctuary in the Beaufort Sea. Some appearances were challenging, such as Dr. Henry Morgentaler's address on "The Continuing Controversy on Abortion," an address prior to which the president, Sarah Band, invited the audience to respect the traditions of the Empire Club and refrain from voicing concerns during the address.

In the midst of the discord and speculation there was always a touch of humour at Club meetings. Charles Pachter recalled the sketches he made of the Queen in Canadian settings, leading up to her visit in 1987. His *Queen on a Moose* featured the Queen taking the salute on mooseback; another setting had the Queen receiving a curtsey from Mrs. E.P. Taylor with a moose in the background; yet another showed a bejewelled Queen in full regalia waving from the back of a CPR caboose hurtling through a stylised Group of Seven forest at night. "One shocked monarchist wrote me suggesting I should go back to where I came from, which was North Toronto." Sondra Gotlieb, whose speech was titled "Wife Of…" related stories about her first days in Washington, as wife of the Canadian Ambassador. While travelling in California with her husband, Allan, she forgot that the meeting with the governor of California was in their hotel room. She had washed out a week's travelling underwear and spread it around on the furniture, while lounging in her housecoat and bare feet. There was a horrified silence as she opened the door to her husband and the distinguished gubernatorial party.

Peter Pocklington, Chairman of Pocklington Financial Corporation, joked about Pierre Trudeau, Canada's hero who could do no wrong. He said "Trudeau was asked the other day by a reporter if it was true that he was born in a log cabin. He replied 'No, you must be thinking of Abe Lincoln. I was born in a manger.'" I'm not saying he has a high opinion of himself, but the other day he was out for his morning stroll—and nearly got hit by a motor boat."

Some speakers had their fun with the difficulty of appeasing the management with a snappy title for a speech. Peter Desbarats, Ottawa Bureau Chief, Global Television, told of a friend who, when asked to speak to a group in Victoria, said his title would be "Artists and their Love Affairs." The organizer told him that since the audience would be over age 65 and liked their topics to have to do with British Columbia, his title would be inappropriate and so he had taken the liberty of changing the title to "Artists and their Love Affair with British Columbia," a subject upon which the speaker was then obligated to hold forth. Robertson Davies, whose speech was initially titled "How a book gets written," also had to change his title as, he said, Mr. Jackman told him "Pull yourself together....you don't expect anybody to turn out to hear that do you?"

Strangely, there was one subject that made such an insignificant impact that it was not mentioned until a year after it took place. In 1973 a speaker congratulated the Club for coming into the twentieth century, having allowed women in as members the previous year after seventy years of operation.

THE ECONOMY ENTERS A NEW DECADE
January, 1970
Dr. Arthur J. Smith, Chairman of the Economic Council of Canada

In the past twenty-five years, something like a revolution has taken place in the field of 'looking ahead'—perhaps particularly in the field of 'economic looking ahead.' It used to be considered the main task of economists to explain what had happened and why it had happened. But increasingly it has become their responsibility…to foretell what would happen and why it might happen, or what should happen and how it could be brought about.

BILINGUALISM; A PRESCRIPTION FOR NATIONAL UNITY
January, 1970
The Hon. Jean-Luc Pepin, PC, MP, Minister of Industry, Trade and Commerce

Sociologically Canada is multi-ethnic, multi-cultural, multi-lingual, multi-everything you want; but politically and constitutionally it is bilingual and bilingual in French and English only. You may very well tell me that it is more useful to speak Italian than French in Toronto and you may very well tell me that it is more useful in Vancouver to speak Chinese than French. I might even agree but this will not change anything. You will not learn Chinese if you are in Vancouver and you will not learn Italian if you are in Toronto because you know damn well the Italians here are going to learn English as are the Chinese in Vancouver. Immigrants, while fortunately retaining many cultural traits from their homelands, are expected to integrate…into one of the two linguistic streams.

THE POLITICS OF QUEBEC—TODAY AND TOMORROW
February, 1970
Claude Ryan, Publisher, *Le Devoir*

Another aspect of Quebec's politics is the great importance which French-Canadian voters attach to the personalities of the leaders. The most successful men of the last 25 years in Quebec's political life have been Maurice Duplessis, Jean Lesage, Daniel Johnson, Jean Drapeau, Lucien Saulnier and Pierre Elliot Trudeau. You will easily grant that each of those men had a strong personality. But each was also, in his own way, a moderate; that is to say, a man with no rigidly pre-conceived dogmas as to how problems should be solved. In Trudeau's case, for instance, I can say that thousands of voters who would have disapproved of many of his statements and attitudes if they had come from a different leader, were swayed to his cause by his overwhelming personality.

THE WHITE PAPER ON TAXATION: WHAT ELSE IS NEW?
March, 1970
The Hon. Eric Kierans, PC, MP, Minister of Communications

The White Paper [of Finance Minister Benson on tax reform] is a good paper in the view of those of us who have worked on it, and on the Carter Commission. Certainly, it can be modified in some respects. But, when you bring your arguments to us, don't bring them simply from the point of view of the particular interest you represent....Tell us what are the objectives that you want to see dropped....But most of all tell us what image of this country we should really be working from....Then I think that you and I and my colleagues can conduct a very satisfactory discussion about the ways of generating revenue that will achieve the kind of Canada we are seeking.

THE APOLLO XIII MISSION
August, 1970

H. Ian Macdonald, President, The Empire Club of Canada:
Although I had concluded my term (1969–1970) in the spring of 1970, I had already invited Captain James A. Lovell to speak to the Club on August 18, 1970, and Harold Cranfield asked me to take responsibility for the meeting. This was only a few months after the miraculous return of Apollo 13 (and long before the present movie). I recall Jim Lovell telling me that he had to make some 67 manual calculations in order to bring the flight home—and a mistake in any one would have doomed them to remain in outer space.

Captain James A. Lovell, Jr., Commander, Apollo XIII

If we are to maintain the earth as a livable dwelling place for mankind, we must learn to view it as a whole, we must understand that our existence depends upon the delicate balance of nature, and that this balance includes not only all of mankind, but all of living things. We must know the intricate relationships and interactions between planet earth and a dynamic solar system, particularly the sun. To obtain this knowledge and understand it requires a sustained programme to develop the science technology necessary to reveal what man's limited senses and capabilities cannot reveal unaided. We are concerned today with the threat of pollution to our environment. We have become more keenly aware of environmental pollution from the view we have from space as observed from manned and unmanned space craft....The growth of the world's population and its attendant demands for food, potable water, shelter, transportation, communications, means that all nations ultimately must join in managing the use and replenishment of our natural resources.

IMPERIAL LEGACY
October, 1970
The Hon. Mr. Justice S.H.S. Hughes, Judge in the High Court of Justice, Osgoode Hall

You may recall a well-known remark of Goldwin Smith's which went something like this: "I would like to see my country behave towards other nations as an English gentleman behaves towards other men." In my student days a recitation of this sent us all into shrieks of laughter as an example of what an awful snob he was. But on reflection, I feel a little foolish about all that hilarity. Canada has, after all, won golden opinions among the nations for fairness and lack of prejudice. Our way has been the way of moderation, of compromise, of considering other points of view. That is our heritage in a nutshell. Be it so.

COMING DEFEAT OF CANADIAN NATIONALISM
The Super Powers as Empires
November, 1970
Donald Creighton, historian and author

Our generation, and the one which preceded it, were brought up to believe that the hope of the world lay in peaceful internationalism. Now, after a trial of a quartercentury, it has become manifest that the twentieth century's second attempt to found a world order has failed almost as completely as the first. The universal state, or the universal peace imposed by a single great state, are as far away as ever; and instead, regional groupings on a continental scale, aggregations of smaller satellite states usually dominated by a super power, have emerged as the dominant fact of modern political life. These modern super-powers have, in fact, become empires; and it is their rival imperialist aims which most seriously endanger the peace of the world, just as it is their economic agencies, and in particular the so-called multi-national corporation, which form the advance guard of modern technology and threaten to deplete or destroy the dwindling riches of a finite world. It is not nationalism, but imperialism, political and economic, which carries the greatest peril to humanity. And, in the absence of a genuine and effective world order, the only power strong enough to prevent the destructive onward march of imperialism is the national state. This, then, is the dangerous corner into which we have been driven by recent events. On the one side is the steady advance of American power; and on the other the alarming evidence of national division and weakness. What confronts us is either the break-up of our country or its continuation as a fragmented, decentralized nation, firmly integrated in the American economic and military empire, with all its assets, down to the last treasures of its birthright, freely expendable in the service of the government and people of the United States. Our only hope of deliverance from this fate lies in the reassertion of Canadian nationalism in its first and integral form. The vain and perilous pursuit of dualism, which was not an original object of Confederation and has nearly brought about its undoing, must be abandoned. One nation, not two nations in one, can alone maintain an effective defence of Canada.

THE ART GALLERY OF ONTARIO—ONTARIO'S GREAT ASSET
October, 1971
Edmund C. Bovey, Past President of the Art Gallery of Ontario

Mr. Moore is giving to the Art Gallery of Ontario, and to Canada, a priceless collection of his sculptures and drawings. But, and perhaps this is equally important, with the Henry Moore collection, and the other gifts that I have mentioned, we were given something additional; the much needed stimulus required to work towards enlarging the gallery's facilities, and to help bring to the AGO the recognition it deserves; that is, an art gallery of international calibre and renown. I feel it says a very great deal for Canada, and for the Art Gallery of Ontario in particular, that this famous artist should wish to entrust an important collection of his works to us, making our city one of the very few world locations where the creative genius of Mr. Moore may be viewed and studied under ideal conditions.

WHERE ARE WE GOING?

October, 1971

The Most Rev. and Rt. Hon. Arthur Michael Ramsey, PC, DD, DCL, DLitt, **Archbishop of Canterbury, Primate of All England**

Well, there are so many generalizations about youth and youth are very, very much maligned. No doubt the now young generation can be criticized just as our generation can be criticized in turn. I only want to note [a couple of] things that I believe are really true and important about the people we call the young generation. First of all is this: That they won't take things on authority just because they have been handed down and because they have been told. No. They will take things they discover to be true from their own experience and we just have to face the fact that that is so. The upshot is that when it comes to Christianity young people don't take Christianity as a traditional thing handed down to them, especially if it is put to them in a negative form of you mustn't do this and you mustn't do that. I believe that young people can respond wonderfully to Christianity if it is put to them as an exciting adventure, serving God and serving humanity in ways that they are going to discover for themselves. Let them have their adventure and bless them with it. The second thing that I haven't the slightest doubt is true amongst young people; it is true in England and I haven't the slightest doubt it is true in Canada and most other countries: There is in young people an intense care about human suffering and the desire to serve those who suffer and to care for them and to help in heart-breaking human situations. I believe that the young people today have that sense far, far more than young people had when I was one myself and that is a very great quality and a great ground of hopefulness for the future. In religious terms they will understand Christianity only if there is a strong emphasis on the practical outcome of religion, practical service. The second great commandment of love and service to their neighbour.

CANADA AT THE CROSSROADS
October, 1971
The Hon. Robert Stanfield, PC, QC, MP, LLD, Leader of the National Progressive Conservative Party and Leader of the Opposition.

There must be a realization that the purpose of any government, large or small, must be to serve the people, not to serve itself. It is not the function of government to stifle initiative; it is its function to encourage initiative....Above all it isn't the function of government to become the major growth industry of the nation....The major ingredient in internal economic development as well as in external economic co-operation, is confidence....Confidence in oneself, confidence in the society, confidence in the government and in the men who run it.

THE WORLD TODAY
January, 1972
The Rt. Hon. Lord Thomson of Fleet

It is no good my giving off a lot of false optimism about this Middle Eastern deadlock. A huge and hitherto unbridgeable gulf of mistrust exists between Israel and the Arab States. The Arabs believe that Israel is aggressive and expansion-minded. The Israelis believe that the Arabs are implacably devoted to the extermination of Israel as a nation. President Sadat has said that if the beginnings of a settlement do not emerge by the end of 1971, and that date has now passed, then war is the only alternative. I think we have to remember that when Egyptian statesmen talk like this, their belligerency is often intended for home consumption, and that the words do not necessarily mean what they appear to say. But the danger is that one day such words, whatever the intentions behind them, will be too strong, and will lead inexorably to action. If that should happen, then the menace, with the Soviet Union backing the Arabs, and the U.S. backing Israel, is of a world war with superpowers intervening. I still do not think this is likely, but there is no doubt that the Middle

East, together with the India sub-continent, is one of the hot spots of today's world. But in ten years things may look different in a lot of places. There will almost certainly be a new leader of China; I think the transition will be peaceful. There may be a change in the leadership in the Soviet Union and in the attitudes of the elite groups. The United States will, I'm sure, have recovered from some of its more serious traumas. Europe will be an infinitely stronger power. Its star is rising rapidly even now, after years of dissension; it may be we are witnessing the beginnings of an economic and political renaissance in Europe. Anyway, I hope you'll ask me back in 1982 to see if I am right and to tell you where I've been and how I see it.

HOW THE AUTHOR REACHES HIS PUBLIC
March, 1972
Robertson Davies, BLitt, LLD, DLitt, DCL, FRSC, **author and Master of Massey College**

You have been told that my subject is "How the Author Reaches His Public." I assure you this title has only a general relationship to what I am going to say. One of the most difficult things about making speeches is finding titles for them. A few weeks before the speech is due, the president of the club or the chairman of the Speakers' Committee calls and says: "What is the name of your address?" You reply: "It has no name." He says, rather sternly: "Well then, what is it about?" In this case I told Mr. Jackman it was about how a novel gets itself written. "Pull yourself together," he said; "you don't expect anybody to turn out to hear that, do you?" I replied modestly that I was always surprised when anybody turned out to hear me under any circumstances. But he was firm. He wanted a catchy title. I pondered for a few days, and called him. "What about, How the Author Reaches his Public?" I said. I had no delusions whatever that it was catchy, but at least it was a title. He very generously accepted it. So here I am, and here you are, and we must get on with our business. Authors are not very much in the public eye, unless they are in trouble because of some gigantic imposture about a book they haven't written, or should not have written, such as a biography of Howard Hughes. Occasionally they are deemed to be of interest if they are being divorced, especially if the cause is cruelty. There is a widespread idea that authors are absolute devils in their matrimonial lives. Sometimes the newspapers carry reports of an author's death. These often run like this: "The unknown man of shabby appearance who was knocked down yesterday by a pizza delivery van has at last been identified as Lanugo Inkhorn, an author once popular but long forgotten. Identification was possible because the sum of forty-seven cents, which was found in his pocket, tallied exactly with Inkhorn's 1969 royalties, which had been paid to him last week by a Canadian publishing firm, now under American domination." When authors die they are frequently described as "once-popular" or, more often "well-known in the thirties." It is unheard of for an author to be popular at the time of his death. This is part of the tragedy of my profession.

THE YEAR BOOK
Annual Meeting, 1972
Past President John Griffin

One unchanging Canadian institution that keeps track of the changing world is The Empire Club Year Book published annually and without interruption since 1904. In it we find the record of our times, not as written later by an historian but as put on the record by the do-ers of our era.

SOME COMMENTS AFTER ONE YEAR'S CONTEMPLATION
April, 1972
The Hon. John P. Robarts, PC, QC, LLD, former Prime Minister of Ontario

I find an increasing dislike for the tendency that I see creeping in whereby it is being openly stated that decisions in the public field are being made purely against the standard of what effect it will have in the next election. I am afraid that there is a greater tendency for that standard to be used in the minds of men who are truly professional politicians, than with the type of man that I suggest I think we need, who simply comes and goes and does his best and really is not too desperately afraid of being defeated at the polls in case he should go wrong.

THE THIRD WORLD
May, 1972
His Eminence Paul-Émile Cardinal Léger, CC, LTH, JCL, STD, LLD, DCL, DLitt, KHS, missionary priest in The Republic of Cameroon, and former Cardinal Archbishop of Montreal

These then are the main lines of a picture concerning the Third World which I would like to impress upon you. It is a world of poverty, hunger, sickness, a population explosion and a lack of resources which is causing the gap, or better the gulf, between the white nations and those of the rest of the world, to grow even larger. It is a gulf which is known about, which is resented, and the resentment is being exploited. Something must be done about it if we are to avoid a catastrophe on a global scale. Whether this catastrophe is actually provoked by the increasingly depressed people of the Third World themselves, or whether their misery is used by other power blocs, with different ideologies, does not matter very much, for it will be the end of our world as we know it.

NEW DIRECTIONS IN FOREIGN POLICY
September, 1972

Joseph Potts, President, The Empire Club of Canada:
"It is very good of you to join us today after that magnificent game you
played yesterday against Russia...sorry that wasn't you, but I think we are all
very pleased about that. However it is very good of you to take time out of
your busy schedule to be with us." To which Trudeau responded: "I haven't
taken any time out of my schedule; this is my schedule" and the crowd roared
with laughter. And this was in fact in the middle of the 1972 election campaign.

The Rt. Hon. Pierre Elliott Trudeau, PC, QC, MP, LLD, FRSC, Prime Minister of Canada

Well, to go on to another example, I begin by saying that it
required no original thought to accept the proposition that
Canada's interests would be served well if our relations with the
Soviet Union, this joint neighbour to the north, could be
improved, if they could be placed upon an open and businesslike
basis which would provide an opportunity for friendship, to
replace the distrust, the suspicion and the fear of the past. That
proposition has been well accepted for many years. We don't
claim credit for that proposition but we do claim credit for the
courage to test it out and for the resolve to put it into effect. And
what's been the result? We haven't been forced to surrender any
of our principles or values. We haven't found ourselves conced-
ing any strongly held beliefs, except perhaps the belief that we
could take on the Russians very easily and lick them at any game
we wanted to play. But we have gained a great deal. We have
gained pride in the realization that we have contributed considerably to the reduction of east-west tensions. We have gained
from far-reaching and still extending exchanges of information
and experience. We have gained the possibility of having this
communication between experts and scientists in fields which
are as divergent as gas pipelines and Arctic icebreakers. We have
gained assurance that Canada, because we have seized the initiative for friendship, will enjoy a favoured position as a supplier of
wheat to the vast Soviet market. We have gained, perhaps even

more important still, in hundreds of individual cases the joy and the relief of seeing families reunited, this reunion of families and relatives which had been denied for years. The opportunity of leaving the Soviet Union and of taking up residence in Canada. And we gain interest because they, too, at the other end, the other government, the Soviet Government, wanted to respond to the overtures for friendship and when we were asking them such a humanitarian thing as to make progress in the reunification of families, they obviously couldn't say "no."

HOMAGE TO A.Y. JACKSON
October, 1972
John W. Fisher, SM, LLD, former Commissioner, National Centennial Administration

A.Y. Jackson. He was a builder. He was an interpreter who wasn't scared to go into the toughest places. He had no time for the soft life. Had he been born a hundred years earlier, assuming that he had the same assortment of genes in his system, I think he would have been an explorer and probably a great one; because where he went he always wanted to go further, always that curiosity, and in his little book, *A.Y's Country*, in his little book he explains "I always wanted to see what lay beyond," so he went to Yellowknife and he was curious then to go further, to Eldorado, to see what lay beyond. And finally he got up to the very Arctic, to the roof of the world itself. So now we have this wonderful parade of Canadian names which are very Canadian and in everyone of them he's painted. Just listen to the roll call and that will bring back Precambria, The Shield, the wilderness, the land of our forefathers and the land still in the forefront. Listen to the names—Labrador, Tadoussac, Saguenay, Baie St. Paul, Gatineau, Georgian Bay, Algonquin, and that lovely one Algoma, and tough ones Noranda, Abitibi, and then those beautiful strong names out west, Great Bear, Great Slave, Lesser Slave, Eldorado, Norman Wells, Radium and then the Whitehorse, the Yellowknife, the Valley of the Peace, Athabasca, the Yellowhead

Pass, the Kicking Horse Pass, the Crow's Nest Pass, Okanagan and Skeena in the land of the totem poles. It's an incredible life. We're here to wish him a Happy Birthday. I'm not going to do that....I can't wish A.Y. Jackson a Happy Birthday because a birthday celebration connotes that you are going to give the celebrant a present and any gift that I could give him in words, in comparison to the gift that he has given Canada, would be so minuscule it would be ludicrous. Therefore, all I'm going to say about A.Y. is that I think a hundred years from now people will say A.Y. you came too early, you didn't stay long enough. Birthday gift, he has given us the gift of the portrait of our country from the French side and the big, lone land side. He gave us a portrait in perpetuity. A.Y., or Jacqui, as they call him in French, or if you play that word carefully "j'acquis" also means to acquire and if anybody didn't acquire but gave it was A.Y. So to A.Y., Alex, Jackie, Dr. Jackson—a demain.

FREE ENTERPRISE IN CANADA
One Canada
November, 1972
Réal Caouette, MP, Leader of the Social Credit Party of Canada

If we really want the people of Canada to know of their two official languages, we have to start the first year at school....A kid at six years of age will learn any language....I see the future of Canada when we decentralize from Ottawa and give more autonomy to the provinces from coast to coast....I hear people say...'Quebec is not like the others.' In 1968, for instance, Mr. Stanfield came out in the Province of Quebec so to get more votes and he came with that...the policy of two nations. The French-Canada and the English-Canada....The night of the election he had four seats...I came in the same province, in my own province, with one platform—one Canada—not ten, not two, not three, one Canada....We came with fifteen seats....Tommy Douglas came. He was the NDP leader. He says, 'Quebec, oh you are not like the others so we'll give you a special status.' [He gained no seats.]

THE END OF THE WORK ETHIC
November, 1972
Professor H. Marshall McLuhan, CC, MA, PhD, Director, Centre for Culture and Technology, University of Toronto

To live in the present, or to take today now, involves acceptance of the entire past as now and the entire future as present. Science fiction doesn't really measure up to the everyday reality because the real has become fantastic. The future is not what it used to be, and it is now possible to predict the past in many scientific senses. With 'carbon 14' tests available, we can now predict why we shall have to re-write most of the past, simply because we can see much more of it simultaneously....We are living in a situation which has been called 'future shock.' Future shock in fact is 'culture lag,' that is the failure to notice what is happening in the present.

LAW REFORM AND THE TRANSITIONAL MAN
December, 1972
The Hon. Mr. Justice Patrick Hartt, Chairman, Law Reform Commission of Canada

Because law, good law, must reflect the collective experience and values of a society, it changes slowly. Human societies need time to digest their experience and the law follows behind, changing always a little more slowly, still trying to avoid fads and new values that might be rejected when their novelty wore off.

ENOUGH IS ENOUGH
January, 1973
David Lewis, QC, MP, Leader of the new Democratic Party of Canada

If I will not be thrown out for saying so, may I take the liberty of congratulating this Club for having become a Club of the Twentieth Century and being ready to admit ladies as members....I am sure that with the deafening applause of this audi-

ence, I say to the corporate welfare bums, 'enough is enough.'
Welfare is for the needy, not the powerful.

THE PRICE OF UNITY
February, 1973
Claude Ryan Publisher, *Le Devoir*

Just as English is destined to be the predominant language in
other provinces, French must also become to all practical purposes the predominant language in Quebec. This has long been a
fact of life in the operations of the Quebec Government....In
many large financial, and commercial and industrial concerns,
especially at the middle and top management levels, leaders in
this sector have long been predominantly English-speaking.
They have behaved too often as if English must be the only
instrument of communication both internally and external-
ly....The massive orientation of immigrants towards the English-
speaking minority rather than the French-speaking majority
must in large measure be attributed to this fact....Thousands of
Montrealers of Anglo-Saxon background have left Quebec in the
last few years....Others think that they can maintain the same
stance as in the past and can cling to the interests they have
established in the province without changing their fundamental
attitudes. These are destined to live in prolonged and tragic dis-
comfort.

GETTING OUT FROM UNDER
April, 1973

Joseph Potts, President, The Empire Club of Canada:
It is my understanding that our guest today is not one who is easily shocked!
Nevertheless, I must confess that the tactics, to which I resorted, in inducing
her to accept my invitation were shocking to say the least. I had tried the
orthodox approaches in an endeavour to track her down—telephone calls
during normal business hours in and about Toronto and New York City—but
with no appreciable success. My wife was a co-conspirator, as is usually the
case in my little escapades, so when I reached for the telephone one morning
at about 7:30, she exclaimed, "You're not going to call Margaret Atwood in
New York at this hour?" to which I replied "But of course." In the result I
aroused our guest from her slumbers, talked to her when her resistance was
low, and told her all kinds of wonderful things about the Empire Club—all of
which were true. She told me she was intrigued with my proposal, that she
would have to break some self-imposed rules as to her own conduct, but
finally she succumbed and graciously accepted.

Margaret Atwood, Writer in Residence, University of Toronto

That account of how I come to be here was more or less correct.
I explained to Mr. Potts at eight o'clock in the morning that I
don't make speeches and anything I had to say might be rather
disconnected. He said that was alright because they just had
Marshall McLuhan. I also understand that Mr. Potts is a fund
raiser for the Liberal Party and having been subjected to his
technique, I now understand why the Liberal Party has so many
friends. He also kind of indicated that he wanted some sort of
title for what I was going to say so he could put it on the program, so I made one up. He then sent me a little red book and in
this little red book there were the speeches of everybody else
who had spoken at the Empire Club plus photographs of them
all with their mouths wide open. Then after taking a look at the
speeches I realized that every single one of them was on a heavy
political trip of some kind so I thought that I couldn't speak on
"Getting Out from Under" or everybody would get indigestion.
So this speech is now untitled. The prospect of speaking at this
organization once I had woken up later in the day I found quite
intimidating partly because *The Globe and Mail* phoned and

asked me for my text. And I said "Text?" And secondly because Mr. Potts proudly informed me that the Empire Club had just let women in last year. And this reminded me of when I used to be a student at Harvard. There was a kind of sombre hall where they all used to eat dinner and before they let women in there if a woman ever showed her nose during the luncheon proceeding they would all throw buns at her. So I thought you know that there might be a danger that some of these bun-throwing tendencies had lingered on at the Empire Club. But then I thought about that and I thought well if they're going to throw anything I would rather that it be buns than plates or forks.

DEMOCRACY IN INDIA
June, 1973
Mrs. Indira Gandhi, Prime Minister of India

Non-alignment was decried by some fundamentalists as a refusal to make ethical choices. We did make ethical choices. That is why we are non-aligned. It was difficult to regard the transitory power factions of the postwar world in terms of moral imperatives. Fortunately the essentials of non-alignment have at last come to be accepted by others. The age of crusades seems to be ending, at least outwardly. Detentes have attracted powerful adherents but detentes should lead, not to compacts for the sharing of power, but become the starting point of a new international endeavour to improve the human ambience, be it the removal of poverty, the reduction of terror and violence, or the restoration of the purity of our environment. We do not seek conventional military strength. We are not interested in becoming a power, major or minor, and certainly not a nuclear power. The founding fathers of our nation asked the question: Can India become a modern nation without sacrificing harmony and human values, without being caught up in the pursuit of possessions? The answer is: India can and will and this is what we are working for. India has given much to human civilization. Even in the dark age of colonial subjection, we had men of radiance. A nation which comprises one-seventh of mankind must have some contribution to make. It can do so when its millions are given the opportunity of developing their personalities. The transfer of scientific knowledge has brought with it a strong imitative propensity. Increasing awareness of conditions elsewhere has spread dissatisfaction with conditions at home, but I see also a tremendous upsurge of confidence and creative endeavour in our young people.

THE WORLD OF 1975
Diplomatic Gifts
June, 1973
William Rees-Mogg, MA, Editor, *The Times* of London

We had an unfortunate Ambassador [in Washington] who got things wrong with the press....He was telephoned and asked what he wanted for Christmas and innocently enough replied. He tuned into the radio the next day to hear the following statement read out: The Russian Ambassador says that for Christmas he wants peace on earth. The French Ambassador wants friendship between nations; but the British Ambassador wants a box of crystallized fruit. The British Ambassador was the only one of the three who got what he asked for.

ARCTIC GAS: A GIANT OF NECESSITY
January 1974
William P. Wilder, Chairman, Arctic Gas Study Limited

In terms of energy supply, Canada may well be the envy of the industrialized nations of the western world. We are the only such nation which today produces as much energy as it consumes. Our present supply constraints are not a result of inadequate energy production, but inadequate transportation facilities. As such, present supply constraints are likely to be temporary. But we will soon need new energy supplies. We will have to tap our frontier oil and gas reserves in the Arctic and offshore regions: our enormous resources of heavy oil and Athabasca tar sands and similar deposits; our coal deposits, which offer potential supplies of synthetic gas and petroleum fuels.

UNIVERSITIES: WHO NEEDS THEM?
February, 1974
H. Ian Macdonald, Deputy Minister of Treasury, Economics and Intergovernmental Affairs, Government of Ontario and President-elect, York University

Looking forward, I believe that we face some fundamental battlegrounds in Canada that will command all the intellectual muscle we can muster:
- The road to national unity remains as treacherous as ever before....
- The outcome of the basic uses to which we put our non-renewable resources will determine our long term future and relationship to the world.
- The question of human settlement, in all its complex parts....
- The importance of planning the landscape to suit the full needs of everyone rather than the selfish interests of the few....
- The issue of the balance between work and recreation will have profound economic and social consequence.
- The questions of who should be educated, how far, in what direction, for what, and paid for by whom....
- The process of humanizing government and...bringing it closer to people....
- Retaining and enhancing a compassionate society in Canada.

BUILDING MARKET POWER INTO CANADIANS AS CANADA GROWS
Our Acquisitive Nature
February, 1974
Louis O. Kelso, attorney and economist, San Fransisco

Nobody is going to change the acquisitive instinct of the human being. Marx predicated his whole philosophy of Communism on the idea that if you lived under totalitarian socialism long enough it would purge you of your acquisitive instinct. It is like sending a bunch of sailors off to sea and saying that if you stay out there long enough, you will lose your sex urge.

THE DOCTOR'S DILEMMA—CIRCA 1975
January, 1975
Dr. Bette Stephenson, President, Canadian Medical Association

During the year 1973 at least 43,000 abortions and probably closer to 50,000 were carried out on Canadian women. In British Columbia, for every four children born, one fetus was aborted. I hope that those figures will give you reason to pause, for they illustrate the dismal failure of our totally inadequate educational and family planning programs. In many large Canadian hospitals the excessive caseload has made the role of the legally required therapeutic abortion committee well-nigh impossible. Thoughtful and concerned physicians continue to serve on these committees on a voluntary basis because it is the only way in which the needs of their patients, the needs of society, and the demands of the law can be met.

RECESSION, INFLATION, AND ENERGY
April, 1975
Dr. John R. Bunting, Chairman, First Pennsylvania Banking and Trust Company

The future has changed….We in the States have turned from being essentially a very optimistic people to…a somewhat pessimistic nation, in the space of about a year and a half. To some extent I think this is a reflection of the Watergate trauma….I would say that the number one factor producing this innate feeling that something fundamental has changed has to do with oil, and specifically of course, the quadruple price of oil. Until the Arab and Israeli war of fifteen months ago, you in Canada may have known that oil was finite and not infinite, and there were some college professors in the United States who knew it, and some scientists too, but the great body of the American people felt, I think, that oil had a kind of infinite supply....As long as Detroit is still manufacturing the gas guzzlers, as long as we're still heating all of our major buildings with oil, as long as our public utilities are 70 or 80% on oil, we will have to import too much oil.

CANADA'S ECONOMY—CAN WE ADVANCE BACK TO REASON?
The Academic President
April, 1975
H. Ian Macdonald, President, York University

Since we have just concluded a rather severe budget, I understand better the story of a mother going upstairs at nine o'clock one morning and saying to her son who was languishing in bed: 'You must get up and get along to the university.' He replied: 'Mother, I just can't face it. You have no idea how miserable it is there. Everyone hates me—the professors hate me, the administration hates me, and even the students hate me.' However his mother persisted [and] in a fit of indignation and frustration...she exploded 'Get up and on your way to the university—you're fifty years of age and you're the President!'....The Canadian economy....is not moving! And yet a magnificent journey still lies ahead for Canada if we can rev up the engines, keep down the price of fuel, encourage the helmsman to steer the smoothest course, and urge all hands to be more moderate in wanting to enjoy the benefits of the Promised Land before we have arrived.

ANNUAL MEETING
1975
H. Allan Leal, on election as Club President

The Empire Club is an honourable, an old, and a good society. It is not good because it is old. It is old because it is good.

THE HEIRS OF RUNNYMEDE
September, 1975
The Rt. Hon. Margaret Thatcher, PC, MP, Leader of the
Opposition, British House of Commons

I have always felt that it is the task of politicians to be two or
three years in advance of public opinion; to be able to foresee
dangers, to warn about them, and then to guard against them.
This, it seems to me, is the essential task of a leader—not to follow public opinion from the back, but to lead it from the front.

THE ROLE AND FUNCTION OF THE
OMBUDSMAN
November, 1975
Arthur Maloney, QC, Ombudsman, Ontario

[A certain guest speaker] had far too much to drink. He could
barely be heard and he went on interminably. When he sat down
he leaned over to the chairman and said, 'How was I?' The chairman thought for a moment and said 'You were Rolls Royce!' The
Chairman's wife leaned over and said, 'How could you say that
to him....That was the worst speech I ever heard.' He said, 'I did-
n't lie to him. He was well oiled, barely audible and lasted forever'....The inequality of the contest that I used to experience as a
lawyer in the courts between the state on the one hand and the
accused person on the other never ceased to amaze me. I would
go into court, day after day, defending an individual charged
with an offence and see arrayed against him a skillfully prepared
case, prepared by trained detectives, experts in handwriting and
ballistics and all the fields of expertise involved....The person on
the other side was invariably alone. He had only me or one of
my colleagues going for him....It is the same kind of inequality
now that the citizen, when he speaks alone, experiences against
the great structure of government and the bureaucracy.

LEADERSHIP IN CANADA TODAY
November, 1975
Flora Macdonald, MP

Governing, as it is practiced at the federal level in Canada today, has come to mean no more than making yes or no decisions between alternatives put forward by civil servants or by an alarmingly swollen cadre of private advisers. Our leaders have not involved themselves in identifying emerging problems in time to deal with them before they become crises. They have not taken the trouble to set a tone in the country, by word and example, which would ensure the development of a general public will to support measures which are necessary.

THE COMING YEAR—1976
December, 1975
The Hon. William G. Davis, QC, LLD, Premier of Ontario

Quite frankly, I don't think Canadians have got the message concerning the importance of energy conservation, to say nothing of economic restraint, as have our neighbours to the south. From what I read and hear, most Americans have come to realize that "the party's over," at least for the time being, and they're prepared to make sacrifices. Their wage settlements on average are running considerably below the 20 to 80% demands we've become accustomed to hearing in Canada. For the most part they've learned to live with reduced speed limits, because in many states some two years ago the reality of the energy crisis was brought home to them when they were lining up in their cars for hours on end to get a gallon of gas.

UNIVERSITIES—SOME CRISES OF MISUNDERSTANDING
January, 1976
Dr. Donald A. Chant, Vice-President and Provost, University of Toronto

Governments, Canadian society as a whole, and to some extent our universities themselves, seem to have forgotten some of the true roles of universities as institutions....To create new knowledge and understanding, to transmit these things through education, and to act as repositories for them....Many employers look upon a Bachelor's degree as a necessary prerequisite for the job market. Few young people or their parents would disagree. These pressures and attitudes have focused great attention on universities as centres of training, and obscured their roles as centres of learning and research.

A CANADIAN ANTI-INFLATION PROGRAM
January, 1976
John L. Biddell, FCA, Regional Chairman for Ontario, The Anti-Inflation Board

People have been complaining about government spending since we all came out of the log cabin era and set up government departments to do things we want done but don't want to do for ourselves....The private sector measures the success of its own employees by their contribution to productivity and profits. We may as well recognize that much of what we ask government to do cannot be measured by those yardsticks....However....We must first develop a much better set of employee incentives and much better labour-management co-operation in the private sector before we can expect to impose it on government service.

THE MONETARY MUDDLE
February, 1976
Nicholas L. Deak, President, Deak and Company

Not long ago I had the pleasure of introducing the Finance Minister of South Africa at a monetary conference in Lausanne. When he finished his speech he said, "Ladies and gentlemen, now that I have finished my speech, I would like to say something"....Just yesterday, our Secretary of the Treasury, Mr. Simon, made the following statement: "A government that taxes away more than half of what [the people] earn has robbed them of a great part of their economic freedom." Can there be any doubt that when our economic freedoms are destroyed, our political and personal freedoms will not long survive.

BASIC TRUTHS OF THE MIDDLE EAST CONFLICT
March, 1976
His Excellency Mordechai Shalev, Israeli Ambassador to Canada

The Arab States have not yet accepted the existence of a free and independent Jewish State in the land of Israel as an unalterable fact. All the wars that they have launched against us, all the propaganda campaigns that they are conducting, all the anti-Israel resolutions that they are steamrolling through the United Nations and its various agencies, all derive from a basic Arab purpose, to eliminate the State of Israel from the map of the Middle East....There is no peace in the Middle East, no peace between the Arab States and Israel, because the Arab States do not want peace.

BRITAIN TODAY
September, 1976
The Rt. Hon. James Callaghan, PC, MP, Prime Minister of Great Britain

The present preoccupations of the major industrial countries of the world are to achieve a rate of growth in our economies that can be sustained whilst at the same time overcoming inflation and reducing unemployment. As individual countries our economies do not always move in step. Although that is not necessarily a disadvantage, for my country it is a matter of concern at the present time that the rate of growth of industrial activity in a number of other countries is slowing down, for at this very moment our economy is beginning to grow faster. It will be important to ensure that all our countries maintain a rate of economic growth that can be sustained in the longer term. Both Canada and Britain must play an active part in international discussions to achieve this end.

TORONTO—MAJOR LEAGUE BASEBALL FOR A MAJOR LEAGUE CITY
February, 1977
William Karn, Club President, introducing Peter Bavasi, General Manager Metro Baseball Ltd.

April 7, 1977 will usher into our fair city a new era in ornithology. Metro bird watchers in their thousands have already subscribed for advantageous season perches in the enlarged CNE sanctuary, which will hopefully be swept clear of snow by that date, to welcome the Toronto Bluejays as they migrate from sunny Dunedin in Florida, chattering and scolding all the way, to carry Toronto—a major league city—forward into major league baseball.

REFLECTIONS FROM WASHINGTON
March, 1977
His Excellency J. H. Warren, Ambassador for Canada to The United States of America

In part because they assume that Canada is a land much like their own, Americans find it difficult to grasp that a group of people, even of different culture and tongue, would wish to forego the potential of the broader horizon for what they would see as the disadvantages of a more limited, if culturally and linguistically more homogeneous, status. There has also been a feeling in the United States, as in other countries, that Canada is fortunate among nations, has much of its destiny yet to be fulfilled and remains a land of great opportunity for those who were born here or through immigration have had a chance to share in the Canadian adventure. Measuring these prospects against the problems and limitations present in so many overseas countries, Americans and other foreigners are bound to find it difficult to understand why any group in our country would wish to put the future at risk, their own, and that of their fellow Canadians. At another level of perception, and although this is unspoken, Americans are, I believe, concerned about a diminution of stability in Canada, and hence in North America, should the separatist forces in Quebec gather in strength and the separation of the province become a realistic possibility. The prospect of stability being imperilled in a friendly neighbouring country which stands both between the Lower 48 and Alaska and between their country and the Soviet Union is, I believe, not something Americans wish to contemplate.

FOUR MONTHS LATER
Quebec Separatism
March, 1977
The Hon. Jacques Parizeau, MLA, Minister of Finance and Minister of Revenue, Province of Quebec

I suppose everyone recognizes the importance of the election that took place on November 15, and we will probably need, every few months, both inside and outside Quebec, to survey the paths followed and the views ahead until such time as a political conclusion is attained....I think that we, as Quebeckers, have now reached the point of no return. I am deeply convinced that we can manage on our own. The referendum will be the test. I sincerely hope that in this process of the emergence of a new country, we can keep with our closest neighbours, the confidence, the good faith and the common interest that history, geography and economics have bestowed upon us.

CANADA, QUEBEC, AND THE CONSTITUTION
April, 1977
Senator Eugene Forsey, QC, PhD, LLD

Can Quebec legally secede from Canada under our present constitution? The answer is no....Is there any way in which Quebec could constitutionally get out of Canada? And the answer is yes....There would have to be an amendment to the British North America Act, passed by the British Parliament....The answer to the question "Could Quebec legally and constitutionally secede?" is yes, provided all the other provinces consented, or nearly all the provinces....I am convinced that we need a strong Canadian state. I am horrified by the decline in the sprit of national pride, national belief in our country, by the rise of provincialism, regionalism, all over the country....I hope very much that we shall succeed in recreating where it needs to be recreated, strengthening where it is weak, the spirit of Canadianism, the devotion to this country, a devotion transcending all our local loyalties, all our ancestral loyalties, all our linguistic loyalties, a spirit which will enable us to realize...the magnificent future that awaits this country if only we will keep our heads, and use our heads, and use our hearts.

NORTHERN FRONTIER—NORTHERN HOMELAND
May, 1977
Mr. Justice Thomas Berger

A gas pipeline will entail much more than a right of way. It will be a major construction project across our northern territories, across a land that is cold and dark in winter, a land largely inaccessible by rail or road, where it will be necessary to construct wharves, warehouses, storage sites, airstrips—a huge infrastructure—just to build the pipeline. There will have to be a network of hundreds of miles of roads built over the snow and ice. Take the Arctic Gas project: the capacity of the fleet of tugs and barges on the Mackenzie River will have to be doubled. There will be six thousand construction workers required north of 60 to build the pipeline, and twelve hundred more to build the gas plants and gathering systems in the Mackenzie Delta. There will be 130 gravel mining operations. There will be six hundred river and stream crossings. There will be pipe, trucks, heavy equipment, tractors and aircraft.

THE LORD MAYOR OF LONDON
August, 1977
The Rt. Hon. The Lord Mayor of London, Commander Sir Robin Gillett, Bt.

I said to a young policeman, "Did you have a good view? Were you on duty somewhere where you could see the Queen on Jubilee Day?" And he said, "No. We were all told to get out of it." I thought this was a bit strange, so I asked the Commissioner of Police, "Were there no policemen?" And he said, "No, there weren't. The Queen doesn't like having policemen near her when she's doing a Walkabout. She thinks they get in the way! They're taken out well ahead of her, and they only return once she has passed." Now that tells us something. Where else in the world would a head of state walk so freely amongst her people? There was no need for any policemen because they love her like you wouldn't believe. Let me leave you with that thought. There is a place in this world for people who are not constantly involved in active politics, who are there to set an example—leadership by example and not by precept. And in his humble way, that is what the modern Lord Mayor tries to do for his City. The Queen does it, superbly, for the whole Commonwealth. We are very proud of her. She's ours. But she's yours too.

JOURNALISTIC FREEDOM AND RESPONSIBILITY
December, 1977
A.W. Johnson, President, CBC

First, I profoundly believe that the fourth estate...the press...the media...whatever you want to call it, is a crucial element in the cement that holds together our democratic society. In our increasingly complex society the media constitute the only way the mass of people can find out what's going on, can communicate with each other, and can communicate with their government and their government with them. In short, without free, independent media, no democratic society can survive. My second point really flows out of my first. Because the media are so crucial, so fundamental to democracy, I believe the media must be socially responsible. I have not the slightest doubt that freedom of the media requires a sense of public responsibility on the part of the media. My third point is that I believe the demands on the media are rising faster, and public expectations of the media are rising faster than the capacity of the media has grown to meet them. We must do more to match our performance with the demands and the expectations. My fourth point is that if public credibility and public trust in the media decline, public resentment will follow and so will a search for mechanisms by which the media can be guided, even directed, to meet their social obligations. And to some this even suggests government intervention—something which is manifestly unacceptable if we are to maintain the free and independent media which are so essential to freedom of speech and discussion.

DAVE BROADFOOT'S CANADA
March, 1978

Peter Hermant, President, The Empire Club of Canada:
I asked Dave Broadfoot to give a speech on comedy and not a comic speech—
there is a difference. It was so we could listen to a comedian instead of just
asking him to entertain the audience, although he did that too. He is a
Canadian icon.

David Broadfoot, comedian, celebrity

Just last week, I was asked to appear on a talk show and to read
out the winning jokes in a national joke contest. Fortunately I
got there an hour and a half before show time, so I read through
the jokes they were asking me to do, and almost without exception they were put-downs of minorities—either Ukrainians,
Pakistanis, French Canadians or Newfoundlanders. Talk about
divisive. Whether I was right or wrong, I thought I had no alternative but to refuse to participate. The only group that I dare to
put down are Anglo-Saxons, because I am one. I feel I have a
right to do that. For instance, there is new evidence that Adam,
the first man who ever lived, was an Anglo-Saxon. Who else
would stand in a perfect tropical garden, beside a perfect naked
woman, and eat an apple? I can rationalize that. I can say I'm
making fun of myself. But in a country where divisiveness is
rampant I don't feel that it's a comedian's job to contribute to
the problem. I want to contribute to the solution. And the best
way I can do that is to do my job well. My job is to make people
laugh and I do that best by giving voice to the various controversial issues that come along in our country, in the person of my
alter ego, the leader of the New Apathetic Party, and member for
Kicking Horse Pass.

CANADA, THE CROWN AND CHAUVINISM
October, 1978
Laura Sabia, journalist

[We are] complacent, lethargic Canadians, under the spell of
flower power.…We have spent nearly two billion dollars to make

this country bilingual, only to pronounce it a total failure and an utter disaster....I'm a firm believer in learning a second and third language. I speak three of them. I am bilingual. French was my first tongue. I also speak Italian. But you cannot legislate bilingualism. You can foster it effectively through the educational system, slowly. It may take twenty-five years, but that's the way to go....I am an unashamed, unabashed chauvinist, a demonstrative patriot. I'm a monarchist and proud of it. I make no apologies. My father was an immigrant who pulled himself up by the bootstraps, from shovel and wheelbarrow to bulldozer and crane. He incessantly extolled the wonders of a country that had given him the opportunity to succeed. He passed that passionate love on to his children. When, as children, [in Montreal], we came to him and told him that our French and English playmates were calling us names, he would say. "I'm the Wop. You're Canadians and don't forget it, and don't let anybody ever call you anything else."

QUEBEC UPDATE
October, 1978
Claude Ryan, Leader of the Liberal Party, Province of Quebec

The transition from the relatively comfortable role of the critic to that of the political leader is not an easy one by any account. Politics has its great moments of exhilaration, solidarity and triumph. Next to religion, I like to say, it is by its very nature the loftiest occupation....But it is also an extremely tough world in which only two species seem able to survive; those who are content with following the tide of the day without ever really committing themselves, and those who are really strong and dedicated to the pursuit of noble and deep seated convictions, and in addition, have a lot of luck working for them. In my case time alone will tell if I can survive.

UP THE EMPIRE—INTERBREEDING FOR A BETTER WORLD
November, 1978
Ben Wicks, political cartoonist and author

Brig. Gen. Reg. Lewis in introducing political cartoonist and author Ben Wicks said: "Members and friends of the Empire Club: Our guest speaker, Ben Wicks, and myself have at least two things in common—we are both Canadians, new Canadians, if you like; and we were both born in England. Indeed, Ben Wicks might share in common with me what I share in common with many other people from the United Kingdom in that we have some of the blood of each of the four nations that make up Great Britain. Each country has a distinct national characteristic. For example, there are the Scots. They religiously keep the Sabbath and for that matter anything else that comes their way. Then there are the Welsh. They pray upon their knees and upon their neighbours. Then the Irish—the Irish really do not know what they want but they are perfectly prepared to die for it. Then there are the English. The Englishman is a selfmade man, thereby absolving God from an awful responsibility."

It is not enough to love Canada like a mistress, and whisper about her in the back alleys. If you're going to love this country you should shout about it—like a wife you're proud to take out in the daylight. Bring out your thoughts. My wife and 1 came here in 1957. Those exasperating, dull, lovable, silly, decent, tolerant and generous people—Canadians—took us in. They didn't have to, but they did. Before I finish, I want to add this one word. I get lots of arguments in the newspaper, and letters, and criticism about what I draw and what I talk about. I don't care. You can curse me. You can swear at me. You can threaten me. You can say what you like. But don't tell me to go home. Because here I am home.

1979—THE YEAR OF THE REFERENDUM
December, 1978
Peter Desbarats, Ottawa Bureau Chief, Global Television
Network

For centuries Quebec had never been a full and willing participant in our national life. The shock of the British victory in 1759
and separation from France was followed by a long period of
mutual suspicion between French and English. Confederation,
for many French-speaking Canadians, was at best a necessary
expedient. There was little sea-to-sea idealism in
Quebec....Gradually the ethnic balance in Montreal shifted
towards the French as French Canada itself shifted from a rural
and conservative society to an urban society with typically
North American aspirations. In the sixties French-speaking
Quebeckers, or more accurately French-speaking Montrealers,
were no longer content to have their progress dependent on the
goodwill of their English-speaking neighbours....At first, optimists on both sides...felt that mutual development was possible,
but that wasn't realistic. Eventually it became clear that gains by
the French-speaking group would be made to some extent at the
expense of English-speaking Montrealers....Those who stayed
saw their business activities curtailed, their community institutions starved for funds and the value of their homes decline.
These have been the real victims of the Quiet Revolution in
Quebec....I would like to see a referendum in Quebec that really
means something. After all the turmoil and struggle of the past
twenty years in Quebec I would think that the people of that
province had earned an opportunity to choose...to choose an
option for Quebec.

CANADA AND ITS LAND FORCES—A FRENCH CANADIAN SOLDIER'S VIEW
What Does Quebec Want?
February, 1979
Lieut. General Jean Jacques Paradis, CMM, CD, Commander, Force Mobile Command

As a French Canadian and a soldier, the very thought that divisions within my country could spark a violent confrontation among its people is repulsive, and it is a prospect that must be devoutly rejected by all Canadians....The distance is short between disenchantment and outright discord. How far is it between discord and violence?....The almost patronizing and perennial question "What does Quebec want?" I suggest has been heard often enough and there are sufficient elements of an answer by now. Perhaps it is high time for asking "What does Canada want?"....What are all those noises we hear about nationalism, separatism, federalism, sovereignty association, if not one massive appeal from a threatened minority that craves for recognition and respect, for equal opportunity to develop, to be happy and prosper in the land their forefathers helped to open and to build Canada.

SCIENCE: THE HIDDEN MAINSPRING
March, 1979
Dr. John Tuzo Wilson, Director, Ontario Science Centre

It was the development of the steam engine rather than any change in financing which made growth possible. The steam engine provided the first source of cheap and abundant synthetic power with which to produce goods in abundance and transport them quickly....Cheap energy has been the source of our prosperity and it is now vanishing. It is not capitalists that are in short supple. It is resources. Adam Smith was the author, but, more than anyone else, James Watt was the creator of the Wealth of Nations....Many...leaders have come to believe that laws, edicts, taxes and financial manipulations are more important than production. This ability of economists to put the cart before the horse and then forget the horse is one of the tragedies of our times....Once an invention or discovery has been made, managers, bankers and lawyers move in to exploit it and build an industry. Generally they are not the original inventors, but they make more money, seem to exercise more power and appear to be more glamourous and important than the true creators of wealth.

LIMITED CHOICES: CANADA'S NEEDS AND FOREIGN OIL
October, 1979
Wilbert H. Hopper, Chairman and Chief Executive Officer, Petro-Canada

Incredible as it may sound, the true petroleum era—the period during which it has been the prime source of commercial energy for most nations—began no more than twenty-five years ago. The primitive use of oil encompasses all of recorded history but it has been only in our lifetime that it achieved such universal importance. It is certain to remain significant throughout the next quarter-century. But by the end of that era we are likely to have become accustomed to the appearance of alternative forms of energy. When that time comes, many of our current concerns will have faded. But we cannot leap over time. There are tough years ahead, when nations will compete to obtain their oil from whatever amount is placed in world trade. It is on the next decade that I want to focus your attention. Issues of economic and social progress, of war and revolution—or peace—may depend on how carefully we appraise our risks and our opportunities. It is a task which confronts virtually all nations. The industrial world, and most of the developing countries, will remain dependent on imported oil as their predominant source of energy. "Imported" is another way of saying most nations will have to have access to someone else's oil. The federal government has set the end of the next decade as a goal for attaining self-sufficiency in oil. But in the intervening years we shall pass through a time in which our continuing dependence on imported oil will be a vital consideration in all that we do—as businessmen, bankers and as government. The need for imported oil will be a factor in all our relationships, domestic and foreign.

THE CONCERT HALL AS AN ARTISTIC INSTRUMENT
November, 1979
Isaac Stern, violinist

Artistic excellence, enquiry and profit do not run in the same league. Like everything else, culture must be paid for. As we pay for education, medical services, mail services—and all of those are supported—so too must cultural efforts be supported. In a very real sense, the support of the arts gives an artist or an artistic concept the right to fail. We must not demand that they always succeed. For this I would ask that some attention be given, as the hall [Royal Thomson Hall] nears completion, to a performing fund, and that those who are knowledgeable in that area be made responsible for the discretionary use of those funds. The effort of making a hall like that pay for itself is going to be a rather difficult one at best. Serious music is not and never has been, as you well know, a profitmaking undertaking. It is necessary to support it massively. It would be only too easy for the directors of the new hall, at the moment called the New Massey Hall, to take the path of least resistance and allow as many pop and rock groups to come in as want to because they attract a very large audience and they make a lot of money. But shall they be the measure of all the care and attention and artistic thought that went into this soaring new building, the care for the musicians and patrons and acoustics? Is it for that reason that it was built?

ON A WORKING HYPOTHESIS
January, 1980
The Hon. René Lévesque, Prime Minister of Quebec

I was led to understand that traditionally your two clubs [the Empire and Canadian Clubs] are quite separate, each holding on to its full sovereignty. And yet sometimes it is found possible to merge your sovereign entities to such contracts of association. I know this probably will not be the most fruitful of such occasions, but let me hope, at least, that it will not sour you on such a promising, modern, up-to-date trend....At any rate, some time in the spring, the people of Quebec will be asked to give us a clear mandate to negotiate a new partnership. It will be a partnership, not a rupture. If a rupture should come, it will be because the basic democratic structure of both our societies cannot stand the pressure of change. But for the moment, what we are talking about from the heart as well as the mind—you only have to look at the map to see our intertwined realities and to know that these are required on both sides—is a new partnership with the rest of Canada....I have no illusions about convincing many people here today. But please believe me when I say that I came here with the abiding faith in the possibility of minds opening on both sides to the promises of a new, joint future.

GOVERNMENT AND THE ARTS
February, 1980
Mavor Moore, Chairman of the Canada Council

But I honestly believe that the whole system of support for the arts in this country rests upon the maintenance of an independent board of public trustees. One of the country's leading arts columnists last year called the Canada Council "the most democratic and efficient means of allocating funds to the arts." A recent editorial in the *Ottawa Journal* said: "Its integrity and independence have never been in doubt; the great flowering of the arts in this country is in significant part the result of its efforts." There is much in the system to improve, and we are working hard on it. But we should be very careful indeed before we emasculate or strait-jacket a system that has worked well and responsibly, that is strongly defended by the arts community, and that has been imitated and envied in other advanced countries. The Canada Council is not a give-away to others but an investment in ourselves.

ISLAM: MYTH AND REALITY
February, 1980
Dr. Hadia Dajani Shakeel, Associate Professor, Department of Middle East and Islamic Studies, University of Toronto

Decades of political, economic and religious changes in the Muslim world culminating in the Iranian Islamic revolution, the recent Grand Mosque rebellion in Saudi Arabia, the Camp David agreement and the tendency to normalize relations between Egypt and Israel, the oil policies of some Muslim countries and their impact on Western economies; these changes along with what has been seen recently as the resurgence of Islamic fundamentalism, the attempts to build the so-called "Islamic Bomb," and perhaps of special importance to us here, the ever increasing Muslim presence in Canada, the U.S. and Europe, have arrested global attention arousing concern about the rising tide of Islam. International responses to these happenings have been expressed in a variety of manners—ranging from threats of military intervention in some Muslim countries to counteract political upheaval and preserve Western interests in the area, to the actual invasion of Afghanistan by the Soviet Union, to talks of economic sanctions against some Muslim countries. On the positive side, more interest has been expressed in understanding the factors underlying these changes as well as the state of Islam and its future prospects.

BLOCKS TO NATIONAL UNITY
The Will to Survive
October, 1980
The Hon. Frank Miller, Treasurer of Ontario and Minister of Economics

Sir John A. Macdonald said that Canada was a "triumph of politics over geography"....When we formed this country, we ignored the tremendous impediments to its creation. We built railways that ran east-west across the roughest terrain in the world. North-south would have been more logical. We protected fledgling industries with tariff barriers and this increased the price of goods to Canadians. It would have been cheaper to form an economic union with the United States. And we gave the central government the right to move money from the richer provinces to the poorer ones so that all parts of Canada could be provided with reasonable levels of social and government services....Canada was not a logical union. It was a creature of people with...a strong will to survive as a separate political entity on the North American continent....What these motives produced is a country based on the concept of economic equality and sharing that is unique in the history of modern nation-building.

PARTNERS IN FREEDOM
October, 1980
The Hon. Jean Casselman Wadds, Canadian High Commissioner to the United Kingdom

Half of the world has no tradition of democracy. Of the remaining half, fifty per cent are part of the Commonwealth, not only a Commonwealth of Nations but a commonwealth of freedom.

BASEBALL TODAY AND TOMORROW
Baseball Talk
November, 1980
Bowie Kuhn, Commissioner of Baseball

[Baseball] has contributed in terms of descriptive words and metaphors to our language. For example, we call something we like a 'hit.' The man who fails has 'struck out' or at best 'doesn't get to first base.' A person who is wrong or indiscreet is 'way off base.' When we are unprepared, we are 'caught out in left field.' and if you cover every contingency you 'touch all the bases.' Our salesmen in industry 'make pitches'....An unfortunate mistake is a real 'blooper.' A person who behaves eccentrically is a real 'screwball.' When we refuse to get discouraged it is because we'll 'get our innings.' If you are getting pressure from both sides you are the victim of a 'squeeze play'....When you compete outside your class you are 'not in the same league.' A man who is willing to co-operate is 'willing to play ball with us.' The fellow who operates against big handicaps has 'two strikes against him'....When you understand quickly you 'get it right off the bat' and when someone asks you an embarrassing question he has 'thrown you a curve'....When success is assured you are 'home free.' When you are alert you are 'on the ball.' When you defend someone you 'go to bat' for him.

WHAT EVERYONE SHOULD KNOW ABOUT THE SUPREME COURT OF CANADA
March, 1981
The Rt. Hon. Bora Laskin, Chief Justice of Canada

There was some grumbling during the constitutional discussions about some of the Court's decisions affecting the exercise of provincial powers, but there could have been equal grumbling from the federal side. Constitutional issues are always sensitive ones, and if there is overreaching by either Parliament or a provincial legislature it is the Court's duty to pull them back.

Governments are better advised to draft their legislation with less bravado than to run the risk of overstepping the limits of their powers. What was dismaying to me as I watched and read about the constitutional proceedings that took place last year was the total misconception that so many ministers and first ministers had about the Supreme Court. They treated it in political terms and, fallaciously, regarded it as a federal institution on a par with the Senate. Let me say, as forcibly as I can, that the Supreme Court of Canada is not a federal institution; it is a national institution and its members are under no federal allegiance merely because they are federally appointed. Just as there is no federal allegiance, there is no regional allegiance and no political allegiance. If the ministers and first ministers had a better understanding of the character of our work, they would have realized that there is very little that is regional in that work. Essentially, we deal with national issues, with matters of general public importance that have no special regional connotation.

HOW STANDS OUR HOME AND NATIVE LAND?
April, 1981
Charles Lynch, political analyst

As we have prospered, we have become more and more critical of our own country. Lacking foreign enemies—and we are almost unique in the world in that respect—we have turned inward on ourselves....We have separatist movements, or incipient ones, everywhere from Newfoundland to Vancouver Island....Everybody wants out, to some extent, except Ontario—and all the others seem to want Ontario out! We're....the only country in the world that I have known in my lifetime where you can stand up and say, "The country stinks!" and everybody else says 'Great! Fantastic. Tell us More.' In the majority of the countries in the world you would be arrested....We have created a framework of freedom greater in its capacity to accommodate difference than any other country in the world, great enough even to contemplate free discussion on the merits of ending the country altogether.

THE FUTURE IS NOT WHAT IT USED TO BE
April, 1981
Charles F. Baird, Chairman and CEO, INCO Limited

In the last century Victorians looked with Tennyson 'into the future' and, like him, saw "all the wonders that will be"....Confidence in the future faded after World War I. Paul Varley, French poet and author, expressed...his doubts about these changes: "The trouble with our times is that the future is not what it used to be"....By the 1960s Broadway was expressing its somewhat jaundiced view of the future in a more forthright style with the play "Stop the World I Want to Get Off"....One common thread runs through almost all scenarios about the economic future of the Western industrial countries....Record levels of inflation, a continuing series of energy price hikes, growing balance of payments deficits, fluctuating exchange rates, rising unemployment and stagflation continue to erode the economic vitality of most countries.

THE CHRYSLER SYNDROME
Dedication to Growth
October, 1981
Lee A. Iacocca, Chairman of the Board, Chrysler Corporation

Given an adequate supply of money at a reasonable rate, the businessmen of both our countries can attack the economic problem where it counts—on the revenue side. Consumers will buy cars and housing. People can be brought back to work again. Factories will reopen. Government revenues will rise to equal expenditures. The Canadian dollar will be worth a dollar again. Inflation will decline and our economies will grow. That is bipartisan economic policy at its best. It does not correct U.S. problems at Canada's expense, at Germany's expense, or at the expense of the deprived people of all nations. It unites all people, north and south, industrial and rural, rich and poor, union and non-union in a common effort to restore the free world's economies to a position of strength again. There is no other way.

We must never again accept double digit inflation as a fact of life. We must never force Canada to run up its prime rate to twenty-two per cent to stop the flow of money to the United States. We must never accept the principle of a "zero sum" society which dictates no more growth, and no more jobs. The economic pie must be enlarged so that all our citizens can share the challenges and the rewards of investment and hard work. That spirit of dedication to growth is what made your country great, and it is what made my country great. It's time to rededicate ourselves to that goal again, for the sake of generations yet to come.

THE CANADIAN DREAM—WE MUST WAKE UP TO ENJOY IT
The Free Fantasy
January, 1982
A. Jean de Grandpré, Chairman and CEO, Bell Canada

I fear that our political leaders have spent an inordinate amount of time bringing [constitutional reorganization] to the present stage, when we should have been putting at least an equal amount of time into our intellectual resources, planning and introducing measures which would be reflected in increased economic well-being for the years ahead....A root cause [of inflation]...is "inflated expectations"....During the period of economic boom of a decade or so ago....It was popular to believe that all the needs, fancies or desires of the people could be met on...a "no cost" basis. You remember the political slogans of the day; "Free Education For All," "Free Hospital Care," "Free Indexed Pensions," "Free Medical Services." Everything was free. We were like a bunch of drunken sailors on a buying spree....The sailors were burning hard-earned money; we were buying on credit.

HANGING TOGETHER: CANADA AFTER PATRIATION
February, 1982
The Hon. Thomas L. Wells, Minister of Intergovernmental Affairs and Government House Leader, Ontario

Do you think that Canada will exist as an Atlantic to Pacific nation on February 18, 1992? Probably your answer is "yes." So is mine. But it is not a sure thing....But very soon, the British Parliament will enact a bill...that will become the Constitution of Canada....I will put it to you straight. Our efforts to keep Quebec and Quebeckers as an integral part of Canada must continue. Out new Canadian constitution will give us something fresh to build on. You and I cannot afford to throw up our hands in despair and say that Quebec will never be satisfied, or as some others are quick to say, "let them go." The name of the game is continued compromise and working together.

WHY PAY TWICE? THE COST OF DOUBLE GOVERNMENT
March, 1982
Darcy W. McKeough, President, Union Gas Limited

It is my conviction that there are ways to reduce total government expenditures. I want to talk about one of them. I'll take the next twenty minutes or so to elaborate on my basic message. The message itself is simple and brief. It is this: with a few exceptions, every responsibility currently held at the federal and provincial levels would be handled better, more efficiently, more effectively, more economically and with greater accountability if it were handled by one or the other level, rather than by being shared, or even worse, competed over, by the two levels. We now have eleven departments of labour, eleven departments of agriculture, eleven of industry, eleven of corrections, and the list goes on. In almost every case, we need either one department, with its head office in Ottawa, or ten, one in each of the provinces. We do not need eleven. We must get away from the confusion, the cross purposes, the waste and the sheer ineffectiveness that comes from having eleven.

DO WE NEED DIPLOMACY?
Diplomatic Ingenuity
March, 1982
Lord Moran, KCMG, The British High Commissioner in Canada

One quality diplomats are supposed to have is presence of mind—the ability to react quickly to unexpected situations. Many years ago a British Ambassador to the Sublime Porte at Constantinople, on arriving to present his credentials to the Sultan, found that the final door into the presence chamber was only two feet high so as to compel him to enter on hands and knees, thus demonstrating subservience. Lord Duncannon made no difficulty about this. He went in on hands and knees—but backwards.

NEW DIRECTIONS FOR THE CANADIAN ECONOMY
June, 1982
The Rt. Hon. Peter Lougheed, QC, Premier, Province of Alberta

The real concern over the extent of foreign ownership of our economy has to evolve beyond the simplification of polling Canadians as to whether or not they prefer, for example, to see a larger portion of the Canadian oil and gas industry owned by Canadians. Obviously the vast percentage of Canadians is going to answer "yes" to such a simple question. But recent polls indicate quite a different answer if the question is phrased on the basis of whether or not limiting foreign ownership would lead to fewer jobs for Canadians....The transactions during 1981 by certain Canadian-owned petroleum companies in acquiring the shares of successful foreign petroleum companies in Canada merely resulted in a shift from foreign equity to foreign debt....It is a time for candour—a time to try to explain the complexities and possible negatives of policies like so-called Canadianization.

REMINISCENCES OF THE GROUP OF SEVEN
October, 1982
A.J. Casson, RCA, LLD, artist

In 1926 we went up to Lake Superior. I thought you might like to know what a Group of Seven sketching trip was like. We took the night train. It was in the middle of October. We got off at Port Coldwell about five at night. The train wouldn't stop—it was on a heavy grade—but Harris had given the conductor ten dollars or something to slow it down to twenty-five miles per hour. Because I was the youngest, I was put on the steps to count our baggage coming out. When we got to the right point, I got a shove to jump. Harris had arranged for a couple of section men to put the heavy things on a jigger and take us up the track five miles. Well, of course, that night we had no more time than to get a tent set up, get something to eat, and go to bed. Next morning we set up camp. There was a fireplace and all that to get ready. For two weeks it snowed every night and every morning. We thought that would be fine; light snow was great. But about half-past nine every morning it would rain a bit, which took the snow off. We spent two weeks there. For some people it would be miserable. We had a wonderful time. I have never in all my life been associated with people who were so enthusiastic. Not because they were painting to sell, because there were no sales anyway, but just with straight enthusiasm. It got into your blood. I would go out with them; they would pick their spots, and I would watch them for a whole morning and a whole afternoon and I don't think they would raise their heads. They were concentrating on what they were doing. I was roaming around to see if I could pick up some pointers from them. But they didn't pay much attention. They were busy. But every night when we came back—we had a little stove, a little woodstove, I wouldn't say it was warm but at least it wasn't freezing—they would ask me to show them what I had done that day.

Douglas Derry, President, The Empire Club of Canada:
The Club's 80th year was one of fun and celebration. The 80th anniversary luncheon had Canada's only living father of Confederation as guest of honour. Newfoundland's colourful and loquacious Joey Smallwood finally concluded, "In Newfoundland we are enjoying the richest harvest time that ever was known." Most of the attendees had by then completed their midday harvest and returned to work! Later in the year, members and guests celebrated the Club's anniversary and a membership exceeding 2,800 in University of Toronto's Hart House with the Eightieth Anniversary Tea at which senior past president Sydney Hermant, attired appropriately for the occasion, cut the cake and members and guests enjoyed the Club's own "Empire Blend" of tea. The same week, in celebrating Toronto's sesquicentennial, the Club again looked to the past to hear historian J.M.S. Careless on *The Life of a New City: Toronto, 1834*, an address given from the perspective of a visitor to Toronto at that time.

BEYOND EVEREST
January, 1983
Sir Edmund Hillary, KBE

Thirty years ago conservation hadn't really been heard of. On our 1953 expedition we just threw our empty tins and trash into a heap on the rock-covered ice at Base Camp. We cut huge quantities of the beautiful juniper shrubs for our fires, and on the South Col at twenty-six thousand feet we left a scattered pile of empty oxygen bottles, torn tents, and remnants of food containers. And the expeditions of today aren't much better in this respect either. Mount Everest is littered with junk from the bottom to the top—there are even a few bodies lying around. Since those years I have spent a great deal of time in the Himalayan Kingdom of Nepal. I have learned to understand the people, to enjoy their friendship and cheerfulness, and I have gained an appreciation of some of their problems. One thing that has really concerned me has been the destruction of their natural environment that is taking place. Population pressures are forcing the farmers higher and higher up the mountainsides to find land where they can plant their crops. A large proportion of the forest cover has been destroyed in order to clear land for cultivation, to supply the local people with fuel, and to produce firewood for trekking and climbing groups. The Nepalese are experts at ingenious and laborious terracing of their hillsides, but when the monsoon rains come the surface soil is washed down into the streams; it pours into the great Ganges River, flows out into the Bay of Bengal, and is finally deposited in the Indian Ocean. That valuable soil will never return.

CLEANING UP OUR ACT (THE INCOME TAX ACT, THAT IS)
February, 1983
J. Lyman MacInnis, FCA, President, Institute of Chartered Accountants of Ontario

The [Canadian] Income Tax Act is an unmitigated mess!....It is incomprehensible; yet you and I and every other taxpayer in this country are required by law to understand it....Nowhere in [the Act] is "income" defined. It just sort of seeps in in various places like perspiration seeps through pores in the skin....When you find section 39, you will also find that the fun is just beginning. Section 39 begins with a sentence that has 774 words, 28 commas, and 2 semicolons. Lincoln's entire Gettysburg Address had only 267 words in it. Section 39 has 7 subsections. It refers you to ten other sections which in turn refer you to another forty sections....There is an old saying that an infinite number of monkeys using an infinite number of typewriters would eventually type all the great works. I think they've completed their first one. It's called the Canadian Income Tax Act.

LESSONS FROM CURRENT MISERIES
February, 1983
Michael A. Walker, Director, The Fraser Institute

It comes as no surprise to us that the world price of oil has overshot its true economic level. It overshot because of the intervention of government in restraining price and artificially elevating demand and thereby sending false signals to consumers and producers. The lesson we must learn from this experience is that the intervention of government does not ensure that the impact of any particular unfortunate event will be ameliorated. From our experience with energy policy, we must now acknowledge that involvement of government can make matters tragically worse than they otherwise would have been. I think it is high time we recognized that reliance on market force as a way of solving economic problems is not, as is often implied, naïve, simplistic, or stupid.

NEW KNOWLEDGE, NEW POSSIBILITIES, NEW RESPONSIBILITIES—A CHRISTIAN PERSPECTIVE
March, 1983
The Most Rev. Edward Walter Scott, Primate, The Anglican Church of Canada

I believe that God is, and that God created all that is. In other words I do not believe that the world is an accident. I believe it is a creation....As creatures of God we are accountable to Him....He invites people like you and me, made in His image but imperfect, to be co-creators with Him....Our concept of success in recent years has almost demanded that in order for one side to win, the other side must lose. I think we must recognize that it is a far better situation if we all win. I think we have to quite deliberately focus more attention upon corporate relationships that are win-win, relationships where both parties benefit....We have felt that nature was ours to do with as we wished. Ecological research is beginning to show us that we don't stand over nature—we stand in nature, we are dependent on nature. We must recognize that there needs to be a creative balance between nature and humankind. We must rekindle a respect for nature.

RESPONSIBLE AND PRUDENT ECONOMIC POLICIES
September, 1983
The Rt. Hon. Margaret Thatcher, MP, Prime Minister, First Lord of the Treasury and Minister for the Civil Service of Great Britain

You'll be very well aware, both at the top table and throughout this audience, that inflation, interest rates, levels of taxation are all part of this complex problem. We have made great progress in inflation; so have you. It is very well down. Some progress, but not enough on interest rates and less than we would have wished on reducing taxation. In the last Parliament, because we believed that we had to set out to check the balance between the citizen and the state and that it needed correcting in favour of the citizen, we transferred from the public sector into private ownership companies like Cable and Wireless, British Aerospace, Britoil, The National Freight Corporation; we're ending the monopoly in the telephone industry and the commercial postal services. We encourage the public services to contract work out to the private sector whenever this helps them to cut costs and operate more efficiently. This may seem natural to you; I had to take over a country where the public sector had got far too big, where politicians had to run state nationalized industries and where the time had come really to reverse the trend and put more responsibility and initiative back to the private citizen.

WHAT IS WRONG WITH LOVING CANADA?
The First Photograph
October, 1983
Roloff Beny, OC, LLD, RCA, photographer

At the age of thirteen, I was photographing nature—gopher holes, rattlesnakes, daffodils in the snow—but on May 26, 1939, I took my first people photograph. King George VI and Queen Elizabeth stopped in Medicine Hat—if only on a flag-decked railway siding during their first state visit to Canada. As a King Scout, I was presented to the King…and boldly took a snap! Years later, at Clarence House in London, I met and photographed Queen Elizabeth (now the Queen Mother); her lilac costume and radiant smile relaxed me. I amused Her Majesty by relating this story of the first royal photograph I had ever taken. The Queen Mother asked what kind of camera I had used. When I replied, "A box Brownie," she remarked, "Ahh, and a very reliable camera too." Gathering my courage, I continued and described a new book project—the photographs I had taken of people during forty years and in more than forty countries. I had hoped to open the book with that early—for me—historical photograph but tragically, the negative was long lost. Prophetically, the Queen Mother said, "Surely you will find it, or your mother has hidden it away." One year later, while on location in Spain, I received the news that my mother had died. I rushed home for the funeral. In Medicine Hat, my mother was laid to rest under a veritable blanket of wild roses—her name was Rosalie. Afterwards, friends gathered, among them my former Scout leader, Colonel Bruce Buchanan, whom I hadn't seen for forty years. He had flown from Ottawa, a surprise and a great comfort to me. Quietly drawing me aside, he said he had brought a small gift of sentimental value—and behold, there it was—my lost negative along with a print, hand-coloured by me, of the King and Queen. My friend, having jealously preserved the negative and print for all those years, asked mildly, "Would you like to have these?"

CANADA-U.S. RELATIONS—SOME THOUGHTS ABOUT PUBLIC DIPLOMACY
November, 1983
Allan E. Gotlieb, MA, LLB, Canadian Ambassador to the United States of America

You know, I've come to realize after two years in Washington and extensive travel in the United States, that there is at the heart of our relationship the fact that out there both in the grass roots and in the cities, Canadians are often not really seen by Americans as foreign. We are neighbours, friends, cousins, fellow North Americans; we are Canadians, but we are not foreigners. When Peter Jennings was recently named anchor at ABC, Roone Arledge, head of ABC news and sports, was asked if there was a downside to having a non-U.S. citizen as anchorman of one of the three most influential news broadcasts in the country. I can't recall his precise words but they were something like, "Well, you know, he's not really a foreigner, he's a Canadian." Well, this view of Canadians is an enormous and certainly unique compliment to us. It gives us opportunities and advantages and I will discuss some of these later. But if there is a downside to this view of Canadians—and perhaps there is—it is that if we are often perceived as Americans, then there is surprise when we don't behave like them. The view might then be that we are behaving like confused or naughty Americans or even perverse ones. Whatever the perception, the reasons why we sometimes need to behave quite differently from them is not fully appreciated, and this is why I believe it is essential for Canadians to engage in public diplomacy in the United States; to explain Canada, to encourage Canadian studies in the United States; to export our cultural products and achievements, to create greater understanding of our Constitution, political system, and history. We have to explain these things to understand that we are indeed different, because of our very different geography, our vast expanses, our scattered populations, our thin bank along the border, our regional character and diversity, our bilingualism and multiculturalism, our degree of foreign investment and control. We will always have national policies in Canada—whatever the party in power—aimed at cementing our sovereignty, strengthening our unity, our east-west axis or ties, our transportation links, our access to our North, our languages and cultures; and aimed at enhancing our ability to strengthen our nationhood and benefit our peoples. Americans, with good reason, do not speak of their national unity and their national identity: they never speak of their sovereignty or independence. That is not part of their vocabulary. All these differences spring from the fact that we are different political entities with significantly different challenges and problems to face. It is important for our closest friends, with whom we share most of this continent, to understand that when we Canadians behave differently from them, and when differences create some conflict between us from time to time, the policies from which they arise are not anti-American, not in the least. They are just pro-Canadian.

THE AUTHORITY OF LEARNING
January, 1984
Professor Northrop Frye, CC, DD, LLD, DLitt, FRSC, Literary Critic, Chancellor, Victoria University, and University Professor, University of Toronto

This year, 1984, seems to be the only year that has had a book written about it before it appeared, and discussions of Orwell's 1984 have become one of the most hackneyed themes in current journalism even before we are out of the January of that year. Nevertheless, I insist on beginning with one more reference to it, and for two reasons. In the first place, most of the discussions of the book I have read have failed to grasp its central thesis. Second, that thesis coincides with my own conviction as a student and teacher of English, which I have been trying to pound into the student and public consciousness for nearly half a century....The central thesis of the book is that there is only one way to create a hell on earth that we and our children can never escape from, and that is to smash language. As long as we have the words to formulate ideas with, those ideas will still be potential, and potentially dangerous. What Orwell's state brings in is a pseudo-logical simplification of language called Newspeak, in which, for example, instead of saying that something is very bad you say that it is "double plus ungood." This kind of talk is rationalized as making language more logical; what it actually does is to make it mechanical, like a squirrel's chatter. Orwell devotes an appendix to his book in which he impresses on his reader the fact that the debasing of language is the only means to a permanent tyranny. We can no longer change a world like 1984 when the words that express the possibility of change have been removed from speech.

THE UNITED NATIONS: A CANADIAN PERSPECTIVE
March, 1984
The Hon. Allan J. MacEachen, PC, MP, LLD, Deputy Prime Minister and Secretary of State for External Affairs

Clearly, the United Nations has to do better on high-profile peace and security issues if it is to gain maximum support in the international community and with our publics. We must not, however, fall victim to exaggerated expectations. There is little point in blaming the United Nations for the inability of those who wield a veto to agree among themselves....No other scheme appears feasible and acceptable to the international community. Canadians continue to serve in United Nations' peacekeeping forces and observer missions that are making positive contributions to stability in the Middle East and Cyprus....We should not dismiss the United Nations' function as a useful safety valve. Despite the limitations of the United Nations, I believe the international situation would be infinitely more dangerous without it. The maintenance of peace and security in the United Nations system may capture the headlines, but much valuable work goes on in the technical parts of the system.

CANADA AND THE PACIFIC CHALLENGE
March, 1984
Dr. Stuart Smith, FRCP(C), Chairman, Science Council of Canada

The United States is now, and always will be, our major trading partner. After that, however, Canada's trade with the Pacific is now much larger than our trade with the Atlantic and this trend is rapidly accelerating. Never again will Canada's Atlantic trade be even close to that which we will experience with Pacific nations. The sooner we begin to think of ourselves as a Pacific rather than an Atlantic nation, the better we are likely to do. This should guide the courses we teach in universities and in business schools, the sales agencies and trade offices we set up, the languages and customs that we learn about. The Empire Club might not be the most propitious place to say this, but I have brought along a map which centres on the Pacific; and I would recommend that such a map replace the usual Atlantic-centred one in our consciousnesses.

AS OTHERS SEE US
Speech Writers
November, 1984
Charles Ritchie, CC, author and diplomat

During the last electoral contest a friend of mine was working as a speech-writer for one of the protagonists, and he had a row with his political master, when the politician was making a speech....[The politician] started to read the speech and it began, "There is no easy solution to the twin problems of inflation and unemployment, but I have a few positive thoughts to put before you today." He turned to the next page and the script writer had scrawled "You're on your own now, Mac."

THE RUNAWAY BRAIN
Scientific Illiterates
December, 1984
David Suzuki, broadcaster and author

[Of the issues that daily preoccupy the media] none...in a long-term sense will matter very much. We have spent enormous amounts of time in the media with "who will be the new leader of the Conservatives or the Liberals?" I am sure that within five years few will remember even who the major contenders for the title were and that in ten or fifteen years [their names] will not be very significant in terms of the nature of the society we live in at that time. The fact is that the most powerful force shaping our life today is none of those issues—it is Science....When I was five years old there was [polio and smallpox]....there were no computers...there were no tranquillizers, there were no satellites...no jets...no nuclear bombs...no antibiotics....I am absolutely sure that my daughters will take it for granted that if they want to travel in outer space they will....A few years ago we did a test on fifty MPs and gave them a simple test for their comprehension of science, terms and ideas....Lawyers and businessmen came out absolutely rock bottom. They simply had no idea what the most elementary terms and concepts were. Now these are people who are going to make decisions....About the future of Canada's medical care, about the future of satellite communications, about forests, about our fisheries, about pollution, the impact of computers in the workplace...about our Candu reactor....And the people we elect to look after or consider these are simply not competent to make judgments that have a scientific or technological base....We had better become more conversant with science—each and every one of us.

THE WASHINGTON VIEW
January, 1985
Joe Schlesinger, Washington correspondent

In a democracy a government can only be successful by taking a country in the direction in which it is ready to go.

PRINCIPLES AND APPROACHES
Our Charter
January, 1985
The Hon. John Crosbie, PC, MP, Minister of Justice

My appointment as Minister of Justice can be explained on the same grounds that John F. Kennedy explained appointing his brother Robert. He said: "I see nothing wrong with giving Robert some legal experience as Attorney General before he goes out to practice law." I understand that I do not even have to pass an exam to join the Bar of Ontario, so that I can make my fortune when I go out to practise law....I believe there is widespread agreement that many of Canada's laws are outdated and do not adequately respond to present-day social needs or properly reflect the changed attitudes and values of Canadians....Perhaps the most significant innovation in Canadian law since Confederation was the introduction of the Canadian Charter of Rights and Freedoms in April 1982....Every Canadian who believes a right guaranteed in the Charter is infringed by an existing law has the right to challenge that law in court....Of course the Charter is still very much a work in progress and the full meaning of many of its provisions has yet to be determined.

FORECAST TWO THOUSAND
March, 1985
George Gallup III, Chairman, American Institute of Public Opinion

We are guilty as individuals and as nations of not identifying those "future forces" that will shape our lives, and of planning accordingly. Societies today all over the world are afflicted with a bewildering array of social problems that threaten to undermine the stability of nations. Let us look at the situation in the United States. Crime is endemic....Drug and alcohol abuse are common....One person in five says he knows of at least one case of child abuse in his neighbourhood....An estimated twenty per cent of the U.S. population is functionally illiterate....Cheating is "epidemic and big business"...."Cheating...has become an American pastime." We interviewed 1,346 opinion leaders....These leaders....see the number one problem—the nuclear threat—diminishing in importance by 2000. Thirty-eight per cent see [overpopulation as a threat] by 2000. And environmental pollution jumps from thirty-nine per cent to fifty-five per cent.

FINANCIAL INDUSTRY RESTRUCTURING: A USER'S GUIDE
March, 1985
Allan R. Taylor, President and CEO, The Royal Bank of Canada

On every issue, the acid-test of any move to deregulate or re-regulate is "cui bono?"—Who profits by it? Who benefits?....Unfortunately, so far in the debates on financial industry restructuring we have tended to hear mainly from partisan voices—people who speak only for one segment of the industry; their own sector's market share; or their private corporate interests....Canadian banks are by no means perfect. But we are very good at what we do—delivering a wide range of financial services, to all of Canada and to much of the rest of the world, safely, efficiently and yes, at a profit.

ONTARIO'S TRADING RELATIONSHIPS IN A CHANGING WORLD
Free Advice
September, 1985
The Hon. David Peterson, Premier, Province of Ontario

I know what a very distinguished group of speakers you've had lately....[including] columnist Ann Landers....You know she is besieged by nine million people who want her advice and I'm besieged by nine million people who want to give me advice....One of the great joys of political life is that you're never short of advice; the problem is, which advice to take.

OUR RESPONSIBILITY TO YOUTH
November, 1985
Her Excellency The Rt. Hon. Jeanne Sauvé, PC, CC, Governor General of Canada

It is perhaps the fate of Governors General to be witness throughout their tenure to so much which compels them to [acquire an] opinion, yet to be restricted by the nature of the office in speaking about what they know. A predecessor of mine, who is present, once said that most of the time he was restricted to "Governor Generalities." However, it's the function of Governor General to have some substance. Surely it is worth exploring what he or she may stand for publicly, while keeping it above political controversy. There is one topic about which I need not remain silent I am sure: a matter of such critical importance to this country that I have chosen it as the principal focus and preoccupation of my tenure as Governor General of this nation. You will recall that some of my predecessors to this office have, in turn, encouraged and promoted causes, such as the arts, energy conservation, the family, and so on. I speak, of course, about the youth of this country: of the concern I have for the forthcoming generations and the fact that we, as the current leaders and authorities of the day, should take time from pursuit of our own ambition to nurture, encourage and provide real opportunities for those who will succeed us. This, in many ways, means jobs for the young unemployed.

CANADA-U.K. RELATIONS: A FRIENDLY CHALLENGE
January, 1986
The Hon. R. Roy McMurtry, QC, High Commissioner for Canada to Great Britain

My not-so-well-planned route to London encouraged one of my friends to offer a new definition for a High Commissioner as "one who is denied a job by his provincial colleagues, but who is given employment by the Prime Minister on the condition that he leave the country"....Traditional and sentimental ties with Britain have now to be set against the recognition of considerable changes marked by Britain's increased role in the Europe of the past ten years and also of a Canadian preoccupation with its relations with the United States. The two countries, therefore, tended to grow apart, through no deliberate design, but by force of external circumstances....At the level of public perception, sentiments of active sympathy have progressively given way to active indifference....As a Canadian ever mindful of the enormous and pervasive influence of our friendly neighbours to the south, I strongly believe that we must work to strengthen our other traditional relationships.

SPACE MISSION 41-G
January, 1986

Harry Seymour, President, The Empire Club of Canada:
Canada's first astronaut, Dr. Marc Garneau, put forth a strong argument in early January as to why our 24-year-old space programme must be allowed to develop further, prior to taking us around the world on his 41-G mission.

Dr. Marc Garneau, QC, first Canadian astronaut

I always look forward to the opportunity to speak to Canadians about the honour I felt when I was chosen to fly in space in October 1984 aboard the shuttle Challenger....I went up into space with six other people, which at that time was the largest crew ever to go up into space. There were five men and two women. The women were: Kathy Sullivan—the first American woman to walk in space....The other woman was Sally Ride who was the first American woman astronaut ever to go into space. In all we spent 8 1/4 days in space and went around the world one hundred and thirty-two and a half times....That works out to sixteen times every day....Because you go around sixteen times you have sixteen sunrises and sixteen sunsets.

CANADA 1986: NEW REALITIES
February, 1986
Marie-Josée Drouin, Executive Director, Hudson Institute Inc.

We have entered what I would call a Post-Ideology Period....Many...traditional support systems have more or less disappeared. The family, the school, religion are playing a weaker role in providing support and security to individuals who must deal with change. Political ideology does not appear to be the answer either....Increasingly people are trying to fill the void through personal challenges—search for individual satisfaction…customized this, customized that. Life lived for oneself. The biggest question facing our modern societies is whether this is compatible with the pursuit of the common good.

SHAW FESTIVAL—25TH ANNIVERSARY
February, 1986
Allan Slaight, Chairman, Shaw Festival

Mr. [Clifton] Fadiman tells us that while George Bernard Shaw was still a music critic he was dining with a friend in a restaurant that provided for entertainment an orchestra that was at best mediocre. The leader, recognizing Shaw, wrote him a note asking him what he would like the orchestra to play next. "Dominoes" replied Shaw….A lady, notorious for courting celebrities…sent Shaw an invitation reading "Lady Smithers will be at home on Tuesday between four and six o'clock." Shaw returned the card annotated: "Mr. Shaw likewise."

A SCIENTIST AND THE WORLD HE LIVES IN
November, 1986
John C. Polanyi, CC, PhD, Professor of Chemistry, U of T and Canada's 1986 Nobel Prize Winner

And yet you may know that on the day the bombshell of the prize exploded in my living room, when asked by reporters what would be my advice to a talented and ambitious Canadian scientist, I replied that I would suggest he go abroad. I did not relish giving that response, but, at this juncture in our scientific history, it is the only answer that I can give. In truth, a talented and ambitious scientist would be unlikely to ask me that question, since the answer would be obvious to him. Fortunately for us, there are scientists of very high quality who ignore such promptings, and remain here. Canada, let me tell the Empire and Canadian Clubs, is a wonderful country. People want to live here. Scientists, myself among them, are no exception. We should be clear, however, that these individuals live here at a price to their scientific careers that many will not be willing to pay. We who remain are impoverished by the departure of the others, since the intellectual environment in which one does science is of crucial importance. It is not, I should add, that the numbers leaving are huge. It is just that the marketplace works to ensure that those who leave are often the best.

NUCLEAR WEAPONS AND NUCLEAR ARMS CONTROL: CANADA AND THE WESTERN ALLIANCE IN 1987

January, 1987
The Hon. Perrin Beatty, PC, MP, Minister of Defence

Reductions in nuclear weapons alone are not sufficient to enhance our security. The debate continues to centre on whether it is weapons or people and their political systems that cause conflicts. The truth is it is probably both to some extent. Competition in arms may indeed fuel mistrust, and temporary advantage may encourage adventurism. However, the peaceful resolution of conflicts, and the fostering of mechanisms to bridge the differences that give rise to mistrust and conflict, are absolutely essential if we are to build a better and safer world. If conflicts are to be resolved in non-military ways, then each of us bears a responsibility for encouraging the processes of conflict resolution and peacemaking....As a responsible citizenry, we must face up to the fact that, in this imperfect world, wars continue to occur and nuclear weapons exist on both sides of the East/West divide. The knowledge of how to make nuclear arms cannot be erased, even if existing stockpiles could be eliminated. Our peace with freedom cannot be taken for granted, but must be vigorously defended. Accordingly, it seems to me that both conventional and nuclear weapons, to deter and defend, are going to be here for some time. Further, nuclear weapons, on which we have relied for more than forty years, will continue for the foreseeable future to play a role in maintaining our security.

THE U.S.-CANADIAN FREE TRADE AREA
October, 1987
Ambassador Clayton Yeutter, United States Trade
Representative

We in the United States are pleased with the agreement concluded last Saturday. It culminated 16 months of gruelling negotiations. President Reagan and Prime Minister Mulroney played
active roles throughout the process, first by providing the vision
and then by demonstrating the political leadership necessary to
keep the negotiations on track. Both our governments spent
many long hours setting negotiating objectives and devising
negotiating strategies. And in the final days of the talks, we met
nearly around the clock to complete the agreement. It is not surprising that many details had to be settled at the political level in
the final days; that is the nature of negotiations. But it is important to remember that skilled and dedicated negotiators on both
sides laid the groundwork during the previous 16 months. This
agreement was not cobbled together at the last minute. The
United States government devoted an enormous amount of time
and effort to this negotiation because Canada is our best friend,
closest ally and biggest trading partner. We know that our economic health and national security are inextricably bound up
with the people of Canada. There is nothing in the world equiv-
alent to the political "open border" between the United States
and Canada. Now we are hopefully on the way to an open economic border as well. That would be a truly remarkable achievement for both countries, and each will be far stronger as a result.

CANADA'S FUTURE UNDER FREE TRADE
October, 1987
Ambassador Simon Reisman, Chief Trade Negotiator for
Canada

Ten days ago we reached agreement on the essential elements of
a Canada-U.S. free trade agreement. What was agreed will set the
stage for securing Canada's future as a strong, sovereign and

prosperous nation. Within the next several weeks we will flesh out and put in legal form the agreed elements of the accord. The agreement reached October 3, however, captures the essence of the accord. Let me assure you in the strongest possible terms that what we achieved is a good deal for Canada. And nothing, not even letting the lawyers translate it into their own special language, will change that.

THE ROLE OF THE DEFENCE COUNSEL IN CANADIAN SOCIETY
November, 1987
Edward L. Greenspan, QC, Senior Partner, Greenspan, Rosenberg

Even my own mother is ambivalent about what I do for a living. When she reads about some "horrible" person who has retained me, she can't understand why I would take the case. I've often said Al Capone's mother was more tolerant of her son's profession than my mother is of mine....Project yourself for a moment into the position of a defendant. If you should one day find yourself accused of crime, you would expect your lawyer to raise every defence authorized by law of the land. Even if you were guilty, you would expect your lawyer to make sure that the government did not secure your conviction by unlawful means. You would be justifiably outraged if your lawyer sat silent while the prosecution deprived you of your liberty on the basis of a defective indictment, perjured testimony or a coerced confession. In the movie, *And Justice for All*, Al Pacino was cheered by the audience both in the movie and in the movie theatre when he announced to the jury that his client was guilty. Surely that is not the kind of lawyer you want. You would scarcely want him to decide that these things were "technicalities" and that society would be better off if you were in prison. The most unpopular defendant has the right to expect the same kind of defence you would want yourself. And the role of the defence counsel, the obligation the community places on him, is a societal role—to

defend the constitutional guarantees of presumption of inno-
cence and the requirement that in our democracy no one can
lose freedom unless and until the state can prove guilt beyond a
reasonable doubt. Our community can retain justice and freedom only as long as it gives standing to one person to take, within the limits of the law, the defendant's side in court and to
remind society when the scales of justice are tilting in the wrong
direction. For instance, we live in the Dawning of the Age of the
Victim. You may think the defence counsel will naturally oppose
the interests of the victim. Not true. What we must do is remind
you all the time of the potential danger that fashionable and
trendy ideas might have on the law. Will it upset the delicate balance the justice system desperately tries to maintain. John
Robinette, the dean of Canadian lawyers, says, "It's so easy for
the victim to exaggerate.…I'm not happy about this new rule for
the victim. It worries me."

THE ECONOMY: 1984–1988
February, 1988
The Hon. Michael Wilson, PC, MP, Minister of Finance

And how have we been doing as Canadians? Since 1984,
Canada's growth has led that of all the major industrial nations.
In 1987, our performance surpassed all expectations, buoyed by
strong consumer spending, the highest levels of business investment in six years, and the most housing starts in the last 10
years. When the final numbers are in, the real gain in a national
income is likely to be close to 4 per cent—far ahead of most
expectations.

THE JOURNALIST AS CELEBRITY
June, 1988
Peter Mansbridge, television journalist, CBC National

We in Canadian television journalism are in the big leagues. We
play this game as well or better than anyone else in the world,
and our record shows it. Sure the American networks have more

money and more resources but their journalists are no better. If they were, why would they have to keep hiring Canadians for their top jobs? Why do they often choose our reports over their own when major international news stories occur? Why, when we work jointly in the field with the U.S. networks, do they often use the news pictures shot by Canadian crews over their own pictures? Why? Because we play in the same league and we play as well or better than they do. We are also willing to spend more time analysing issues, events and people, looking at stories in depth. Do you see any of the major American networks following their nightly newscasts with an in-depth analytical broadcast like The Journal? On both sides of the border, there is a serious commitment to covering the news of the day. But the commitment on this side of the border, not just at the CBC, I believe runs deeper. Canadians want more and more reporting on news and current affairs and we're doing our best to deliver it. And when our 24-hour news channel goes on the air—and I am still very positive that it will—our commitment will run even deeper and your desire for even more information will be fulfilled.

RELATIONSHIPS
June, 1988
Ronald Reagan, President of the United States

(The President of the United States and the Prime Minister of Canada spoke after the seven-nation Economic Summit which was hosted by Canada)

The president was introduced by Brian Mulroney, Prime Minister of Canada

Since September of 1984 I have had the distinct pleasure of working closely with President Reagan. In the process, we have become friends. This is not to say that either of us has ever lost sight of the national interest of his own country, but I think that it has helped us to find the mutual interest of both of our countries....The Free Trade Agreement is going to give Canada access to a market of 250 million people, half of them within a day's drive of Toronto, making Toronto the centre of access to the biggest and richest market in the world. It's a good deal, a very good deal for both of our countries.

President Ronald Reagan

Today our relations are better than ever. Over the last four years the Canadian-U.S. partnership has grown and strengthened. In a world that is changing before our eyes, we need each other's friendship as never before. And in many ways, that is what, for Brian and me, the last three days here in Toronto have been about....As you know, we have just finished meeting with the leaders of the five other major industrial democracies....This year's summit was informal yet highly focused....The progress achieved may not be fully evident for months, but it was substantial....In ensuring the security not only of our nations but our ideals, in fighting the drug scourge, in leading the world economy to a future of opportunity and growth—the partnership between our countries is at the centre. It is the example to our allies and the world....Since this is my last official visit to Canada, let me add here publicly to Brian Mulroney, a colleague for four years and a friend for life, a particular thank you. Brian and Mila, God bless you, and God bless you all.

Tony van Straubenzee, President, The Empire Club of Canada:
Robin Younger, CEO of RBC Dominion Securities hosted a dinner at which I begged some of my partners for help. The Hon. Michael Wilson, Minister of Finance at the time, was present as was Jean Claude Blanc from Lausanne, Switzerland. About a month after the dinner Michael telephoned and asked me to take a couple of friends of his to dinner. When he told me they were President Reagan and Prime Minister Mulroney I had to pinch myself to make sure I wasn't dreaming. Jean Claude and I discussed the UBS and Credit Suisse and I happened to ask him why his wife Jaqueline hadn't been at the above mentioned dinner. He replied that she had been in New York shopping with Audrey Hepburn. Miss Hepburn agreed to come to the last meeting of my year on the condition that we raised $100,000 for UNICEF. It was the easiest $100,000 I ever had to raise—and she was wonderful.

MANAGING CHANGE
September, 1988
The Rt. Hon. Brian Mulroney, Prime Minister of Canada

Economically, we know that people, not governments, create wealth....Given a chance, the people of Canada can create economic wealth with the best of them. Canada's private sector, its business people and entrepreneurs ask merely for a good economic climate and fair chance....That government be an ally and not a competitor. We have tried to help that process by acknowledging that government, by over-spending and over-regulating, can frustrate the initiative and enterprise of its citizens....Politicians can be a thick-headed breed—I have found that a thick skin is a more useful attribute—but we do listen, we can hear, and we can learn. Most of us at least have heard the message to stop the bickering and get on with the job of building a better Canada.

BLINKERS AND BOOK BURNING
October, 1988
Esther J. Harshaw, Toronto School Trustee

I understand [that previous speakers this year include] a sex therapist, the Prime Minister, the President of the United States and the head of the Salvation Army....I am gratified that the Empire Club ranks education right up there with the Economic Summit, national politics, sex and religion....Our school system has turfed out some of the fine values you have been able to maintain. You still open with grace. A recent Supreme Court decision does not allow prayers during the school day, because of our code of human rights and freedoms....You sing the National Anthem at each meeting; we might be lucky if our children know the words....In a recent survey over half of our children did not know what the golden rule is....A large contributor to this general apathy is the lack of profile given to education by the national and regional media. It is viewed as a farm system for the major leagues of postsecondary education....But the public school system in Toronto, let alone Ontario or Metro adds up to big business by any standard. In the City of Toronto alone the Board of Education oversees 117 elementary schools and 43 high schools. Canada's largest high-tech manufacturer, Northern Telecom, runs 46 plants worldwide and few, if any, of the plants would house the number of people we house in an average high school.

DEREGULATION AND THE AIRLINE INDUSTRY
January, 1989
Maxwell W. Ward, Chairman, Wardair

Scheduled economy airfare yields are fundamental to airline operations and a generous sprinkling of economy and business class airfares are essential in the passenger mix for a given flight to be profitable. Transforming a charter airline into a scheduled airline, both national and international in scope, requires a fundamentally different fleet of aircraft, and a fundamentally different operating philosophy. A carrier with 36 years of commercial airline experience, of which 26 years is in international service, can make that transition, if it has enough money to fund the transition, but Wardair does not. Acquiring a mix of small, medium and large aircraft, with capacities tailored to meet different route expectations, has become very slow in an aircraft manufacturing industry swamped with orders, and delay eats up money. Computer passenger reservations networks are slow to build and are even more expensive than aircraft. Again, time is money. This is the age of the mega carrier. Airline deregulation has come far too late in the development of the airline industry for entrants to build themselves into airlines of mega carrier status capable of competing in world markets. Canada, with its relatively small population and relatively small GNP, would be better served with two strong competitive airlines rather than with three carriers inhibiting progress of the Canadian industry as a whole. Wardair suspended trading of its stock today, as did Canadian Airlines International.

FOR THE CHILDREN
April, 1989
Audrey Hepburn, actress and Special Ambassador to UNICEF

I saw hundreds of thousands of men and women and children in camps, both in the government north and in the rebel-held south. Camps and now overcrowded towns where hundreds of newcomers arrive every day after months of walking. Many die on the way, phantoms carrying their sick transparent babies, but reaching their destination, urged on by the one human quality which is the last to die—hope. Even if this mammoth operation Life-Line Sudan were only to achieve half its goal due to the countless odds it is up against in a vast country with no infrastructure, few roads to speak of and no communication system, it will have succeeded. Not only in saving thousands of lives, but together with the government, the rebels, the brave, tireless NGOs [non-governmental organizations], pilots, truck drivers, loaders and operation officers, it will have given the Sudan hope, and the United Nations will have proven that only through corridors of tranquillity can children be saved, and only through peace can man survive. There is so much we cannot do. We cannot give the children back their parents, but we can return to them the most basic of human rights, the right to health, to tenderness, to life.

THE BUDGET
May, 1989
The Hon. Michael Wilson, Minister of Finance

Only 20 years ago, Canada had an annual surplus, and our total debt after an entire century of Confederation was only $18 billion....By 1984, the $18 billion debt had risen to nearly $200 billion. And the annual deficit was more than $38 billion....Put simply, we as Canadians were not paying our way for the services we were receiving from government. The reality of a debt that is large and growing is that it places a nation on a treadmill. Each year, added effort is required from Canadians to produce new revenues that merely go to pay the interest on a growing debt. Let's be clear about what it means if we continue, year after year, government after government, to borrow and borrow just to pay debt interest. We would be borrowing from our children, not paying our own bills. It's easy to borrow from future generations because they have no say in the matter. They have no vote. Yet it is they who would have to live with the consequences if we did not act.

CANADA AND JORDAN
The Middle East
October, 1989
His Royal Highness King Hussein of Jordan

The importance of our region, the Middle East, is rooted in the central position it has always commanded between ancient civilizations and as a crossroad between east and west. The huge energy resources that it commands have made it a nerve centre for the world. Perhaps it is the centrality of this region that has caused it to suffer more than its fair share from upheavals and turmoil.

AN INTRODUCTION TO THE PHILIPPINES
November, 1989
Her Excellency Corazon Aquino, President of the Republic of the Philippines

The Philippines is the gateway to Asia. And it is widely believed that the Pacific will give its name to the next age of progress. We feel that Canada would be an ideal partner for the Philippines in stepping into this new era of Asian-Pacific growth. There are strategic reasons for this; not the least of them being the integrity of Canadian enterprise. We want investors who are mindful indeed of a good profit, and regardful as well of the interests of the country. You can go to Asia and step into a totally alien environment or go to the Philippines, be at home in an English-speaking nation, with an honest and hard-working people, and still be right in the heart of the most dynamic region of the world.

On to the 100th Anniversary

Constitutional reform was on the minds of speakers and audiences in the 1990s. Barbara McDougall's title, in what had become a series of soul-searching debates after Meech Lake failed, was "Canada After the Meech Lake Accord: Is the Country Falling Apart?" In answering, of course not, she referred to the malaise of "an endless history of constitutional negotiations." Jacques Parizeau returned to the podium with dire predictions, "Maybe we should simply recognize that the Meech Lake Accord was the last real chance for a compromise between two broad political visions of Canada that gradually veered towards a collision course." He spelled out the meaning of sovereignty-association as he saw it, wherein all taxes, laws and treaties would be made in Quebec for Quebeckers. The Constitution was the topic chosen by Prime Minister Brian Mulroney, who invited comments through Citizens' Forums and various public commissions. He wanted the people of Canada to speak out about the constitution and the country's future.

Lucien Bouchard, back at the podium, now as leader of the Bloc Quebecois, looked to a "yes" vote for sovereignty, then, he said, "I believe that the Bloc Quebecois will be in a position to stand as one of the voices of reason in the months preceding its implementation."

By 1995, as the referendum approached, members were told "We must remind our fellow citizens in Quebec and elsewhere in Canada of how much they would stand to lose, in economic and financial terms, if the separatists were to triumph in the referendum. Let's do away with complacency and arrogance." And after the choice was made by a narrow margin to stay with Canada, Roger Landry, president and publisher of La Presse, looked to the future. "If there were to be a third referendum it would again be French-speaking Quebec federalists who would make the difference....I fear that if there are no substantial changes before the next referendum....then many French-speaking federalists will be inclined to vote "yes." If that happens, history books of the future will justly assign to Canadians of our generation the title of 'quitters'—if not cowards....I invite all Canadians to reach out to Quebeckers in the next few months."

Amid these deliberations there were three particularly inspiring addresses, one by Edmund de Rothschild, one by the Dalai Lama, and one by Terry Waite. Rothschild, then Chair of Care Britain, outlined in 1990 plans to help the Middle East, to bring peace through co-operation with their projects and through aid of many types—a plan to desalt water in Egypt, providing thousand of gallons of fresh water, rebuilding of damaged housing in Lebanon, a program to prevent large areas of Syria from turning into desert, to bring relief to Sudan, to bring water to Israel and the Gaza strip. The Dalai Lama, through an interpreter, spoke of true peace, not the peace of fear as in the Cold War, but a peace through mutual respect.

All who heard Terry Waite no doubt pictured themselves imprisoned for five years in solitary confinement, in the dark, and wondered how they would keep their sanity. It was April, 1995, when Terry Waite came to talk to the Club about terror-ism and his confinement, endured after his encounter with the terrorists in Tehran, Libya and Beirut. His words were and are today, important. He was in the United States at the time of the disaster in Oklahoma and at that time reporters asked him if there was a link to Beirut. He replied that the link is that it is the innocent who suffer, and so the terrorists who perform these acts of outrage are at heart cowards. He raised ques-tions—are we partly responsible when we do nothing to help the poor, or when we provide arms or fail to help improve conditions? And he said that if you set out to achieve a politi-cal end by violence you attract ranks of people with a psycho-pathic disposition.

There was pride when Canadian Astronaut, Roberta Bondar, spoke of the beauty of the planet earth, the changes of light, sometimes golden, sometimes turquoise blue, and the beauty of Canada. "Here I am," she said, "full of pride with a maple leaf on my shoulder and a maple leaf in my heart."

The new Europe was a subject of great interest in the 90s. A year after the fall of the Berlin Wall, Europe's future looked prosperous—a common currency, the Euro, to be adopted, and optimism prevailing. But there were warnings of a struggle ahead with the advent of economic restructuring, in Eastern Europe. A German financier spoke of the transfer payments from West to East in Germany—180 billion D. Marks to East Germany and advised that, "The development in East Germany is not as exciting as people thought it would be. On the contrary it is very sluggish; it's a very depressed area and it will remain so for some time. It is a historic task to clean up all the terrible mess which was left from the previous system over there." Another German said of his country "the people in East Germany, this former Communist GDR [German Democratic Republic], have never experienced a democracy in their lifetime. Except the few people who are in their mid-eighties and grew up before Hitler's dictatorship, they have never experienced a market economy in their lifetime....Today, there is deep disappointment particularly due to the loss of more than 40 per cent of the East German jobs....that have been eliminated because the products that were produced were not good enough for competition with the European Common Market."

Air Canada's financial problems were also a recurring theme. In 1993 President and CEO Hollis Harris talked of the 1$billion offer to purchase the Canadian Airlines international business and to make Toronto a hub city in continental airline traffic.

There were questions with no apparent answer. What will be the unknown consequences of the year turning to 2000? From the mid-90s on the word Millennium was frequently heard. By 1998, the Y2K problem was seen to have potential dire consequences and, "how ironic it is that the economic decision to delete two digits from the date code in the computer programmes, which was taken 40 years ago, in order to save time and money, has now rebounded upon the world with unknown consequences. There may not now be enough time and money to fix it. Much as we secretly believe there is a silver bullet which will solve all our problems, I regret everything I have read to date suggests that this is an impossibility." (This was a spectacularly wrong prediction.)

The Club addressed the subject of health care in Canada with a series of speakers tackling the question "Can We Save Medicare?" This focus was applauded by the Health Minister, Allan Rock. One speaker saw the solution to current problems in integration and teamwork in the health-care system and said, "This is the time for a wake-up call." Lynda Cranston spoke as CEO of Canadian Blood Services, an organization created as a result of the crisis of confidence in the blood supply of the 1980s and 90s. The view expressed was that "The past years have taken their toll on the health professions. Many physicians are disheartened, frustrated, angry or depressed." Another address was on Prevention and Treatment of Strokes. The conclusion to the series was that it is important for an aging population to take an interest in an aging health care system.

The Club heard an emotional address from Hilary Weston, Lieutenant Governor of Ontario, and another question. What can we do about our street people? She told about her visit with some social workers to the area under the Gardner Expressway where 500 street kids live, including an 11-year-old boy from Montreal. "The boy was a runaway from a hospital in Montreal where he was being treated for fractures of both legs. When he learned that his father was coming to see him, he fled from the hospital because it was his father who had inflicted his injuries. Despite his broken legs he managed to beg, borrow or steal enough for the bus fare to Toronto. He is now trying to survive as a squeegee kid." One young man said to her "If you want a job, you have to have a place to live. If you want a place to live, you have to have a job." Hilary

Weston concluded "I can think of no better way to celebrate the new century and millennium that are almost upon us than by investing in all the young people who will take Ontario and Canada into the future."

As the century was drawing to a close, Dr. Jack Granatstein asked his compelling question, "Who Killed Canadian History?" He spoke of a series of essays assigned to an eight-year-old about Canadian history—Champlain's abuse of his 13-year-old bride, the extermination of the Beothuk by white men in Newfoundland, the execution of Louis Riel, the internment of Japanese Canadians, the maltreatment of Canada's first woman doctor by her male peers. He asked why racism, sexism and abuse were the only stuff of history—why not the lives of ordinary men and women, why not how our great leaders changed the course of events. He concluded history is not a grab bag out of which moralising lessons are pulled. "Without a sense of our past, we are like poor souls wandering lost in a forest without a map. Without a sense of our history we have no future."

And with the words of Jack Granatstein in mind, the Empire Club could look back over one hundred years of history preserved in the ideas of men and women of each age, in the form of published speeches, some prescient, some not, but they do represent "a sense of our past."

THE CONTINUING CONTROVERSY ON ABORTION

April, 1990

Dr. Henry Morgentaler, The Morgentaler Clinic

I wish to finish on a personal note. Over the years, many people have asked me, "Why did you decide to expose yourself to so much stress and danger in a controversial cause, and why do you persist in doing so?" The answer, after a great deal of reflecting about it, is the following: I am a survivor of the Nazi Holocaust, that orgy of cruelty and inhumanity of man to man. As such, I have personally experienced suffering, oppression and injustice inflicted by men beholden to an inhuman, dogmatic, irrational ideology. To relieve suffering, to diminish oppression and injustice is very important to me. Reproductive freedom and good access to medical abortion means that women will be able to give life to wanted babies at a time when they can provide love, care and nurturing. Well-loved children grow into adults who do not create concentration camps, do not rape and do not murder. They are likely to enjoy life, to love and care for each other and the larger society. By fighting for reproductive freedom, I am contributing to a more caring and loving society based on the ideals of peace, justice and freedom, and devoted to the full realization of human potential. Having known myself the depth of human depravity and cruelty, I wish to do whatever I can to replace hate with love, cruelty with kindness, and irrationality with reason. This is why I am so passionately dedicated to the cause I defend and why I will continue to promote it as long as I have a valid contribution to offer.

A PEACE-LOVING NATION TAKES A WORLD VIEW

September, 1990

His Holiness The Dalai Lama, Spiritual and Temporal Leader of Tibet

Now, almost the entire Tibetan population is against the Chinese rule, the Chinese occupation and of course, we [want the] legitimate right to demand complete independence. Meanwhile, even day-by-day, inside Tibet the immeasurable human rights violations always happen and to us the marshal law is just another form. In reality, since Chinese occupation, some kind of marshal law always there. You know communist countries, communist system is police state. Some form of emergency is always there. It's always there, some really unthinkable human suffering always happening there. The most serious threat is large number of Chinese population transfer. Now, already the Chinese population number is greater than Tibetan population. (Our population is around six million, we believe.) So, that really is a serious matter. Therefore, outside, I thought I have to speak out from realistic point of view. I always believe the best solution about human conflict is through human understanding. That I believe is the best way. Even you may not achieve 100 percent satisfaction, whatever you achieve, that achievement remain long last. So, therefore I made two proposals in public. I've no other choice except to turn to the world community. So then 1987 and 1988, I made two proposals in public. Then at the initial stage the Chinese government, they rejected my idea, but at the same time they indicated their willingness to discuss about the future of Tibet. Then somehow after last year the Tiananmen Square massacre happened. Then the situation changed. Now they're following a more hard-line policy. So still no formal response to me. So, my part I still stand by on those two proposals. Although on a few occasions I stated, that from our part, we made the maximum concession. Even that was not satisfied with the Chinese leaders. Then from my part now, nothing else to offer.

And instead, we have every right to say some new demand. So that's the situation.

LONG-TERM AID TO THE MIDDLE EAST
October, 1990
Edmund de Rothschild, Past Chairman, N.M. Rothschild & Sons Ltd. and Chairman, CARE Britain Corporate Council

Bankers are normally conservative people. So to try and foretell whether Britain is right to join the European monetary fund or go for something else is far into the realms of hypothesis. Perhaps I could answer my thoughts on this in the following manner. There is an amusing strip cartoon in the *International Herald Tribune* featuring Blondie. In one of them Blondie asked Dagwood, her husband, "What makes the stock market go up and down?" Dagwood replied, "It is simple—inflationary pressures and fiscal instability, also international imbalance and political tension." To which profound words Blondie replied, "As long as you don't know dear, why don't you just say so." I feel that nearly all of us must feel the same as Blondie about the future of any economic policy....But I want to talk about another serious and very dangerous crisis in the Middle East. All my life I have been involved with refugees. I was fortunate to have survived three campaigns during World War II and I witnessed some of the terrible scenes in occupied Europe and Germany. I became treasurer of the British sponsored World Refugee Year and ever since have been trying to help where possible. So, in 1967 after the Six Day War, I wrote a letter to the *Times* outlining a plan whereby 17,000 Arab refugee families could be resettled in reasonable homes south of the Gaza Strip at El Arish. This was taken up with a whole supportive page of the *Times* newspaper. It took me to see Vice-President Humphrey, General Eisenhower and many eminent people including both Mr. George Woods and Mr. Robert McNamara, Presidents of the World Bank. The then British Prime Minister, Harold Wilson, wrote me a six page letter having had his civil servants go into the plan in great depth. His key sentence was "On the other hand, if an overall international scheme for the economic development of the whole area could be elaborated, Her Majesty's Government would certainly wish to consider participation in projects which could lead to the provision of water to assist the resettlement of refugees." Sadly, the three negatives of the Arab League at the Khartoum Conference inspired by Nasser stopped the furthering of this project.

WHAT DOES SOVEREIGNTY-ASSOCIATION MEAN?
December, 1990
Jacques Parizeau, Leader of the Opposition, Province of Quebec

Undoubtedly the Liberal government, elected at the end of 1985, is a federalist government. It must somehow bring Quebec back to the constitutional fold....The Quebec government gambled. It assumed that if it asked from Canada minimal conditions, Canada would respond readily and accept. Political authorities in Canada responded in fact with alacrity. The Meech Lake Accord was signed. It had to be ratified. Finally, it was not....The Premier of Quebec had gambled. The Prime Minister rolled the dice, all to no avail....So we are back to sovereignty and to sovereignty association. We have now reached a point where even those who in no way share these objectives must start figuring the probabilities.

SEASONS GREETINGS FROM THE LIEUTENANT-GOVERNOR
December, 1990
Colonel The Hon. Lincoln Alexander, PC, CC, O.Ont., LLB, LLD, QC, Lieutenant-Governor of Ontario

To be Lieutenant-Governor is a very rewarding and unforgettable experience. I have had the privilege of shaking over 200,000 hands. I've made 650 visits and revisits to villages, towns and cities throughout the province, welcomed 68,000 guests in my suite, attended over 3,700 functions and attended some 220 schools. It ain't easy, but it's fun.

CANADA AFTER THE MEECH LAKE ACCORD—IS THE NATION FALLING APART?
April, 1991
The Hon. Barbara McDougall, Minister of Employment and Immigration

I did ask someone once, a very senior politician, as I was getting launched into politics, if you ever got over being nervous before you speak. He said "No, you don't." And he said, "If you ever do get over being nervous you should quit"....I believe that democracy, untidy as it is, is alive and well in Canada and I have faith that we can develop a process for a consensus that will keep this country strong and united....And we will ensure as leaders of our country that you have the opportunity to pass this heritage and tradition on to your children and to your grandchildren and to all those who will come after.

VIEWING OURSELVES IN A WORLD PERSPECTIVE: THE KEY TO SUCCEEDING IN THE 1990s
Population Explosion
April, 1991
Edward T. Pryor, Director-General, Census and Demographics, Statistics Canada

The population of the world is growing by 95 million people every year; that's three times the size of Canada in a 12 month period....In the time you will hear me speak today, the world's population will increase by 6,000 people....This kind of unprecedented growth—3.5 billion people in the span of a generation—is one of the most crucial events in the history of our life on this planet. It affects the economy, the environment, concepts of nationalism—and even Canada....the last census told us that more than half our entire population was over 30 years old. The population aged 65 and over.... [had] a growth rate twice that of the population as a whole. [This] has disturbing implications on the demands for health care...for pension plans and mandatory retirement legislation when the labour force of young people is shrinking.

TOAST TO THE ARMED FORCES
September, 1991
Major General R.W. Lewis, Past President, The Empire Club of Canada at the Loyal Societies Dinner in honour of Colonel The Hon. Lincoln Alexander

The Armed Forces of Canada have a history best described as a recurrent cycle of significant achievement, debilitating and demoralizing neglect, and prospects of revitalization, the realization of which was often just beyond reach.

CANADA—TODAY AND TOMORROW
September, 1991

His Excellency, The Rt. Hon. Ramon J. Hnatyshyn, Governor General of Canada

The best constitution in the world means little without the will of a people to breathe life into it. The hopes and goals of its citizens must be respected and supported before a constitution can transform a society and itself into more than rhetoric.

THE FINAL DECADE: THE OUTLOOK FOR CANADA
September, 1991
Arthur Mauro, President and CEO, Investors Group Inc.

We are in danger of becoming a nation of whiners, constantly blaming others for our failure. Virtually every day we see another addition to our list of complaints. We are against constitutional change, we are against the GST, we are against high interest rates, and we are against free trade. We are against a high Canadian dollar. But when will someone speak out for what we stand for as well as what we are against? Where is the asset side of this balance sheet? The list of blessings that we enjoy as citizens of the country....The freedom, the opportunity, the social benefits, the incredible achievements of a young country with a diverse and dispersed population?....I hope that we will view the recent past as the dark moment before the dawn. That the divisive spirit evidenced in the Meech Lake dispute will not be repeated. That we will never again see government officials negotiating with armed, masked men, as we did at Oka. That we will never again see our Senate turned into an assembly of unruly and undisciplined children.

NATIONAL UNITY
October, 1991
The Rt. Hon. Brian Mulroney, Prime Minister of Canada

On Wednesday in Montreal, I told Quebeckers that the real choice they must make is between being citizens of Canada or citizens of another country. I made it clear that separation means more economic barriers, fewer jobs and less prosperity. I invited Quebeckers to join with other Canadians to improve Confederation and strengthen the economic union that serves us all. I invite you to do likewise because it is not through cynicism or mean-spiritedness that this great country will be preserved. No single political party, no given interest group, no easy slogan, will preserve Canada. There is no magical solution, no recipe that can easily resolve our problems. Negativism and carping lead only to a dead-end. And so, the only answer is to look within ourselves: each and every one of us will have to do his or her share, with fair minds, generous spirits and open hearts if we are to succeed in renewing Canada. I believe we can succeed.

BREAKING DOWN THE WALLS: CREATING CLOSER NORTH AMERICAN TIES
November, 1991
James Jones, Chairman and CEO, American Stock Exchange

But there is another major advantage of Canada, the United States and Mexico joining forces. Europe's main protectionist concern is Asia, and vice versa. A North American Trading Alliance could become so big and powerful so as to act as a catalyst or balancing wheel between the two and break all the protectionist logjams. We could do business with both, or a multilateral agreement could be the result. Seeing the combined size and economic might of a North American trading bloc, those 19 countries in Europe may see the wisdom of opening their markets to us, or risk being excluded from ours. If we move to create a North American trading bloc, we can approach negotiations about opening up Europe '92 from a position of strength. If we don't work to create a North American trading bloc, we risk going into the negotiations as a weak sister, instead of being the dominant player. The idea behind those negotiations will be identical to the concept underlying my call for the elimination of the regulatory barriers that are keeping financial markets apart. The world has changed. We are more inter-dependent than ever before and the markets—both financial and economic—should reflect this new reality.

HONG KONG: MYTHS AND REALITIES
February, 1992
Peter D.A. Sutch, Deputy Chairman, Managing Director, Cathay Pacific Airways and Chairman-Designate, John Swire and Sons Ltd.

In 1997…Hong Kong will cease to be a British colony and will be redesignated as a special administration of The People's Republic of China….[the] future is dependent on the Territory establishing a workable modus vivendi with China which recognizes both political and economic realities.…The Territory's interests will therefore be far better served by working with the authorities than by provoking constant confrontation with them over issues which we cannot realistically hope to influence....the Territory does not have a mandate to attempt to influence policies in China as though it were a separate sovereign power....Hong Kong is not going to be a democracy in the normal sense of the term....My belief is that the Territory will eventually come to terms with this new way of doing things without unduly disrupting business....The greatest risk for Hong Kong has never been that China would deliberately seek to harm it....[but rather] that China would fail to understand its workings and implement policies which might damage it.

MAKING IT IN THE NEW ECONOMY
February, 1992
Dian Cohen, author and journalist

The truth is Canada's traditional industries are not as important as they once were. The problem here is that too many of us have clung to the illusions of past glory. The fact is that there's a global shakeout going on, and what's being shook out is most of what Canada's good at doing. The corollary is that while about half of our output is no longer wanted by the rest of the world, we're not excellent at making what the world wants....Economists are just beginning to understand that the product cycle has succeeded the business cycle as the main determinant of economic results....As a nation we are not great transformers of raw input into finished products. Rather we are great transformers of harsh landscape into mines, commercial timber operations, oil and gas wells and pipe lines....Just about everything we do economically reflects our complacency that our resource-based economy will always continue. For example, our income maintenance programs are designed to park people outside the labour force....To stand around until whatever they did before becomes desirable again....We don't actively promote adjustment. If we'd had these programs in place a century ago we'd still have a surplus of sailing ship captains.

NAVIGATING TOWARDS A NEW CANADA
March, 1992
Preston Manning, Leader, Reform Party of Canada

To be fair to Mr. Mulroney, Mr. Chretien, and Ms. McLaughlin, all three of our traditional party leaders have warned that as they study their political radar screens they see trouble ahead for the Canadian ship of state. And all three are standing on the bridge, sending out messages "These are your leaders speaking. Pay your taxes that we might spend more. Accept these measures to accommodate the government of Quebec and other special interests. Trust us to amend your constitution." The Reform Party, on the other hand [says] "Spend less and tax us less. Treat us all equally and fairly, no matter who our parents were or where we live."

THE ECONOMY AND THE CONSTITUTION: GETTING IT RIGHT
March, 1992
Allan R. Taylor, Chairman and CEO, Royal Bank of Canada

Canadians must understand that separation without pain is a real-world impossibility. In my estimation the costs of a break-up would be huge and long term. The value of our dollar would drop; our strong currency would be replaced by two weaker new ones. Foreign investment would fall. The internal Canadian market would be shattered, as would our common international trade policy and our stabilizing fiscal structure. The price of this folly would be paid by everyone in Canada.

THE ADVENTURE OF SPACE (A SLIDE PRESENTATION)
September, 1992
Roberta Bondar, Canadian astronaut, payload specialist,
Canadian Space Agency

People ask me what it was like on the morning of the launch. Well this is the exact position we were in during the launch phase. We were on our backs, pointed up towards the sky and when the three main engines fired it was just like the moderate turbulence you get as a commercial airliner comes in to the airport. But when you're on your back, you feel this massive steel structure start clanging on the pad; you realize there's a tremendous force beneath you. And very quickly the next thing you feel is the vibration from the solid rocket boosters. It's like someone taking you by the shoulder and shaking you. Everything is shaking. We have our helmets on but we still hear the noise and for two minutes and six seconds those solid rockets fire, before they burn out and tumble back into the Atlantic. During this time, of course, everyone has their fingers crossed because people know what happened to the Challenger. This is certainly a very difficult time for all of us. This is an experimental system and we have a lot of confidence in its operation but it is not to be taken for granted.

EUROPE AND THE FUTURE
September, 1992
Karl Otto Pohl, former President, Deutsche Bundesbank and
Director, The Horsham Corporation

Ladies and gentlemen, I could entertain you...one or two hours on the very very tricky problems of German unification.
The transfer payments have been widely underestimated. At the beginning there were enormous transfer payments from West to East. There was about 180 billion D. Marks last year, which is five per cent of the GDP of West Germany and almost two-thirds of the national income in East Germany. The develop-

ment in East Germany is not as exciting as people thought it would be. On the contrary, it is very sluggish; it's a very depressed area and it will remain so for some time. It is a historic task to clean up all the terrible mess which was left from the previous system over there. It will take a long time. It will take much longer than any of us expected at the beginning. But I'm pretty sure that finally we will make it and that, I think, is not only of great importance for Germany but, as well, for the future of Europe which, in spite of all the critical events, has a bright future. So that is at least what I hope and I hope I'm not too old to see that during my lifetime.

THE ONTARIO WINE INDUSTRY
March, 1993
Tony Aspler, author, *Vintage Canada* 1993

When I began writing about wine in 1975 the term Ontario wine was an oxymoron. You may remember Ontario wines then were mainly enjoyed by gentlemen who did most of their entertaining standing up in doorways, drinking out of brown paper decanters. The Ontario products they favoured were sweet, highly-alcoholic beverages. Along Parliament Street they were known as "block and tackle wines." You drank a bottle, walked a block and you could tackle anyone....How times have changed. Ontario wines are winning gold medals in international competitions.

THE EMPIRE CLUB—A LOYAL INSTITUTION
October, 1993
Club President, Dr. Frederic Jackman in his introduction of His Royal Highness, Prince Philip

The Club began—and continues—as one of the loyal societies in Canada. Our members are proud to be part of the pre-eminent speakers' Club in Canada. We take no small measure in being the only Club to maintain an accurate record—contained in the annual yearbook—of every address. Our Club is a witness to history—and our history is a witness to loyalty.

THE NEXT GENERATION
The Business of Charity
October, 1993
His Royal Highness, Prince Philip, Duke of Edinburgh

Even though the cost per participant is modest, the Scheme [Duke of Edinburgh's Award Scheme for youth] still needs to be financed. Unfortunately, there is one important difference between businesses and charities. The more successful the business, the more money it makes; the more successful a charity becomes, the more it costs.

CANADA—THIS IS YOUR WAKE-UP CALL
March, 1994
Dave Nichol, President, Dave Nichol and Associates

For every one dollar of new taxes the Canadian government takes in, it spends $1.75. Combined federal-provincial debt will be $700 billion by the end of 1994, or 98 per cent of Gross Domestic Product and in two years economists predict that the government debt to Gross Domestic Product ratio will rise to 105%.

Reflections of a Past President—Dr. Frederic Jackman, President, The Empire Club, 1993–1994
During 1993–1994 we deliberately created a focused series of speeches on a particular topic. "Media and Society" was addressed by four speakers, each from a different walk of life. Former Ontario Premier the Hon. Wm. G. Davis, former Supreme Court Justice, the Hon. Willard Z. Estey, former CBC anchor, Knowlton Nash and Dr. Eric Jackman, Club President and initiator of the series, all spoke. The political, legal and journalistic presentations showed the struggle between the freedom of the press and the right to privacy. The case was made for bridging the gap between the media and society despite the media's fear with libel chill and news blackouts, and society's concern with media accountability and invasiveness. For myself, as President, it was a wonderful series to arrange and in which to participate. Seldom has a current President taken the Club lectern to blow his own horn and create a series in which he was personally interested.

FREEDOM OF EXPRESSION VS. THE INDIVIDUAL'S RIGHT TO PRIVACY

April, 1994

The Hon. Willard Z. Estey, Chairman, Ontario Press Council and former Canadian Supreme Court Justice

The Canadian Charter of Rights...is essentially a product of the English Common Law....Under the Common Law there are two fundamental streams of knowledge and principle. One of them is the ordinary basic rights related to contract, property, criminal law and procedure. The other is the so-called law of Equity—the law of fair play....So, there is a limit as to what you can properly do to curtail publication of a trial, even though the Charter doesn't really impose that limit. Furthermore, there is no Charter right to public access to the trial in the first place— that's Common Law. The accused has the right to a public trial, but what if he doesn't want a public trial? What if he wants a closed trial because he doesn't want his neighbours to know he's a crook? The accused does not have that right, because the Common Law says that the public interest in an open trial is predominant. Therefore, the Court has the power to protect public access to it, but subject to the right of the accused to a fair trial. Both considerations are fundamental to our judicial system, and the court must balance the two principles where they conflict or compete. There have been all manner of attacks on these principles. The Americans have a different viewpoint. Do not forget that the mass of 265 million to the south of us is a highly productive and ingenious force—and they have a lot of fun while they're at it. Their system works for them, so I don't knock it too loudly, but I don't want to adopt too much of it either. Their legal system is not their strongest feature, but it's not as bad as our press leads us to believe. The Americans say it's very difficult to corrupt a juror for the reasons I have given: the oath, the sanctity, the tradition and all of that, so therefore they say the predominant right is access to the public by way of the press. That works for them, even though they have by far the most aggressive press in the world—and by far the best-equipped press, both print and broadcast, in the sense of gathering the information and disseminating the information we call news.

THE MEDIA'S ROLE IN SOCIETY: THE MEDIA VIEWPOINT
April, 1994
Knowlton Nash, CBC broadcaster, journalist, and Chair, The Canadian Journalism Foundation

We're often accused of having delusions of adequacy. One of the most biting criticisms I have ever heard came from Jimmy Carter's Press Secretary, Jody Powell, who said political journalists are "like those who watch the battle from afar, and when it's all over, come down from the hills and shoot the wounded." Actually it's hard to think of a political leader today who doesn't think that way....What we in the media are doing today is, I believe, better than it has ever been. But, as I have said, it's still not good enough. We're far from perfect. In fact it sometimes seems there's hardly enough mediocrity to go around. In the competitive rush to be first, we sometimes are not as thorough as we should be on fact checking....I worry also about too much emphasis on the scoopery and snoopery of the supermarket tabloids—the flash and trash journalism....I worry too about the cynicism of many journalists....I worry that we too often look for good guys and bad guys in black and white simplicity....I worry, also, about the increasing emphasis of theatricality in the news and lessening emphasis on substance....In the American presidential election campaign of 1986, the average sound bite of the candidates on American Network TV was 43 seconds—43 seconds to outline their position on a particular issue. In the last election it was about seven seconds.

CHANGE IN MODERN IRELAND
August, 1994
Her Excellency Mary Robinson, President of Ireland

I come before you today…as a direct witness of the constructive energies and exciting changes which are happening in modern Ireland. I do believe they tell a story of that pluralistic, open and tolerant society I was elected to represent. But of course it is not the whole story. We live in a society and a country which has been scarred by violence for a quarter of a century. Whatever else we can say about that violence I think we have to recognise that it marks—in the broadest sense—a failure of dialogue between diverse cultures, viewpoints and traditions. And rather than dwell on the griefs of the present, which every one of us who has the interests of Ireland at heart must feel, I think it is right to look to the future and reflect in the widest sense on how we can encompass a respect for difference in our democratic values, and how we can commend to our children the view that cultures, traditions, and histories are deepened and not diminished by sharing. I am far from complacent about such a process, but I think we should undertake it as a challenge and a responsibility.

PERSONAL RESPONSIBILITY AND THE MEDIA
December, 1994
John Fraser, author and journalist

We are almost beyond surprise or shock at anything that happens. My profession—journalism—has assisted this apathy by knee-jerking us all into a kind of stupefied cynicism. We are now systematically programmed to see and read about terrible atrocities and catastrophic events…with hardened hearts. This is partly because we simply can't take in the sheer volume of it all any more. It's also partly because our messengers and information services seem somehow to have lost an ability to evaluate the worth and weight of news. Often we don't know whether we're at a tragedy or at a circus in our front row seats at the glorious global village information theatre....Generally, the media is too lazy to start trouble, but—boy—we sure know how to fan the flames. Consumers are also partly to blame. The media has become so powerful in setting a public agenda of shock, inflated trivia and cynicism precisely because it sells so well. The moment it doesn't sell, let me tell you, changes will come swiftly.

ADVICE TO THE FUTURE PREMIER OF ONTARIO
December, 1994
The Hon. Bob Rae, Premier of Ontario

The judgments of others, if always taken seriously, will drive you to distraction. Remember that the media, many of whom are here today (they're my good friends), are not in the governing business. They are in the entertainment business, the information business, the influence business. They have, on the whole, even less of a sense of humour about themselves than politicians, and so leave them alone. Treat them with respect and courtesy because your rudeness or short temper will only lead to further troubles....Politics is not the most important thing in most people's lives....If you don't have a mind of your own, it will very quickly be captured by others who do....Don't be afraid to change your mind when confronted by facts and arguments that are too persuasive to ignore....There are always more good ideas than there is money....Everyone is in favour of restraint in general, but noone likes restraint in particular. Those who benefit from many changes are powerless and disorganized. Those who might lose in any change are invariably powerful and very well organized and, in my experience, very vocal....Remember that a poll will tell you people's first impression of things based on what's on the top of their minds that day and based on what they've just heard. A poll will never tell you...what people will do when they hear arguments. It will never tell you how people change their minds.

THE ROLE OF JUDGES
April, 1995
The Rt. Hon. Antonio Lamer, Chief Justice of Canada

The judge's fundamental duty is to decide the questions before the Court impartially, independently, and according to law. A judge cannot approach a case as a legislature would. The scope of the judge's decision is defined by the question submitted by the parties. The answer which the judge gives is constrained and dictated by the legal context in which the dispute arises....One often hears it said that a majority of the Supreme Court is opposed to assisted suicide, as a result of the Rodriguez decision. But that way of describing the case misses the whole legal context in which the Court was called upon to rule. The legal issue was whether Parliament may, under our Constitution, make assisting suicide a crime....That is what the Court had to decide, not whether assisted suicide was a social good.

A JOURNEY INTO MYSELF
April, 1995
Terry Waite, Emissary of The Church of England

The only way in which, of course, anyone can do that sort of thing, [take captives] is to treat the captives as symbols, symbols of the West, symbols of the rich West, symbols of the affluent West, symbols of the powerful West, against whom the poor seem powerless. Then the terrorist groups spring up and say, "The only weapon we have is terror, and we'll use it." And they use it to devastating effect on the lives of innocent people, who pay the price. They're the ones who pay the price. It could be you tomorrow. It could be any of us. The danger, of course, in terrorist movements, is that if you set out to achieve a political end by using violence, you will attract also into your ranks people of a psychopathic disposition. Perhaps you may be able to reason with the leaders of the group. In fact, it is possible to reason with the leaders of the group, who have decided to use violence as a means of achieving a political end in a number of instances. We see in the Middle East, as we mercifully see in Ireland, a number of instances in which the leaders are beginning to renounce violence and say, "We have to find some other ways of resolving political conflict." And sometimes this political conflict is legitimate. The danger, of course, is obvious. The leaders frequently have lost control of the psychopaths in their ranks, who continue to kill and murder and cause mayhem and trauma to the innocent. That is a fact we have to take into account. It provides not only the victim with great problems and troubles, it provides the leaders of the organisations with great troubles. It says something about violence and the use of violence. Also, these expressions of small groups growing up in society as institutions change and crumble say something as to what we can do and what we ought to do in the face of this problem. In a sense, perhaps it is not too extreme to say that terrorism is, in part, a manifestation of a society that is sick.

THE ACCELERATING PACE OF PROGRESS
May, 1995
Sir John Templeton, Founder, Templeton Mutual Funds

Global restructuring is expected to bring four billion new people into the free-market system, four times the number who lived in free markets just a decade ago. People around the world are beginning to experience more freedom as well. According to a study by Freedom House, 1990 was the first year ever when there were more free countries than not-free countries. It was also the first time there were more people living in freedom than those still under repressive regimes. This trend toward greater capitalism and freedom unleashes tremendous potential for efficiency gains and even greater wealth potential. So does the shift away from regulation and isolation toward free trade. World exports today in real terms are more than 11 times what they were just 40 years ago. Numerous institutions have arisen to protect the principles that have fostered this dramatic growth and to spread the preconditions necessary to continue free trade throughout the world.

LEADERSHIP IN THE THIRD MILLENNIUM
June, 1995
Dr. Billy Graham, evangelist

But what kind of world will the 21st century be? Will the third millennium usher in a golden age of progress and happiness, as some project? In his book *Global Paradox*, John Naisbitt wrote, "We live in a time of great change, a time of new beginnings. We live in a time when many things are coming to an end." One writer in a special *Time* magazine issue on the coming millennium several months ago commented that "our descendants may encounter technological upheavals that could make 20th-century breakthroughs seem tame." Or will it be a time of political chaos or social upheaval or economic collapse or ecological disaster—as others speculate? In the same issue of *Time*, one writer predicted the end of the nuclear family, and another forecast vast hordes of homeless children wandering aimlessly in the streets because they will have nowhere to go.

QUEBEC'S DECISION
October, 1995
The Hon. Jean Charest Leader, PC Party of Canada

But back to our campaign. What is surprising about this campaign is that Mr. Bouchard and Mr. Parizeau have already played the language and culture card in the referendum—telling Quebeckers that if they vote "no" their language and culture in some way, shape or form will be threatened. Anyone worried about a "no" vote weakening the province of Quebec should look at the extraordinary growth that we experienced in the last 15 years. The population of Quebec has grown 15 per cent from six to seven million people and the French language and culture are more secure now than at any previous time in the history of Canada. A whole new entrepreneurial class has risen in the last 15 years and I'm not the one who says this by the way. All I'm quoting and re-reading these days is Mr. Parizeau's speech—one he delivered at the Montreal Chamber of Commerce in

November of 1994, where he describes in very poetic language the great progress that the province of Quebec has made in the last 15 years. And he names all the companies and the entrepreneurs. It's important to remind ourselves of this great leap and progress of this new generation of men and women who came forth because that happened exactly 15 years ago, after the last referendum—when people in Quebec were told by the separatists that if you vote "no" you will weaken the province of Quebec, that this will put us in the position where we won't be able to take our rightful place. Well a whole generation of Quebeckers has proved exactly the contrary. Mr. Parizeau and Mr. Bouchard tell Quebeckers that if they vote "no" they will weaken themselves. Well, ladies and gentlemen, the only people who will be weakened after this referendum are those who made the decision to hold this referendum. The only ones who will be weakened by the decision by Quebeckers to stay within Canada are the separatists themselves, starting with Mr. Parizeau and Mr. Bouchard.

CANADA'S REFUGEE DETERMINATION PROCESS
March, 1996
Nurjehan Mawani, Chair, Immigration and Refugee Board

In 1996, the refugee challenge is without precedent. The numbers are staggering. They continue to grow. Last year, the United Nations High Commissioner for Refugees (UNHCR) reported that there were 27 million refugees worldwide. That is an increase of eight million over the last two years and it represents a 10-fold increase from the Cold-War era. Courtesy of television, we are all witnesses to modern tragedy—chaos in the Balkans, civil war in Sri Lanka, anarchy in Somalia and genocide in Rwanda and Burundi. What you might be surprised to learn is that the top refugee-receiving nations are all thirdworld countries. UNHCR figures from 1994 show that Iran ranked first with 2.2 million refugees within its borders. Zaire ranked second and Pakistan third. The only industrialised country in the top eight was Germany, which had just over one million refugees in the country, of whom 430,000 made their refugee claims in 1994 alone. In comparison, Canada received just 22,000 claims the same year. Our refugee determination process and others like it do not represent the "answer" to the refugee issue. We are a response to only one aspect of an international challenge. More important are the decisions taken by governments around the globe—decisions that attack the root causes of displacement and the social and economic inequities that undermine the stability and development of communities. This requires an international effort of Herculean proportions. Meanwhile, here in Canada, we continue to face the immediate and practical challenge of responding to those in urgent need of our nation's protection.

THE FEDERAL BUDGET
March, 1996
The Hon. Paul Martin, Minister of Finance

It is important to note that today's fiscal progress is much more than simply a federal effort. It is a national effort. It is one that is supported by Canadians across the country and no matter what their political stripe. Every single province and territory in the land now has as its primary goal the return to fiscal health and the results are striking. In 1993, Canadian business and governments borrowed $29 billion abroad. This was reduced to $13 billion in 1995 and it will be reduced again next year and the year after that and the year after that. In fact I was quite struck at the last meeting of finance ministers when we went around the table. Every single finance minister essentially talked about the extent to which they were either achieving budget balance or how close they were getting to it. That was the goal they sought. It is really quite a story for Canada because about a week earlier I had been at a meeting of OECD nations in Europe and there was no such common effort; there was no record of success comparable to that which we had in this country. This is a story that we really have to get out to the markets of the world. Not only the federal government but all of the provinces and territories have really come together and, I believe, in the next couple of years we will have one of the most attractive financial records of any industrial country. That is something of which Canadians can be very proud....Successful countries do a lot more than simply occupy a place on a map. They live in the souls of their people because they are relevant to the betterment of their lives. I believe that the real problem is not that we have failed to meet the goals that we must set. It is that too often we have failed to set the goals that we must meet. With that in mind, I would ask you now: "Is it beyond this country to decide that in 10 years our medicare system will not simply survive but that it will be the most successful in the world, with a record in cure and prevention that is second to none?" I would ask you: "Can we not decide together as a nation that in 10 years from now our streets will be the safest as they can possibly be—not because we have more prisons or more police but because we have addressed directly the sources of crime?" I would ask you: "Can we not decide that in 10 years Canada will be regarded as the world leader in bio-technology, in environmental technology or in the cultural industries of the multi-channel universe? Can we not decide that 10 years from now increasing child poverty rates will be a thing of the past, that illiteracy will be erased from our communities and that when it comes to international tests our students will not only do fine work but they will be among the finest in the world?"

SIZE AND COMPETITION IN CANADIAN BANKING
April, 1996
Helen Sinclair, President, Canadian Bankers' Association

The issue of the banking industry's size clouds the horizon. It threatens to weaken the political will to deal with the financial sector strategically and to do what is right for the country and the banking public. Size according to our detractors is a negative. But size is also about competitiveness globally, and about jobs in Canada. Size is not the be-all-and-end-all to bank competitiveness. Good earnings, increasing productivity, ongoing investment in people and in technology are indispensable.

THE HEALTHY BARMAID, THE NEW MINISTER OF HEALTH?
April, 1996
Dr. Kenneth Walker, physician, medical journalist and author of *The Healthy Barmaid*

The longer I practice medicine the more I am convinced there are two kinds of diseases, those we get and those we make. The secret is in learning how to prevent the ones we make. The Healthy Barmaid as Minister of Health would tell...[us] to buy a bottle of wine....Sir William Osler, one of Canada's greatest physicians, knew the value of alcohol for seniors. He remarked that "Wine is for the elderly what milk is for the young"....The Healthy Barmaid would teach preventive medicine in the schools....Stress that obesity is the number-one killer. [She would] defend Canadian farmers....Foolishly saying no to dairy products, means many people are not getting enough calcium and setting themselves up for broken hip, severe disability or death....[She would] stress that humans deserve the same nutritional treatment as gorillas....Gorillas in captivity get better nutrition than humans. [She would] urge doctors to use heroin [in cancer treatment] which was legalized for medical use in 1984....She would remind the public and her fellow politicians that no country has enough money to give everyone all the health care he or she demands.

A REVOLUTION IN COMMUNICATIONS
July, 1996
Bill Gates, Chairman and CEO, Microsoft

Advances in computer technology represent a revolution in communications...this is going to reshape every business that there is today, and even redefine the way we think of entertainment, the way we think of politics and perhaps most exciting how we think of education. Behind all of this there are some real miracle technologies. There is the miracle of the chip. Every two years, according to what is called "Moore's Law" chips become over twice as powerful and that means that over a period of twenty years you get a thousand times the power you had before. And that's without any increase in cost. In fact, the costs come down at the same time....The potential is not just...a computer on every desk and in every home—but rather that people have computers in their pockets, computers in their cars....So many computers that you don't even think of them being there in the same way that you don't think about electricity or water as things that have transformed the way we live.

BUSINESS EDUCATION IN CANADA: A BLUEPRINT FOR CHANGE
September, 1996
Lawrence Tapp, Dean, Richard Ivey School of Business, University of Western Ontario

Intellectual capital is now the prized resource in our post-industrial economies....Continuous learning is now an imperative for both the organization and the individual....Over-reliance on government funding has sapped our energy and initiative....Greater reliance on other sources—tuition, alumni and corporate support and new revenue centres—will foster competitive excellence by encouraging direct investment in intellectual capital....Most Canadian businesses....had to fight hard to win the competitive advantages they enjoy. They have been buffeted by gale force winds—free trade, recession, globalization, technological revolution—without the insulation of a huge domestic market. They have had to be global both operationally and intellectually in order to survive.

BRITAIN IN EUROPE
Canada and Europe
September, 1996
Anthony Goodenough, British High Commissioner

With 370 million people the EU is the world's largest single market, accounting for well over 20 per cent of world trade. After the U.S. the EU is Canada's largest trade and investment partner. Yet the proportion of Canada's exports which goes to the EU has fallen from 12.4 per cent in 1973 to 6.4 per cent in 1995—despite the EU's enlargement....If Canada had maintained its share of the EU market at 2.2 per cent you would have exported $4.6 billion more merchandise to the EU. According to the Senate Committee Report in rough terms this might have meant about 50,000 more jobs for Canadians....The thought I want to leave with you is the need to strengthen ties between Canada and Europe [and] ensure that our companies on both sides of the Atlantic take full advantage of the enormous potential of each other's markets as we move towards the 21st century.

THE ANXIOUS YEARS: POLITICS IN THE AGE OF MULRONEY AND CHRETIEN
The Free Market
October, 1996
Jeffrey C. Simpson, columnist and author

The free market is the best mechanism ever devised for the delivery of goods and services and for sending signals to consumers and taxpayers to guide their behaviour. But the market cares little for social justice and a cohesive society must search endlessly for a balance between justice and efficiency, rights and responsibilities so that the agency of government is needed to lean periodically against the injustices and disequilibriums caused by the free market.

CONVERGENCE AND DEREGULATION IN THE ENERGY MARKETPLACE
Gaslights
February, 1997
Ron Munkley, President and CEO, The Consumers Gas Company

Try to imagine [Toronto]....in 1848. Toronto had chosen to set up its first street-lighting system with 100 new gas lamps...Put in the context of the time fewer than a dozen North American cities had gas street lighting. Yet Toronto, still a fledging and muddy city on the edge of a forest, was one of them....The company that supplied the gas for those lamps...was my company. By 1848, Consumers Gas had built the first buried water system for the city of Toronto and it was the company that built and supplied those first street lamps with gas....Consumers Gas [now] is a shareholder-owned, largely regulated utility and service company with assets of approximately $3.5 billion....Our company serves over 1.3 million....We'll pay Revenue Canada and the 175 municipalities we serve over $500 million in taxes and we make a profit for our shareholders.

THE MEDIA AND THE UNITY ISSUE
March, 1997
Roger Landry, President and Publisher, *La Presse*

The media are at least part of the unity problem. Journalists who report on politics do not reflect the debate from a completely neutral perspective. They single out the most sensational remarks; that's only natural: they can't always just report the same old platitudes. Since they don't always have time to double-check everything mistakes sometimes slip through. And—let's be honest—they are influenced by their own opinions and interests. Yes, even journalists are human. In the 1970s....Had Premier Lévesque miraculously walked across the St Lawrence River, they claimed the headline in *La Presse* would have read "Lévesque a marche sur les eaux (Lévesque walks on water)," while in the [Montreal] *Gazette* the headline would have been "Lévesque can't swim"...In radio and television news reports, where the average story lasts less than a minute, reporters have no choice but to limit themselves to sound bites—short punchy statements clipped from comments of politicians. On television the practice often adds to the sensationalism. News directors, editors-in-chief and assignment editors also play a major role since they decide....not only on what stories to cover but also the relative importance of each story....The media put all their efforts into covering the very people who accentuate the divisions between Canadians: the politicians. They invest little energy in reporting on Canadians themselves beyond the everyday political squab-bling.

PRIVATE GIVING IN CANADA
April, 1997
The Hon. Henry N.R. Jackman Chairman, The Council for Business and the Arts in Canada, former Lieutenant-Governor of Ontario, Past President of the Empire Club

Volunteerism, as measured by numbers of volunteers, is perhaps three times as great in the United States as it is in Canada. Charitable giving, according to the House of Commons Finance Committee, is also almost three times as great. Canadians give about 0.7 percent of their taxable income to registered charities. Ironically for higher income donors, that is those who make more than $100,000 a year, the comparison shows that Americans give four times as much as Canadians. Similarly in the corporate sector, charitable giving is more than twice as great, relative to our size. Foundation giving in this country is a pittance compared to the United States.

THE CANADA-U.S. AUTO TRADE PACT
October, 1997
Bobbie Gaunt, President and CEO, Ford Motor Company of Canada, Limited

I have come to a company [the Ford Motor Company] with a proud Canadian heritage, a company that has continually strived to earn the loyalty of Canadian consumers for five generations now, and a company whose investments and jobs have helped provide Canadians with one of the highest standards of living in the world. My inheritance from my predecessors and the 17,000 men and women employed by Ford of Canada and our 600 Ford and Mercury dealers has been most generous. They have handed me the reins of an organisation that has just completed the most extensive investment programme, by far, in our 93-year history —nearly $6 billion and 2,000 jobs created in Canada since 1990. In a way, they also have made the job more challenging because of the unprecedented growth in market share and customer satisfaction they have won in recent years. Those impressive achievements pretty well leave me, and our employees and dealers, with a simple strategy—to keep winning. Although no one could have known at the time, the founding of Ford of Canada in 1904 was the beginning of a revolution that is sweeping trade and commerce today, particularly the auto industry. The revolution is called globalisation and it is in full flight wherever you go in the world. When you consider the fact that over the next 100 years, 98 per cent of the world's population growth will take place in Asia, Latin America and Africa combined, it's easy to understand the motivation for globalisation.

CANADA'S FOREST PRODUCTS INDUSTRY
November, 1997
K. Linn Macdonald, President and CEO, Noranda Forest

Again, it's quite simple. The forest products industry, like so many others, is consolidating into fewer, larger players. Canada's largest forest products company is now only the twenty-first-

largest on the world scene. Larger companies can manage industry cycles better and provide improved returns to shareholders
with less volatility. These cycles are not really driven by fluctua-
tions in demand, but rather by surges of new capacity arising as
the fragmented industry rushes to add production capacity with
several companies building or expanding at once. Each surge
effectively lowers unit productivity in the collective industry.
And this, in turn, adversely affects profitability and shareholder
returns. The industry is marching steadily—and some would say
relentlessly—towards this consolidation. In Canada, in the first
six months of this year alone, some 15 mergers or acquisition
transactions valued at almost $6 billion have been announced. A
recent Ernst & Young report described the pressure to consoli-
date: "Shareholders faced with inadequate returns will continue
to pressure companies to restructure operations, sell non-core
assets, and court mergers and acquisitions."

THE SEALING INDUSTRY OF NEWFOUNDLAND AND LABRADOR
January, 1998
The Hon. John Efford, Minister of Fisheries and Aquaculture,
Government of Newfoundland and Labrador

The International Fund for Animal Welfare is against the commercial seal hunt. Its misleading propaganda campaigns have
been economically devastating for aboriginal people who have a
profound dependence on seals. The President of the Inuit
Circumpolar Conference said recently: "Although Inuit were
never directly a target of the anti-sealing campaigns, we became
perhaps their biggest victims....The IFAW propaganda campaign
has become an annual circus of deceit....They use graphic
details to get an emotional response....The seal harvest is not a
pretty sight. Neither is the killing of chickens, or cattle or pigs or
anything else in a slaughterhouse. The only difference is that the
seal harvest is conducted in a public arena—an open space abat-
toir."

GROWING UP DIGITAL: THE RISE OF THE NET GENERATION
February, 1998
Don Tapscott, Chairman, Alliance for Converging Technologies, and author

There is a new medium for human communication emerging and we need to go back to the invention of the printing press to find something similar. [Information highways are] going to fundamentally change the nature of the firm, the way we trade wealth, the way we conduct learning and the way we maintain social development as a society. My wife and I had a couple of kids and we noticed how they seemed to be able to use computers effortlessly. At first we thought our children were prodigies and then we noticed their friends were like them. We thought how odd that all their friends were prodigies. It then occurred to us that something important was happening. A new generation was emerging....These kids are the first to come of age in the digital age.

THE Y2K PROBLEM
May, 1998
Anthony Taylor, Director of Wellington Underwriting, plc Lloyd's of London

Thank you for listening to me and perhaps I can leave you with one further warning. There is a distinct possibility that if we are still using today's Windows, DOS and Unix-based systems in 40 years' time, there will be another date problem. The problem is that on 19 January 2038 at 3:14:35 a.m., the number of seconds since January 1970 will exceed 2,147,483,647. This is the largest number that can be stored in a 32-bit processor, used commonly for storing time information in the aforementioned systems. Of course, we won't he using them then... will we?

WHO KILLED CANADIAN HISTORY?
September, 1998
Dr. Jack L. Granatstein, Director and CEO, Canadian War
Museum

We marked the anniversary of V-E Day in Canada but there were
no crowds of 500,000 in our streets. There were no banners as
there were in Holland saying "Bless you boys" in English. The
Dutch who had to be liberated, who had lost their freedom,
remember. Present-day Canadians, I regret, if they ever knew
that there had been a Second World War, probably remembered
only that this country had been unkind in the way it treated
Japanese Canadians. How could this have happened? Who killed
Canadian history? The second formative event in pushing me to
write this book came when a very good friend showed me five
essays written by his eight-year-old son at a private school. Brad,
eight years old, was in grade two and he was being taught
Canadian history. If he had been in a public school he wouldn't
have been. In a private school he was and I suppose that's a good
thing but what concerned me was what his essays were about.
Five essays from a first introduction to Canadian history. The
first one concerned Samuel de Chaplain's abuse of his 13-year-
old bride; the second, the extermination of the Beothuk by the
white man in Newfoundland; the third, the execution of Louis
Riel by the Government of Canada; the fourth, the maltreatment
of Canada's first woman doctor by her medical peers; and the
fifth, the internment of Japanese Canadians. That was Canadian
history as presented to an eight-year-old child by his teacher.
Our history, Canada's history in other words, was about sexism,
racism, and the abuses of government. Nothing else. There was
no attempt to have a chronology, a basic tool of Canadian history or any other. There was no attempt to put events in context.
There was no attempt to balance evil with good. Instead inci-
dences were pulled from the past and stuffed down children's
throats to prove a point that a particular teacher deemed important. Why? How could this have happened? Who killed Canadian

history?....So who killed Canadian history? Who are the guilty people? You and me by not paying attention to what was going on in the schools we sent our children to, by voting for school trustees and MPPs who have literally no interest in education. Who can resurrect Canadian history? Again you and me by demanding changes, by voting for those who promise to restore the past, the understanding of the past for the present, because if we can do that then maybe we just might have a future.

LONDON: READY FOR THE EURO
November, 1998
David Clementi, Deputy Governor, Bank of England

We hope that EMU will be a success. The British Government is in favour of joining EMU in principle. The Government has made it clear that it sees no constitutional bar to British membership. There are advantages. For example, the introduction of the single European currency will help to complete the Single European Market. The uncertainty associated with investment decisions within the euro area will be reduced. Europe will continue its consolidation as a major trading bloc. And the euro will create deeper and more liquid financial markets....But there are also risks. For example, will the U.K. economy be able to live comfortably with euro interest rates on a permanent basis? And if problems emerge after EMU begins, will a 'one-size-fits-all' monetary policy be adequate to deal with them, particularly if there is insufficient flexibility in product and labour markets? A related concern is the high level of unemployment in some continental European countries, and the differing rates between them. Consequently, the British Government has set a number of economic tests to ensure that, before the U.K. joins EMU, there will be sustainable convergence between the U.K. economy and the euro area. At the moment, short-term interest rates in the U.K. are approximately twice the core European level. So the U.K. will not join EMU at the outset. But financial market firms in London, whatever their nationality, see the euro as a key part of their business. With our support at the Bank of England, they have been actively preparing for the introduction of the euro. London thrives on liquid markets, regardless of currency. The introduction of the euro is therefore a major opportunity for London.

HEALTH CARE: WE CAN'T GO ON LIKE THIS. IS THERE A WAY OUT OF OUR HEALTH-CARE DILEMMA?
November, 1998
Dr. Bill Orovan, President, Ontario Medical Association

To begin with, discussion among Canadians about health care is based on the widely held belief that we have the best health-care system in the world. But what if that is not true anymore? As a matter of fact, I believe it is not true anymore. Ask the people who were being driven around Toronto recently in ambulances looking for an emergency room with an empty bed. Ask them whether we have the best system in the world. Ask patients who have waited six months, 12 months, 18 months for a new hip. Ask them if we have the best health-care system in the world. For those who must wait anxiously for brain surgery, psychiatric care, dialysis treatment, or heart treatment, for those who are put on a three-month waiting list for an MRI scan when they could drive to Buffalo with VISA card in hand and have it in a day. Ask them if we have the best health-care system in the world. Is it acceptable that elderly patients may wait one or even two years for cataract surgery? Is it acceptable that women with breast cancer can wait 13 weeks or more for access to definitive treatment? Ask them if we have the best health-care system in the world. Yet, despite these harsh realities we remain the envy of many world communities, some of whom have taken the best parts of our system and adapted many of our practices to their own circumstances, making it better and easier for people in their countries to get the treatment they need. To many of those governments, health-care delivery is an evolutionary process of continually adapting to new circumstances and integrating new medical and structural innovations.

CANADA 1999—ONE CANADIAN'S PERSPECTIVE
June, 1999
The Rt. Hon. Ramon J. Hnatyshyn, former Governor General of Canada and Counsel, Gowling Strathy & Henderson

A few years ago, a friend of mine who worked in the Archives in Saskatchewan came across the homestead certificate of my grandfather, Michael Hnatyshyn, by which he received the title for his homestead. My grandfather arrived in Canada neither speaking nor writing English or French and accordingly signed the homestead papers with his mark. These documents caused me to reflect upon and appreciate the legacy of my forebears and the extraordinary opportunities afforded by our wonderful country. My grandparents were determined that their children would have the education they were denied and, their son, my father, through the sacrifices made by his parents, graduated in law from the University of Saskatchewan and became the first ever Saskatonian to serve in the Senate of Canada—and I, a grandson, have been honoured to have served in the Parliament and Government of Canada and as Governor General.

CANADA'S ACTIONS AGAINST LANDMINES
June, 1999
The Hon. Lloyd Axworthy, Minister of Foreign Affairs

Back home last week after a nightmare that forced him to flee his house, that separated him from his family, that destroyed his possessions, Rifat Morina, a Kosovo Albanian, thought he was safe. Safe to rebuild his life, safe to find his wife and children, and safe to look however tentatively to the future. However in an instant, he was denied even this meagre hope. Mr. Morina stepped on a landmine. He lost his leg, leaving him maimed forever—a brutal, permanent and daily reminder of the human cost of this conflict. Another life senselessly shattered by landmines. In Kosovo NATO prevailed over evil. However, Mr. Morina's experience underlines with devastating clarity that for him and hundreds of thousands like him the ordeal is far from over. In their understandable eagerness to return home, many more ordinary people will suffer like Mr. Morina. Anti-personnel [AP] mines are strewn by the tens of thousands across the countryside, poisoning the land from which Kosovo's people derived their sustenance. They are at once the cruel instrument and the bitter legacy of conflict and hatred.

MALICE IN BLUNDERLAND
Canada—Expectations and Reality
November, 1999
Alan Fotheringham, author and columnist

A hundred and thirty-two years ago when this country was born, foreign observers looked at us and said: "Now here's the perfect chance for a new young country. It's being built on the stability of the British parliamentary system with the advantage of French culture and with an injection of American efficiency." Every single one of you in this room today knows where we are in 1999. We have a country that's built on the stability of the French political system, with American culture and British efficiency.

PRAIRIE AGRICULTURE: AN IMPORTANT PART OF CANADA'S FUTURE
February, 2000
The Hon. Roy Romanow, Premier of Saskatchewan

Well friends I once ended a speech by saying: "To make a long story short…" and somebody from the back of the hall said: "Too late for that Roy." And maybe that's the case here but just very very briefly let me close by saying thank you all for coming here and a special thanks for the honour of speaking to the Empire Club. I believe this Club was founded in 1903 two years before my home province joined the Confederation. I know that as we approach our centennials both the Empire Club and Saskatchewan can look back on our histories with pride and forward to our futures with optimism and confidence. I truly believe that once the people of this part of the world and the people across our nation understand the case that we're trying to make—a case for fairness, for equitable treatment, a case for neighbours working together as Canadians always have, with a bright economic future—I'm convinced that indeed that future will be bright. Not just for our farmers, not just for our province or our region, but a bright and marvellous future for all Canadians and for Canada. We ask nothing more than the opportunity to contribute to it and to be a part of that bright future as we have been in the past.

THINK BIG
A Personal Decision
March, 2000
Preston Manning, MP, Calgary Southwest and Leader of the Official Opposition

Speaking personally—and only with regard to my own position as Leader of the Official Opposition—I do not think it possible to do the best I can as both Leader of the Opposition and an Alliance leadership candidate over the next few months. And so today I have advised our caucus that once the referendum results are known and I formally launch my leadership campaign, I will step aside as Leader of the Official Opposition in order to devote the maximum amount of time and attention to the voters in our leadership election.

THE ROLE OF POLICE IN SOCIETY
May, 2000
Julian Fantino, Chief of Police, Toronto Police Services

Let me remind everyone that a mere 12 years ago, police officers in Canada knew very little about "crack cocaine." Some of us heard about it. We had very little awareness of the havoc it was beginning to generate in some neighbourhoods in some of the major American cities. Until we began to see it surface in Canada we did not even know what it was, how it was made, the depth and organisation of distribution, and most certainly had little experience about the degree of violence it generated. A short 12 years later, whole communities have become crack cocaine battlefields where the dealers are ruthless, well-armed, highly organised and their victims are children, families and the well-being of community life. As well, we know from experience that 50 to 70 per cent of all community-based crime—break and enters, robberies and the like—are drug-related. In the United States, and although admittedly to some lesser degree in Canada, an entire generation of inner-city children has grown up thinking that guns, drugs and violence are all there is to life. Regardless of crime statistics, my concerns have been more than validated by the stunning incidents of gunfire, murder and havoc that I personally witnessed this past Easter weekend.

CELEBRATING CANADA'S OLYMPIC PARTICIPATION
June, 2000
Carol Anne Letheren, Chief Executive Officer and Secretary General, Canadian Olympic Association

At the Olympic Games there is something called the Olympic Village, the secure zone in which the Olympic athletes, their coaches and their officials live. The village is a very special place for them and not many other people have the opportunity to go inside it. But they certainly stand outside it. They stand outside the village in droves. They come by foot, they come by subway, however they can get there. They are there to talk to, touch and smile at the young people who are in that village and about to compete for their country. I don't think they care whether those young people can run fast, throw heavy objects, jump high or hold their breath for a long time under water. That is not why they're standing outside the village. They're standing there because those young people set phenomenal goals. They steadfastly move toward those goals and never veer from them. Often those goals are goals that are totally unattainable. But nevertheless, they set them. And often they achieve their goals under what I would consider very adverse circumstances. They are people who make the human spirit soar. What they stand for is beyond and above their phenomenal talent as athletes.

POLITICAL AND ECONOMIC EVENTS IN THE RUSSIAN FEDERATION
December, 2000
His Excellency Mr. Vladimir V Putin, President of the Russian Federation

Ladies and gentlemen, Canada and Russia are the world's largest federations. One economic advantage is economic flexibility because federalism makes it possible to even out the social economic possibilities of different areas and makes it possible to provide all Russian citizens, irrespective of their place of residence, with equal starting opportunities. Furthermore, the economy of the provinces is always a good proving ground for the most effective and progressive federation-wide models and a testing ground for running strategic models for the economic development of the entire country. This is only part of the multitude of virtues of a federation. I am sincerely convinced we have much in common. Of basic importance is that we are not only aware of our obvious achievements, but seriously and openly discuss the pain spots. A successful roundtable on the problems of federalism was successfully held here in Canada. The leaders of Canada's provinces and of Russia's regions, as well as leading experts in both countries attended. I think we must listen to their opinions. Such interstate discussions need to be made regularly, and held both on Canadian and Russian soil. Russian-Canadian co-operation is in my view absolutely unique. We are working together on the so-called Northern dimension, a project for the joint development of the Arctic, its social component, support of the indigenous peoples of the North and the preservation of their cultures, traditions and language. All this is equally important for Russia and for Canada. This is supported by a whole series of joint cultural, educational and other humanitarian programmes for the indigenous peoples of the North.

GOOD JUSTICE: A GLOBAL COMMODITY
April, 2001
The Rt. Hon. Madame Chief Justice Beverley M. McLachlin,
Chief Justice of Canada

The more I learn of the challenges developing countries face in establishing the rule of law, the more impressed I am with the importance of a fair and transparent legal process and an independent judiciary. Indeed, I am convinced that if fair processes and an independent judiciary can be established, good laws are sure to follow. A young judge in China who had trained abroad put it to me succinctly. "Once we establish judicial independence for commercial matters, fair process in matters of human rights will follow." This led me to ponder the history of our own rights. In England, an independent judiciary and fair legal system came long before democratic government and full recognition of human rights. Could it be that the best way to bring about progress toward democracy and universal human rights is to first and foremost establish open and independent courts? The idea that the humblest person can go to the court, be listened to and receive a fair and impartial decision against a more powerful person or even the state is an empowering idea. Once people understand they have this power, can democracy and human rights be far behind?

THE CANADIAN EXPERIENCE: LESSONS FROM THE CANADIAN HISTORY PROJECT

June, 2001

Mark Starowicz, Executive Producer of the CBC's "Canada: A People's History"

I've been obsessed over the past four years with trying to distill the Canadian experience and to find what shaped us. Here are some of the thoughts that came out of our four-year adventure. The first common denominator to all Canadian communities is the rejection of class, rank and hierarchy, and the insistence that everyone possesses the same rights. It's striking....The second common denominator you can't escape from is the profound effect of climate. It is striking how we are shaped by the winter. As individualistic as we are, it is ingrained in the Canadian experience to collaborate as communities....Third, I am struck how we are an archipelago of distinct communities....Everyone has a very clear idea where home is. A key to understanding the Canadian political process is that this country is very much a parliament of individual communities and identities, a community of communities as Joe Clark said, which will bristle at any infringement of their community rights, probably more than any country in the industrialised world....Fourth, and above all these common denominators, was this: Almost everywhere we went, almost any diary we read had the common experience of refuge. Almost all of us, apart from the First Nations, have at the core of our being the experience of refuge....When the Canadian history series was aired last September, I learned the biggest lesson of all, which I will share with you. We would have been satisfied with half a million viewers. The first episode got 2.5 million viewers. And with every ensuing episode it was like being hit by a hurricane of letters, e-mails and phone calls. The book of the series, which cost $69, became the best-selling non-fiction book in Canada. The web site was swamped. The video boxed set had to go into four printings. In my wildest prayers I never imagined that we would be able to say that Canadian history documentaries, two hours long, beat the Stanley Cup Playoffs and the Olympic opening and closing ceremonies. It was the most viewed documentary in the history of Canadian television, even going back to the days when we only had one channel in this country. The myth that Canadians were not interested in their history died that night—October 22, 2000. What emerged instead was that we had starved Canadians of their history. We had so deprived them of their stories and their experiences, and substituted an imported system of American mythology, that we had deluded our own people, through omission, into believing they didn't have one. That is the single staggering lesson to be taken from this project.

TERRORISM IN THE MODERN AGE: THE EVENT AND THE RESPONSE
November, 2001
Norman D. Inkster, President, KPMG Investigation and Security Inc.

In the 20 minutes of attack on the World Trade Center more casualties were caused than by the World War II bombings of Rotterdam and the attack on Pearl Harbor combined. The combined losses in those two World War II events approximated 3,200 people while the losses of September 11 are close to 6,000. For the first time in history the North American continent was attacked successfully. Fifteen thousand children lost one or more parents. It is little wonder that our confidence has been shaken and our complacency has disappeared....The battle against terrorism will take time and perseverance. There is no prospect of a simple solution, especially since the root causes behind these terrorist acts are unlikely to be removed by military action alone. Inevitably, therefore, the issue of terrorism will impact upon our political, social and economic environment for a long time to come. And that means that the terrorists have already won a major and enduring victory.

"THE FRIENDLY DICTATORSHIP"

November, 2001

Jeffrey C. Simpson, National Affairs Columnist, *The Globe and Mail*

Only 61 per cent of those on the voters' list in 2000 bothered to cast ballots. That participation rate puts Canada near the bottom in terms of voter turnout in western democracies. Voter participation has been falling in many western democratic countries, but it has fallen farther and faster in Canada than anywhere else. Another obvious fact is the documented decline in respect for politicians of all stripes. They are now held in only slightly higher esteem than used-car salesmen. Parliament itself is regarded as an institution of national scorn, where MPs too often are seen to be conducting themselves like kids embroiled in a schoolyard fight. Ordinary MPs, reduced to partisan role-playing rather than genuine legislating, are frustrated with their lot and citizens are frustrated with them....Within the parliamentary system, as it has evolved in Canada, the prime minister is like a Sun King. He is all-powerful. The Canadian prime minister has more unfettered power within this system than any other leader in a democracy. Put another way, he faces fewer checks or balances to that power than any other leader. We think of our system as parliamentary government, but what we really have is prime ministerial government within the trappings of a parliamentary system....So what is to be done to make the system more representative, democratic, accountable and transparent, while retaining its virtue of being effective? How can we try to re-engage Canadians in their political process? I do not have all the answers by any stretch of the imagination. Competitive party politics are indispensable, and that means, as I said, people on the right and left of the political spectrum recognising that they have to fit their policies to the complexities of the country, rather than squeezing those complexities into ideology. If they do not move towards mainstream Canadians, they will remain with influence but without power. A change in attitudes would also help, especially in respecting Parliament and the capacity of MPs to periodically be seen to exercise their independent judgment. And we need to improve the representativeness of our political system. We could change the voting for the Commons by instituting the Australian ballot that would ensure that every MP receives at least a majority of votes. Instead of voting for just one candidate, voters would list their candidates in order of preference. If none receives half the votes, the second preferences of the lowest candidate would be redistributed, a process that would continue until someone gets half the votes. We also need an elected Senate. Canada is the only federation in the world without an upper house that is elected or appointed by the states or provinces. The Fathers of Confederation made one big mistake by opting for an appointed Senate. It lacks legitimacy, does not represent the regional dimensions of Canada, and does not provide a check or balance against the power of the prime minister.

CANADA AFTER SEPTEMBER 11
December, 2001
Rex Murphy, Writer and Broadcaster, CBC

My association with the Newfoundland Liberal Party, disastrous though it was, has some explanation. It was the result of a severe blow to the head. Fortunately the head in question wasn't mine. It was Brian Peckford's. Those of you with a retentive memory may remember at one point Mr. Peckford had a slightly extravagant fantasy at the cost of $28 million of forcefully making Newfoundlanders vegetarians of the cucumber order. Our province spent $28 million in an attempt to grow cucumbers in a climate that contains neither soil nor light and attempted to market that idea among the most relentlessly and proudly carnivorous people on the face of the globe....The intensity of dedication to a type of cause that reaches such spectacular limits of committed action is something to which we have not been accustomed on our part and the intrusion of September 11 was a wild reminder that the tensions that exist on the planet can find their eccentric or singular or particular eruptions and none of us are closed to it. Here in our country, if we are to have some sort of response, it has to be contingent upon our own understanding of ourselves and that's the last thing I have to say. I think it is the very contained, the very diminished, the inadequate understanding we have of where we are in a world that's become more busy and more threatening. It is incumbent that we know ourselves. We have shrunk our politics and our politics itself has shrunk to faction. The parties have shrunk to their own business and to their business only. We are a mightily un-idea'd political system. Look again at the business of the federal parties. The four main questions facing the Canadian citizen today are purely questions of motion or inertia. When is Jean going? Will Stock be allowed to say? Is Alexa still there? And is Joe ever going to leave? We don't need a Parliament for this. We need a good travel bureau....In summary, it is impossible to contain all of the events that flowed from that particular moment of September 11, but if it does have some dividend to pay to us it should make us more vibrantly self-conscious of those things that are of deep worth here and strengthen our resolve to articulate what they are so that they might be protected and advanced. Harnessing the total energy of the nation on a common idea, a common Canadian project, is the greatest way to protect what it is that we are and to have something for which all citizens would widely agree to celebrate.

NATIONAL DEFENCE: A LITTLE COMMON SENSE
April, 2002
Desmond Morton, Professor of Canadian Military, Political and Industrial Relations History, McGill University

One by-product of the September 11 events was an apparent rediscovery of the fragile state of Canada's national defences. Canadians were shocked and appalled that we had such pathetic military resources to apply to President Bush's war. Why the

shock? The facts of post-Cold War military shrinkage and obso-
lescence have been published widely for years. Pre 9-11, the last
major poll of national issues revealed 70-per-cent awareness that
Canada's defences were feeble—and a comparable reluctance to
cure the problem with taxpayers' money.

OLD FORMULAS—NEW VISION
January, 2003
**Sally Armstrong, author of *Veiled Threat: The Hidden Power of
the Women of Afghanistan* and currently serving as a special
UNICEF representative in Afghanistan**

The world community came together after World War II and
created the United Nations so that we would never have another
Hitler in our midst. But in fact we have never got rid of these
egomaniacs—what followed were Idi Amin, Pol Pot, Karadiche
and bin Laden. The fact is the UN was created for a post-World
War II world. It simply isn't working as well as it needs to today.
And yet we fear upsetting the status quo more than we fear the
disastrous consequences of leaving it alone. It takes awesome
moral courage to go against the grain. We used to think the end
of the Cold War would mean peace in places like the Middle
East, Eastern Europe and Africa. But we couldn't have been more
wrong. Instead we got a confounding collection of pot-boiling
civil wars that erupted throughout those regions. What's happened since almost makes one nostalgic for the good old days of
the Cold War. During the eighties, classical humanitarian aid
was viewed both as a universal right and as a politically neutral
good. After the Cold War ended, that gave way to what's become
known as the new humanitarianism. But in this revamped relief,
bandits steal the food deliveries, war lords kidnap humanitarian
aid workers, and rogue presidents put conditions on the humanitarian aid. It is still seen as a substitute for the concerted political action that is the real requirement. Somehow, we cannot get
to that political action. Why? At least part of the answer lies in
the way the United Nations is structured. Although it's practical-

ly heresy to say it, one needs to look at the United Nations Charter itself....States are seldom held accountable for ignoring their international obligations. And the complicated rules at the UN make it nearly impossible to change that....So why can't we change it? Most people say it would be disastrous to reopen these documents. Is there a suggestion that what we are dealing with instead is not disastrous? Some say the world cannot afford these changes. Consider this: the U.S. and the Soviet Union spent $10 trillion on the arms race during the Cold War. The World Bank says it would take $1 trillion today to wipe out world poverty. Indeed that is a lot of money. But the alternative is vastly more expensive. You think we can't afford it? There's more money in the world today than there has ever been. But it's concentrated in fewer and fewer hands. More decisions are made in Davos Switzerland than at the United Nations....There's a giant global chess game going on in Afghanistan today. Playing on one side are the fundamentalists who want a destabilized central government, war lords controlling pockets of turf throughout the country and silencing women. They are well funded by places like Iran, Saudi Arabia, and Pakistan. Playing on the other side is the international community that made a *de facto* promise to the people of Afghanistan—let us invade your country to get rid of the terrorists and your life will be better. The promised funds from the international community have not arrived in sufficient quantity to make that change. What happens in Afghanistan will affect the entire region, maybe even the world. We simply have to demand that the UN find better solutions. There are droves of clever, highly experienced, well meaning officials at the UN who know what to do. They haven't so far got the courage to do it. But like I said, it takes awesome moral courage to go against the grain. It's tough to take a stand, to brave the disapproval of your colleagues, the censure of your friends, the wrath of society. It's been said that moral courage is a rarer commodity than bravery in battle or even great intelligence. Yet it is the one essential vital quality for those who seek to change a world that yields most painfully to change.

COMBATING TERRORISM AND WEAPONS OF MASS DESTRUCTION

April, 2003

The Hon. James A. Baker III, former Secretary of State, United States of America

At the outset, let me make one thing very clear. I know the policymakers in Washington very well, and I talk to them from time to time. But I am speaking for myself today and not for the administration.... Make no mistake about it: "Winning the peace" makes the allied military efforts more difficult. This is because, in addition to defeating Saddam's army, the allies must to the extent possible limit civilian casualties and minimize damage to the country's infrastructure. And the allied military deserves great credit for its success thus far in achieving these additional objectives. But these are just the first steps in winning the peace. What should the United States and the allies do next? Fortunately, we have a road map. The Council on Foreign Relations and the James A. Baker III Institute for Public Policy of Rice University recently published "Guiding Principles for U.S. Post-Conflict Policy in Iraq." The report's most important point is that the allies ought to avoid imposing a solution on Iraq from the outside. Reconstruction models for post-war Japan and Germany are unhelpful because, as "Guiding Principles" says, we want the Iraqis to be "a liberated, not a defeated, people." This argues against a long-term U.S.-led occupation or U.S.-imposed post-war government. Instead, the Iraqi people should take charge of their own country as quickly as possible. At the same time, the allies should promote a vision of a representative Iraqi government committed to federalism, human rights, a free-market economy, peace with its neighbours, and the absence of oppression of its citizens. In the first few months, however, there will be little alternative but to put an allied military commander in charge of an emergency government. Chaos will follow unless the allies quickly establish law and order, and begin dismantling Saddam Hussein's system of repression. The allies will need to begin identifying and bringing to trial war criminals and human rights violators, including those responsible for any atrocities against allied troops in the current conflict. Iraqis will also need food, water, and medical assistance. Humanitarian relief operations should begin as soon as possible. Last Friday's decision by the UN Security Council to resume the "Oil for Food Program" will make this vital task much easier. Canada, needless to say, can play an important role in this relief effort.... Perhaps an even greater risk is internal instability—the anarchy that might accompany an outbreak of ethnic and political score-settling. Allied troops will be needed in all major population centres. At the earliest opportunity, the military governor should surrender control to an interim government that would be internationally supervised but run by Iraqis—a government of, by, and for Iraqis.... If all goes well, a fully sovereign Iraqi government can assume control as soon as possible, although this could take a year or more to occur.... Looking forward, the United States and its allies will also need to achieve substantive progress towards resolution of the Arab-Israeli dispute. As all of you know, the tragic conflict between Israelis and Palestinians continues to elude resolution. But I believe that there exists a window of opportunity similar to the one that existed in the aftermath of the Gulf War in 1991. At that time, we used that opportunity to convene the Madrid Peace Conference, the first-ever face-to-face meeting of Israel and all of its Arab neighbours. Today Washington has a similar vehicle—in the form of the so-called "road-map" made public by President Bush two weeks ago—that can help move the stalled peace process forward. So, too, will the appointment of the moderate Mahmoud Abbas as Palestinian Prime Minister. Of course, the United States cannot "create" peace in the Middle East; only Arabs and Israelis can do that. Washington's responsibility is to help them. Above all else, we need to remember certain truisms about this dispute: (1) Only the U.S. can effectively act as an honest broker between the parties. (Special relationship with Israel.) (2) There can be no military solution to this conflict. (3) A political process and dialogue are essential, and whenever the political process breaks down, there will be violence on the ground. (4) And this Catch-22 applies to the dispute. And that is this: Israel will never enjoy security as long as she occupies the territories, and the Palestinians will never achieve their dream of living in peace in their own state as long as Israel lacks security! (It's a tragic version of the old chicken-and-egg problem.)....Iraq, North Korea, the Arab-Israeli dispute, and tensions in our old alliances (not to mention the war against terrorism). All of these issues challenge the United States, working with its friends to provide leadership in a dangerous and complex world. And, as the war in Iraq so dramatically demonstrates, leadership is not about making easy or popular decisions. It is about making right decisions, no matter how difficult they might be.

CANADA DAY
June, 2003
Peter Mansbridge, Chief Correspondent, *CBC Television News,* Anchor, *The National* and Host of *Mansbridge One On One*

Some would argue that for Canada, the 20th century began in 1896. That's when Wilfrid Laurier was elected prime minister. And it seemed to herald the end of a difficult economic period and the start of a new prosperous period. It was Laurier, of course, who uttered the prediction that has haunted us as Canadians for 100 years. The twentieth century, he said, would belong to Canada. The general consensus is that he was wrong. The century did not belong to us. And because we did not live up to Laurier's vision, some reach the conclusion that the last hundred years added up to a failed century....Well, not too long ago, a beer commercial seemed to strike a certain chord among us. Joe Canadian going on a rant about what a terrific people we are, but able to do it only by comparing us to Americans and by railing against their stereotypes of us. We aren't all loggers. We don't eat blubber. We're good at hockey....I think in some ways it was more sad than funny. Can you imagine a U.S. beer commercial making a big deal about not all Americans wearing 10-gallon hats, not all Americans singing *Yankee Doodle*, and they're all really good at baseball. Of course not. They'd be talking about their heroes, their legends and their heritage. We should do that too. For example, 100 years ago Canada was molding some remarkable men and women. There was Emily Murphy. Thirty-four years old. Proving herself over and over until she would become the first female judge in Canada and the entire British Empire. Maude Abbott. Thirty-three years old. Studying and researching until she would be recognized as a world authority on congenital heart disease. Clarence Hincks. Seventeen years old. One day he would visit what they called a "home for the incurable," a place of horrors for the mentally ill. He would be so appalled at what he saw that he would create the Canadian Mental Health Association, dedicated to training doctors and promoting education on mental health issues. Agnes Macphail. A 12-year-old. She would become the first female member of Parliament. And she would do that by overcoming some determined resistance. She would be heckled without mercy, but she would keep her wits about her and win most battles. At one rally, a heckler shouted, "Don't you ever wish you were a man?" and Agnes Macphail looked at him and said, "Yes, don't you?" There was an 11-year-old named Fred Banting living on a farm in Ontario with his parents and five older brothers and sisters. He would grow up to make one of the most important discoveries in medical history—insulin—which saved literally millions of lives. And a five-year-old toddler in 1902, his name Lester Pearson. He'd grow up to win a Nobel peace prize and become prime minister. Not one of them contributed to a failed century. In the last decade of the last century I had the distinct honour of covering the 50th anniversary of D-Day and the 50th anniversary of VE Day. We did the D-Day anniversary from France, VE Day from Holland. On each occasion, I walked through cemeteries where Canadian soldiers are buried. Row after row after row. And I felt as if I owed it to each person buried there to read the inscription on their tombstone. But after a while it becomes too difficult. For every tombstone has an elementary mathematical calculation staring at you. Subtract the year of birth, from the year of death. Inevitably, the answer is far too small. Sixteen. Seventeen. Eighteen. Nineteen. Sometimes a little higher. You cannot help but choke with emotion....So in these new days of a new century, we must recognize the shining examples of our past and then build on our success. This country is nurturing a new generation of innovators, humanitarians, even politicians who will make us better. To believe otherwise is to ignore what we have accomplished and to surrender to a pessimism unworthy of a great nation....It is no sin to be what most of us are— decent, hardworking, tax-paying Canadians. The sin is in believing that that is enough. That if you look after yourself and your family you have made your contribution. I don't think it is enough. We can give more. We owe it to the society that produced us.

PRINCE ANDREW
June 2003
Prince Andrew, His Royal Highness, The Duke of York, KCVO, AdeC

We have been celebrating the 50th year of the Queen's accession last year in the Golden Jubilee celebrations and most recently we gave thanks in Westminster Abbey for the 50th anniversary of the coronation. I want you to think for just one moment what it must have been like for a 26-year-old to come to the throne of England. The daunting prospect ahead of her must have been almost too incredible to contemplate. We have now been ruled over by her for 50 glorious years and I want to share with you some of the ethos that has rubbed off on me that might help to shed light on the monarch and her exquisite leadership. I am the first child to be born to a reigning monarch since Queen Victoria in the 19th century. Life for me began in Buckingham Palace and it is my home. It is a strange place to be brought up in if you think about it for a moment; an office by any other description. My mother was determined that we should have the same chance to be a family as anyone else. But, there were significant differences that I can remember. For example, I remember that if I didn't get up for breakfast at the appointed time it was allowed to go cold and then was taken away by the staff. Now this was a very good first lesson in life. First in order not to starve you had to be on time for meals, but much more importantly, your life depended on many other people and there is a loyalty to that service of others not to make their life more complicated than it already was with all their other duties. The understanding that others were just as, if not more important than, you was a lesson well learnt and never forgotten. I remember that my mother despite all the many different duties she had to do would always make time for us in the morning and evenings so that we always spent quality time with our parents. I did start life at a time that children were still seen and not heard, but as time has passed this has changed! My early educational influence was from the philosophy of Kurt Hahn. My mother did not have this influence but I suspect my father had something to do with it. Hahn did not simply believe in education as filling the brain with academic knowledge. He worked on the principle of acquiring knowledge and experience and educating the whole person. He stressed "the importance of purposefully directed experience as a part of a whole education." And if there is one thing that I have learnt most it is that understanding failure is as important, if not a much greater lesson than, understanding success. Also coming from the privileged position I was brought up in, Hahn's philosophy was to free the sons and daughters of the wealthy and powerful from the limitations of privilege. It might perhaps be an old fashioned view, but one that has certainly lasted the test of time with me. Having grown up in this environment it was no wonder that I joined the Royal Navy. But far more importantly it became clearer to me during my time in the service just what it meant to be in a position of responsibility or command in a far lesser way than my mother. I had the privilege to command one of Her Majesty's ships for nearly two years. In that time I came to understand the nuances of leadership and command that my upbringing and education had prepared me for. When in command of a ship you are almost a god as your word is the law. The understanding of how to wield this power is the greatest lesson I could have learnt.

The Empire Club of Canada is grateful to the following sponsors of the Centennial Gala Luncheon in the presence of His Royal Highness, The Duke of York. A portion of the proceeds from this luncheon was donated to The Empire Club of Canada Foundation in support of the publication of this centenary book.

The Dominion of Canada General Insurance Company

IBK Capital Corp.

GlaxoSmithKline

AGF Management Limited

Margaret & Wallace McCain

Ontario Power Corporation

RBC Financial Group

The Canadian Federation of Independent Business

Aon Insurance Managers Ltd.

AstraZeneca Canada Inc.

BMO Nesbitt Burns

Fasken Martineau Dumoulin LLP

George Weston Limited

Gowling Lafleur Henderson LLP

Magna International Inc.

Mercedes-Benz Canada Inc.

SpencerStuart

TD Bank Financial Group

The Movie Network

The Queen's York Rangers
(on behalf of Colonel Liliane MacDonald Steward

Rogers Communications Inc.

Past Presidents

1903–1905	Brig.-Gen. The Hon. James Mason, KStJ
1905–1906	Rt. Rev. William Clark, DD, LLD, DCL
1906–1907	J. P. Murray, JP, FREL
1907–1908	J. F. M. Stewart
1908–1909	D. J. Coggin, MA, DCL
1909–1910	Elias Clouse, MD, CM, LFPS Glasgow, LRPS Edin.
1910–1911	J. Castell Hopkins, FRS
1911–1912	F. B. Featherstonhaugh, KC, MBE
1912–1913	Rt. Rev. James F. Sweeny, MA, DD, DCL
1913–1914	The Hon. Mr. Justice James Craig, KC
1914–1915	Lt.-Col. R. J. Stuart
1915–1916	Albert Ham, MusD, DCL, FRCO
1916–1917	James Black Perry
1917–1918	Norman Sommerville, MA, KC
1918	F. J. Coombs
1919	R. A. Stapells
1920	Arthur Hewitt
1921	Brig.-Gen. C. H. Mitchell, CB, CMG, DSO, LL D
1922	Sir William Hearst, KCMG, KC, LLD
1923	Ellis H. Wilkinson
1924	William Brooks
1925	Rev. R. N. Burns, DD
1926	Col. A. E. Kirkpatrick, Hon ADV, VD
1927	Col. Alexander Fraser, LLD, ADC
1928	Robert H. Fennell, KC
1929	Hugh S. Eayrs
1930	John D. M. Spence, KC
1931	H. G. Stapells, QC
1932–1933	Col., The Hon. George A. Drew, PC, CC, CD, QC, LLD
1933–1934	Major James Baxter, MC
1934–1935	The Hon. Mr. Justice Dana H. Porter, CJO, QC, LLD
1935–1936	J. H. Brace
1936–1937	Major G. B. Balfour, KC
1937–1938	Major R. M. Harcourt

1938–1939	J. P. Pratt, QC
1939–1940	F. A. Gaby, BASc, DSc
1940–1941	The Hon. G. Howard Ferguson, PC (Can.), KC
1941–1942	C. R. Sanderson, MA, LLD
1942–1943	John C. M. MacBeth, KC
1944–1945	Charles R. Conquergood
1943–1944	W. Eason Humphreys
1945–1946	Eric F. Thompson
1946–1947	Major F. L. Clouse
1947–1948	Tracey E. Lloyd
1948–1949	T. H. Howse, FCIS
1949–1950	H. C. Colebrook
1950–1951	Sydney Hermant
1951–1952	D. H. Gibson, CBE
1952–1953	John W. F. Griffin
1953–1954	Arthur E. M. Inwood
1954–1955	James H. Joyce
1955–1956	C. C. Goldring, DPaed, LLD
1956–1957	Donald H. Jupp, OBE
1957–1958	Lt.-Col. W. H. Montague, OBE
1958–1959	Maj.-Gen. B. J. Legge, CMM, CM, KStJ, ED, CD, QC
1959–1960	Harold R. Lawson, FSA
1960–1961	The Hon. Alexander Stark, QC
1961–1962	Dr. Z. S. Phimister, LLD
1962–1963	Dr. J. Palmer Kent, QC
1963–1964	Major Arthur J. Langley, CD
1964	The Rt. Hon. D. Roland Michener, PC, CC, CMM, CD, QC
1964–1965	Col. Robert H. Hilborn, MVO, MBE, CD
1965–1966	Col. E. A. Royce, ED
1966–1967	R. Bredin Stapells, QC
1967–1968	B. Graham M. Gore
1968–1969	Edward B. Jolliffe, QC
1969–1970	H. Ian Macdonald, OC, KLJ, BCom, MA, BPhil, LLD
1970–1971	H. V. Cranfield, MD, FRCP(C)
1971–1972	Col. The Hon. Henry N. R. Jackman, CM, KStJ, OOnt, BA, LLB, LLD

Past Presidents *(continued)*

1972–1973	The Hon. Mr. Justice Joseph H. Potts, OStJ, CD
1973–1974	Robert L. Armstrong
1974–1975	Sir Arthur R. T. Chetwynd, Bt, SCM, KCIJ
1975–1976	H. Allan Leal, QC, LLD
1976–1977	William M. Karn
1977–1978	Peter Hermant
1978–1979	Maj.-Gen. Reginald W. Lewis, CM, CMM, CD
1979–1780	John A. MacNaughton
1980–1981	Reginald Stackhouse, MA, LTh, PhD, DD
1981–1982	Brig.-Gen. S. F. Andrunyk, OMM, CD
1982–1983	Henry J. Stalder, BSc, DBA
1983–1984	Douglas L. Derry, FCA
1984–1985	Catherine R. Charlton, MA
1985–1986	Harry T. Seymour, PEng, FFAF
1986–1987	Nona Macdonald
1987–1988	Ronald Goodall, FCA
1988–1989	Tony van Straubenzee
1989–1990	Sarah Band, DStJ
1990–1991	Major The Rev. Canon Harold F, Roberts, CD, BA, MDiv, AdeC
1991–1992	John F. Bankes
1992–1993	Robert L. Brooks
1993–1994	Col. Frederic L. R. Jackman, CStJ, PhD, LLD
1994–1995	John A. Campion
1995–1996	David A. Edmison
1996–1997	Julie K. Hannaford
1997–1998	Gareth S. Seltzer
1998–1999	George L. Cooke
1999–2000	Robert J. Dechert
2000–2001	Catherine Steele
2001–2002	William Laidlaw
2002–2003	Ann Curran

Index

Speaker	Page number

Speaker	Page number

Speaker	Page number

Speaker	Page number

Speaker	Page number

Speaker	Page number